ENGLISH EPIGRAMS

SELECTED AND ARRANGED

WITH INTRODUCTION, NOTES, AND NOTICES OF THE EPIGRAMMATISTS

BY

W. DAVENPORT ADAMS

AUTHOR OF "DICTIONARY OF ENGLISH LITERATURE," "FAMOUS BOOKS," ETC.

GEORGE ROUTLEDGE AND SONS

LONDON: BROADWAY, LUDGATE HILL
NEW YORK: 416 BROOME STREET

Republished by Gale Research Company, Book Tower, Detroit, 1974

Library of Congress Cataloging in Publication Data

Adams, William Davenport, 1851-1904, ed.
  English epigrams.

  Reprint of the 1878 ed.
  1. Epigrams, English. I. Title.
PN6281.A15   1974   808.88'2   74-7039
ISBN 0-8103-3700-2

PREFACE.

THIS is an attempt to provide for popular reading a representative collection of English Epigrams.

The volume differs from its predecessors—first, in consisting wholly of the work of English writers; secondly, in the arrangement of contents under the heads of certain special subjects; and, thirdly, in the exclusion of mere *jeux d'esprit*, professing to be epigrams, but having none of the characteristics of that kind of verse.

A certain number of epigrams which have been translated or imitated from foreign writers are given in the form of an Appendix: in some cases, for the sake of illustrating the general literature of epigram; in others, because some of the most familiar couplets in the language have been derived from a Greek, a Latin, or a French original.

Other features of the book will be discovered in the endeavour made to trace the authorship of a number of epigrams which are generally given as anonymous; in the presence in the work of contributions from the pens of living writers; and in the fact that a large number of the epigrams here given now figure for the first time in a collection.

In the arrangement of the volume generally, the chronological element has been occasionally introduced,—as, for example, in Books I. II. and XI., where there is interest and instruction in observing the gradual course of epigram through a long range of years, and in noticing the difference of style and tone. Elsewhere, the object of the Editor has been to place in juxtaposition epigrams which illustrate one another either by similarity or contrast.

In the Introduction will be found a brief, but it is hoped useful, sketch of the rise and progress of the Epigram. The epigrams themselves are accompanied, where necessary, by notes, critical and explanatory; a few particulars of the lives of the Epigrammatists are given in another section; and, by appending full indices of authors, subjects, and first lines, an effort has been made to render rapid and easy the consultation of particular passages.

No pains, in fact, have been spared to attain accuracy and completeness, and it is hoped that the result will meet with the approval of both the public and the critics.

W. DAVENPORT ADAMS.

CONTENTS.

	PAGE
PREFACE	iii
INTRODUCTION	vii

BOOK I.
HISTORICAL AND POLITICAL 1

BOOK II.
ON BOOKS AND AUTHORS 47

BOOK III.
ON THE CHURCH AND THE CLERGY—UNIVERSITIES AND SCHOLARS 87

BOOK IV.
ON MEDICINE AND DOCTORS—THE LAW AND LAWYERS . 114

BOOK V.
ON CELEBRITIES, AND OTHERS 131

BOOK VI.
ON INDIVIDUALS, AND TYPES OF HUMAN CHARACTER . 151

BOOK VII.
ON WOMEN 195

BOOK VIII.
ON MATRIMONY 214

BOOK IX.
GENERAL 233

BOOK X.
MISCELLANEOUS 252

BOOK XI.
COMPLIMENTS 274

BOOK XII.—APPENDIX.
TRANSLATIONS AND IMITATIONS 311

NOTICES OF THE EPIGRAMMATISTS 349
INDEX OF WRITERS 377
INDEX OF SUBJECTS 383
INDEX OF FIRST LINES 397

INTRODUCTION.

THERE are few subjects on which wider difference of view exists than on that of the nature of an Epigram. To a certain extent, indeed, there is a tolerable consensus of opinion. It is agreed on all hands that it should be brief, and witty, and pointed. One writer describes it as

> A dwarfish whole,
> Its body brevity, and wit its soul.

Another compares it to a bee, and says

> The body should always be little and sweet,
> And a sting should be left in the tail.

A third likens it to a wasp,

> With taper body, bound
> By lines not many, neat and round,
> All ending in a sting.

A fourth to a needle,

> With point and with eye,
> A point that can wound,
> An eye to look round,
> And at folly and vice let it fly.

A fifth compares it to a jelly-bag, and advises us to make it

> at top both wide and fit
> To hold a budget full of wit,
> And point it at the end.

So far, all is plain, but the description is after all a vague one. Much is said about "point," but nothing of the nature of it. We are indeed taught to dedicate the epigram to wounding "folly and vice," but that is obviously too limited an aim.

As a matter of fact, the English epigram has exhibited in the course of its career a remarkable variety of characteristics. At one time it has consisted of a moral sentence—fitting, indeed, but not particularly pointed :—

> A just man's like a rock that turns the wroth
> Of all the raging waves into a froth.
> *(Herrick.)*

At another, it has been devoted to the celebration of a lady's charms—a celebration sometimes witty, sometimes only elegant and refined :—

> For Phœbus' aid my voice I raise
> To make the charms of Celia known;
> But Phœbus cannot bear to praise
> A face that's brighter than his own.
> *(Relph.)*

Now, it is found utilized as the vehicle of coarse abuse directed against persons or communities and classes. For example :—

> "Why tax not asses?" Bob did say:
> "Why, if they did, you'd have to pay."
> *(Anon.)*

Or :—

> A single doctor like a sculler plies,
> And all his art and all his physic tries;
> But two physicians, like a pair of oars,
> Conduct you soonest to the Stygian shores.
> *(Anon.)*

Sometimes it is merely the form chosen in the versification of a witty saying :—

> When Charles, at once a monarch and a wit,
> Some smooth soft flattery read, by Waller writ,—
> Waller, who erst to sing was not ashamed
> That Heav'n in storm great Cromwell's soul had claimed,—
> Turned to the bard, and with a smile said he,
> "Your strains for Noll excel your strains for me."
> The bard, his cheeks with conscious blushes red,
> Thus to the King return'd and bow'd his head :
> "Poets, so Heaven and all the Nine decreed,
> In fiction better than in truth succeed."
>
> (*Anon.*)

Frequently it is nothing but the introduction to a pun :—

> When ask'd by Allen t' other day,
> What fish I fain would face,
> Turbot, I said, was my delight!
> But Allen swore 't was *plaice*.
>
> (*Croker.*)

Too often it is but the means adopted for uttering a mere impertinence :—

> James Allen Park
> Came naked stark
> From Scotland,
> And now he goes
> In very fine clothes
> In England.
>
> (*Anon.*)

It has ranged, in fact, from grave to gay, from lively to severe; and in arranging the following collection I have felt bound to give a few specimens, at least, of all or nearly all of these varieties.

The question of what an epigram ought properly to be is quite another matter. We may accept the universally accepted rule, that it must be brief, and must be witty, and must be pointed. But it must be more than that. It must be not only strong at the conclusion, but strong everywhere; there must not be a word too many, or a word too few; nor must there be, indeed, a word out of its place. Moreover, an epigram must have but one idea, and the object of the epigrammatist must be to express that idea in the briefest and the wittiest way, reserving the sting of it to the last.

Then come the further questions of the point and of the subject. Are puns, for instance, allowable in epigram? I should be inclined to answer—Yes, if the wit does not consist in them, and them alone. The mere play upon words ought not to be sufficient, unless there is wit, too, in the idea that animates the epigram. Then the pun may justifiably be used to point the thought. Unquestionably, however, the point which does not rest upon a pun is keener and much more legitimate than the point which does. Keener, also, and much more legitimate, is the point which rests upon the witty application of a well-known phrase, or on the amusing juxtaposition of opposed ideas. The variety of possible point is really only circumscribed by the range of wit itself, which, in its turn, is limited only by the range of our ideas. Barrow has told us in a famous passage how wide that range is, and it is therefore all the more regrettable that so many of our epigrammatists should have been content to turn their wit so much to punning merely.

As for the subjects of an epigram,—here, too, the field is wide enough, even if we adopt the modern view, and restrict the epigram to compliment and satire. The popular notion will not, indeed, admit the idea of compliment; but that is a restriction which the most stringent should decline to make. Insist, if you please, upon brevity, and wit, and point, as the characteristics of this form of verse; and exclude, if you please, the moral or sententious epigram, which consists only of an elegant idea elegantly stated. That may be conceded, though hardly by the lovers of the Greek Anthology: it is very different, however, from tabooing the epigram of compliment, in which wit is as available and as effective as it is in the epigram of satire. Who shall say, for example, that Luttrell's couplet on Miss Tree, the singer, is not as truly epigrammatic as Rogers's distich on Lord Dudley? Both give the pleasure that wit always gives: they fulfil the requirements of epigram, and are admissible accordingly.

For the moral and sententious epigram of the Greeks I am not, personally, inclined to argue. Beautiful and admirable in itself, it seems to me outside the range of epigram as conceived, and, as a rule, produced by modern writers. It lacks the one great quality of point, which is really the distinguishing mark of modern epigram. I confess I do not see the utility of a learned resuscitation of the primitive epigram—suited as it was to the genius of its inventors, and unsuited as it is to the genius of the moderns. It was more than suited to the Greeks; it was to them in the position of a necessity. They had a passion for the commemoration both of persons and events; their notion of perpetuation was to work by means of stone, either in the way of monument or statue; and, working in a difficult material, they were naturally led to express their feelings with the greatest possible brevity. To brevity succeeded the elegance that comes of intelligence and practice; the mere inscription (*epigramma*) rose into a work of art; and the Greek epigram was soon launched upon a successful career of about a thousand years.

It would be a mistake, of course, to conceive of the Greek epigram as being wholly moral or sententious. At least a small proportion of the Greek Anthology is as bitter and unrefined in tone as anything produced by Martial; the personalities are as keen, the general characterization is as vitriolic. Specimens of this class of work are given in Book XII., and I need only refer here to the names of Lucillius, Lucian, Palladas, and Rufinus as those of masters in the art of witty and pointed epigram of the modern stamp. Unquestionably the great bulk of the Anthology is of a very different character; but so much critical abuse has been directed against Martial, for what is termed his prostitution of the epigram from its original purity, that it is only fair to show how much in this, as in other departments of literature, the Romans were indebted to the Greeks.

Martial himself must always be interesting to the student, not only for the intrinsic merit of his work, but also because of the immense attraction he has always had for English writers. There is often the danger of describing as of English origin distichs or quatrains which owe their inspiration, directly or indirectly, to the Roman satirist. This is a testimony at once to the literary genius of Martial, and to the invariable characteristics of high civilization in all times and climes. Human nature is everywhere the same, and always most strikingly so where the conditions under which it exists are similar. Thus, the biting monographs of Martial appeal as irresistibly to us as they did to the Heywoods and Haryngtons of earlier generations. It is certain that they settled the future of epigram with a decisiveness to which there is hardly a parallel in literature. We could not now return to the purely idyllic epigram if we would; Martial has set his mark so firmly that it cannot be obliterated. Yet, on the whole, one cannot help regretting that this should really be the case. It is not necessary to join in the indiscriminate detraction which the poet has suffered at the hands of certain censors, but it is impossible to deny that he has done considerable harm by his example. His great fault is that he lacks so terribly the virtue of urbanity,—that his work is so coarse in sentiment and style. His weapon is the sledge-hammer, when it might have been and ought to have been the rapier.

> As in smooth oil the razor best is whet,
> So wit is by politeness sharpest set;
> Their want of edge from their offence is seen,
> Both pain us least when exquisitely keen.

Martial, unfortunately, paints with a big brush, and his effects are consequently broad and glaring. This may be owing partly to the people among whom he lived and for whom he wrote. A corrupt age produces a corrupt literature, and the age of Martial was rotten to the core. Yet a man of genius should rise above his time, and that Martial failed to do so is greatly, indeed, to his discredit. He might have done so much for epigram by imparting to it buoyancy and grace. As it is, his imitators have naturally exaggerated his worst qualities, and damaged his reputation and their own.

The Latin epigram so far surpasses its Greek rival that it has lasted from Martial to our day. More and Owen wrote in it, the latter notably; in fact, we have in Owen the ablest epigrammatist of the Middle Ages. The continental writers did little with the form save ape their Roman model; whilst in Scotland, on the other hand, George Buchanan and Ninian Paterson, to name no others, rivalled the ingenuity of the English and Welsh Latinists. Of more recent years, Vincent Bourne, of whom Cowper thought so highly, stands out from among the cultivators of Latin verse as pre-eminently the best modern worker in the pointed epigram. With all these writers we have, however, little to do. They had no influence upon the English epigram, except, perhaps, to retard its growth; notwithstanding that it is to More we owe (if Warton be correct) the first original epigram in English. That epigram finds, of course, its place in this collection; but, except as being the foremost of its kind in point of time, it has little interest or value.

For the first man who wrote English epigrams in any numbers and of any importance, the student has to go to John Heywood, the author of no fewer than six hundred epigrams of varying degrees of merit. These, as might be expected from their numbers, are but rarely good; none of them are polished, but some have considerable piquancy of a quaint and rough-and-ready kind. Here, too, the stroke is from the shoulder; there is no delicate running through the body. The time was a coarse one, and its wit was coarse. Heywood's is almost primitive in its simplicity; it has none of the subtlety of the finest satire. Still, his epigrams are striking as almost the sole product of his century, and as the earliest systematic treatment of that form of verse which had been attempted by an English writer. They could only have been written by a scholar—a comment that may also be bestowed upon the epigrams of Ben Jonson, which exhibit now the merits of the Greek, and now the demerits of the Roman manner. Specimens of the former style are undoubtedly in the great majority. Indeed, few more exquisite things have been composed than some of Jonson's sentimental epitaphs. His satiric efforts are chiefly in the direction of personal characterization, and have much of the vigour as well as of the rudeness of his Roman prototype.

Sir John Haryngton was the first English epigrammatist who struck a purely modern note, as in the lines on treason, which all know by heart. Even he, unfortunately, was affected by his study of the works of Martial—a study of which such couplets as that on "Smug the smith" are a direct and unfortunate result. You see exactly the same thing in Herrick, of whom it must, nevertheless, be said that, like Jonson, he had the Greek spirit more largely even than the Roman. To the latter element in his work we owe such strictures as those on "Rook" and "Urles," whilst it is to the former that we owe the numerous charming compliments scattered over his delightful pages. Some of these little trifles are pure epigrams—perfect in style, and tone, and point, and as much informed by wit as could possibly be desiderated. In the matter of inscription, too, how greatly he is to be admired! what flawless cameos of fancy he has carved out for our edification! In this direction he seems to me quite unsurpassed by any other English poet, in at once the grace and the variety of his achievements.

Donne wrote a page or two of epigrams, a few of which still linger in the public memory. Their chief merit is that they are quite original—more conspicuously of English growth, perhaps, than those of any earlier writer. Dryden produced some epitaphs which are remembered, and Marvel a quatrain on Charles II. which has equal currency; but neither can be called an epigrammatist in the sense of having made a study or a practice of the form. Rochester deserves the appellation more than many of his contemporaries; and so does Suckling. Each, like Donne, has a distinct style of his own, not due to classic models. Tom Brown, who wrote so sharply about Dryden, had also a true native ring about his lines; but they have generally vigour without polish, force without the power of attraction.

The age of Anne was fruitful in cultivators of the epigram. Of these the most prominent and most prolific was Prior, who devoted himself chiefly to satirizing matrimonial cares and the weaknesses of fashionable ladies. There is a certain sameness in his work, but much of it is really excellent, having elegance of style and ingenuity of fancy. Swift was happiest in personal description; Pope most successful in his epitaphs, with which he took great pains, and for which he was greatly celebrated even in his day. His miscellaneous epigrams, it is needless to remark, are exquisitely pungent. Among other and less noted epigrammatists of the time were Atterbury, Budgell, Addison, and Aldrich. The tendency of all of these was less towards the epigram which aims at human follies than towards that which fixes on the blots in individual character.

The same tendency, unfortunately, may be seen perpetuated in the writings of the following generation—a generation which yielded to the list of epigrammatists such names as those of Aaron Hill, Josiah Relph, Horace Walpole, Lord Chesterfield, Lord Lyttelton, Dr. Johnson, David Garrick, and Oliver Goldsmith. Of these Garrick was one of the most fertile and most piquant. All were purely English in their work, their style being marked by a lightness and an ease to which the Roman was entirely strange. Walpole, Lyttelton, and Chesterfield distinguished themselves specially in the line of compliment, as became such distinguished members of "Society." Relph, on the other hand, revived the waning glories of what may be designated typical satire. To Dr. Johnson we owe the amusing burlesque of epigram as then in vogue, contained in the following quatrain:—

> If the man who turnips cries,
> Cry not when his father dies,
> 'T is a proof that he would rather
> Have a turnip than a father.

Goldsmith wrote less of this description than might have been anticipated. His lines to Iris are exceedingly vivacious,

Introduction.

but miss being an epigram by reason of their number. Besides, they have too much of the nature of a "surprise" to be admissible.

We come now to the vigorous tirades of Burns and the poignant diatribes of Porson. Sheridan delights us only occasionally in a form of literature in which he was well qualified to excel. Landor puts vigorous satire into classic shape. Moore scatters in every direction his witty social squibs. Rogers amuses himself by dissecting the follies of his intimates. Byron rails against his friends and relatives. Luttrell puts amiable witticisms into verse, whilst James Smith scatters puns in all directions. Hook follows in the same satiric rut, and so does Jekyll. Coleridge shows how largely wit can coexist with high philosophy, and Erskine illustrates the ready repartee that haunts the bar. At no time was epigram so common, or so excellently done, as in the days when George IV. was king. It was not particularly elegant or refined, but it was at least pointed : it was never dull. Political feeling entered largely into its composition, nor was literary jealousy entirely absent from it. It had plenty of variety, and if classic only to a very limited extent, was invariably effective, and sometimes, at any rate, so pungent as to deserve, and possibly to secure, permanency of existence in our literature.

Of later days the blaze of epigram has been somewhat dimmed. Mansel produced some excellent specimens of academic wit, and Hannay revelled in a few couplets of the Martial order ; whilst Shirley Brooks—the typical journalist of modern times—turned out epigrams in almost every form with a fecundity only equalled by their brightness. Still more recently, Mr. Garnett has added to some admirable versions of the Greek some hardly less admirable examples of his own powers of epigram.

It must be confessed, however, that as an art the culture

b

of epigram has died out. Epigrams are still written, and this volume (I think I may venture to say) contains some good samples of the latest work in this department, from the pens of Messrs. H. J. Byron, Frederick Locker, Austin Dobson, Edmund Yates, and Ashby-Sterry. Still, epigram-writing as a *métier*, or even as a practice, may fairly be said to be no more. Nor is the "reason why" by any means difficult to seek. The fact is, that the wit which was once upon a time thrown into the shape of couplet and quatrain is now thrown into the shape of prose, and appears day by day in the columns of our magazines and newspapers. Epigrammatic verse still makes its appearance now and then in comic journals, but it is confessedly not of a high class. Epigrams are not to be composed by order or the dozen; and yet comic journals, like other publications, must be filled. We have not the time, now-a-days, to elaborate verse into brief forms which shall endure. The literary class is called upon to produce daily an amount of pabulum which effectually prevents the prosecution of a study like that of epigram in its pure and lasting forms; and if pure and lasting epigrams are to be written at all in future, it must needs be by the men who have the leisure, as well as the capacity, to produce them.

That the decay of epigram is to be regretted will, I think, be the feeling of all true lovers of literature. Apart from its value as a moral agent—as a castigator of individual, national, or universal vices—it has an historical and a literary interest which every one would be glad to see preserved. It is fitted by its form and essence for the transmission of feelings and ideas which cannot elsewhere or otherwise find the same felicity or permanence of expression—felicity, because what is briefly is necessarily more keener and acutely stated than it could be in an ampler way; and permanence, because an epigram is necessarily treasured and remembered where an epic or even a lyric is forgotten. It is, therefore, greatly to be hoped that epigram has, after all, a future of prosperity to look for. If its Past should appear to any one to have been less brilliant than it might have been, it should be observed—on the part, at any rate, of English writers—that much of the power which might have shown itself in epigrams preferred to display itself in epigrammatic poetry. If Dryden wrote few epigrams, he wrote great satires; and what is a satire but a succession of connected couplets? As it was with Dryden, so it was with Pope; and so with Churchill, with Byron, and, in our own day, Mr. Alfred Austin. It is useless to quarrel with the satiric wit which prefers to exercise itself in poems; and yet there can be no question that in preferring the poem to the epigram the satirist may earn for himself a higher literary place, but he certainly deprives his work of the wide popularity and general currency which epigram, if adequate, commands.

ENGLISH EPIGRAMS.

BOOK I.

Historical and Political.

I.

ON THE HOUSE OF COMMONS.

When lately Pym descended into Hell,
 Ere he the cups of Lethè did carouse,
What place that was, he callèd loud to tell;
 To whom a devil—" This is the Lower House."

William Drummond (1585–1649).

[John Pym, the great Republican leader, whose life has been eloquently written by John Forster, died in 1643. He was naturally the object of much detestation on the part of so keen a Royalist as Drummond.]

II.

ON CHARLES II.

Of a tall stature and a sable hue,
Much like the son of Kish, that lofty Jew,
Ten years of need he suffer'd in exile,
And kept his father's asses all the while.

Andrew Marvel (1620–1670).

[Charles fled from England after the battle of Worcester in 1650, and, after a ten years' sojourn on the Continent, during which he held a small court of somewhat needy adherents, was restored on May 8th, 1660.]

III.

A MOCK EPITAPH, WRITTEN ON THE DOOR OF CHARLES II.'S BEDROOM.

Here lies our sovereign lord the King,
Whose word no man relies on;
Who never says a foolish thing,
Nor ever did a wise one.

John Wilmot, Earl of Rochester (1647–1680).

[Charles, says Mr. Green, was "too humourous a man to care for the pomp or show of power, and too good-natured a man to play the tyrant."]

IV.

ON WILLIAM III.'S FOREIGN WARS.

The author, sure, must take great pains
Who fairly writes the story,
In which of these two last campaigns
Was gain'd the greatest glory.

For while he march'd on to the fight,
  Like hero nothing fearing,
Namur was taken in his sight,
  And Mons within his hearing.

Sir Charles Sedley (1639–1728).

[Mons was certainly taken (in 1691) whilst William looked on, but this was only because he had but a small army to oppose to 100,000 Frenchmen. Posterity has done justice to William's powers as a general, as well as to his capacity as a statesman.]

V.

ON A REPRESENTATION OF WILLIAM III. AS THE HERO OF THE "ÆNEID."

Old Jacob, in his wondrous mood
  To please the wise beholders,
Has placed old Nassau's hook-nosed head
  On poor Æneas' shoulders.

To make the parallel hold tack,
  Methinks there's something lacking;
One took his father pick-a-back,
  The other sent his packing.

John Dryden (1631–1701).

["Old Jacob" was Jacob Tonson, the publisher, who, without Dryden's consent or knowledge, caused an artist to "adorn" the poet's translation of the "Æneid" with pictures of Æneas in which the features of the hero strongly resembled those of the King, whom Dryden hated. It is recorded that the King appreciated the compliment, whilst the epigram is sufficient testimony to the poet's feelings in the matter. The allusions are to Æneas carrying his father Anchises on his back from Troy, and to William's treatment of his royal father-in-law.]

VI.

The Miracle (1707).

Merit they hate, and wit they slight;
They neither act nor reason right,
    And nothing mind but pence.
Unskilful they victorious are,
Conduct a kingdom without care,
    A council without sense.

So Moses once and Joshua,
And that virago Deborah,
    Bestrid poor Israel;
Like reverence pay to these! for who
Could ride a nation as they do,
    Without a miracle?

John, Duke of Buckinghamshire (1649–1721).

[The Duke would appear to have been a sympathizer with the peace party, in opposition to the coalition of Whigs and moderate Tories which supported Marlborough in his home and foreign policy. The Ministry which was in power in 1707 hardly deserved the ridicule here cast upon them.]

VII.

The Balance of Europe (1715).

Now Europe's balanc'd, neither side prevails;
For nothing's left in either of the scales.

Alexander Pope (1688–1744).

[Pope here refers to the state of Europe, after the treaty of Utrecht, as one of peace resulting from general exhaustion—"which," says Professor Ward, "was not the case."]

VIII.

INSCRIPTION ON A PUNCH-BOWL

In the South-Sea Year (1720), for a Club, chased with Jupiter placing Callisto in the Skies, and Europa with the Bull.

Come, fill the South-Sea goblet full,
The gods shall of our stock take care;
Europa pleas'd accepts the Bull,
And Jove with joy puts off the Bear.

Alexander Pope (1688–1744).

[There can be no doubt that the now familiar terms of "bull" and "bear" had their origin in the year of the famous "South-Sea bubble."]

—o—

IX.

ON THE STATUE OF GEORGE I. BEING PLACED ON THE TOP OF BLOOMSBURY CHURCH.

The King of Great Britain was reckon'd before
The head of the Church by all Protestant people;
His Bloomsbury subjects have made him still more,
For with them he is now made the head of the steeple.

Anon.

—o—

X.

ON THE EXCHEQUER AND ITS CUSTODIANS.

From sunset to daybreak, when folks are asleep,
New watchmen are 'pointed the 'chequer to keep;
New locks and new bolts fasten every door,
And the chests are made three times as strong as before.

Yet the thieves, when 't is open, the treasure may seize,
For the same are still trusted with care of the keys.
From the night to the morning, 't is true, all is right;
But who shall secure it from morning to night?
     Samuel Wesley (about 1692–1739).

[The allusion is probably to the supposed illegal use made of the secret-service money by Sir Robert Walpole.]

—o—

XI.

ON THE REPEAL OF THE GIN ACT.

Deep, deep in Sandys' blundering head
 The new gin project sunk;
"O happy project," sage, he cried,
 "Let all the realm be drunk.
'Gainst universal hate and scorn,
 This scheme my sole defence is,
For when I 've beggar'd half the realm,
 'T is time to drown their senses."
   Sir Charles Hanbury Williams (1709–1759).

[Sandys, when Chancellor of the Exchequer, succeeded in carrying, in 1742, the repeal of the act passed in 1736 for the imposition of certain duties on spirituous liquors.]

—o—

XII.

TO AN OFFICER IN THE ARMY.

God bless the King—I mean the Faith's Defender;
God bless—no harm in blessing—the Pretender;
But who Pretender is, and who is King,
God bless us all—that's quite another thing.
      John Byrom (1691–1763).

["Intended," the title tells us (*Poems*, 1773), "to allay the violence of party spirit" at that time.]

—o—

XIII.

ON THE NATURALIZATION BILL.

With languages dispers'd, men were not able
To top the skies, and build the Tow'r of Babel;
But if to Britain they shall cross the main,
And meet by Act of Parliament again,
Who knows, when all together shall repair,
How high a Castle may be built in air!

John Byrom (1691–1763).

—o—

XIV.

ON ADMIRAL VERNON'S APPOINTMENT TO PRESIDE OVER THE HERRING FISHERY (1750).

Long in the senate had brave Vernon rail'd,
And all mankind with bitter tongue assail'd;
Sick of his noise, we wearied Heav'n with pray'r,
In his own element to place the tar.
The gods at length have yielded to our wish,
And bade him rule o'er Billingsgate and fish.

Horace Walpole, Earl of Orford (1718–1797).

[Vernon sat in the House of Commons as Member for Ipswich, and made himself conspicuous by his rancorous speeches.]

XV.

ON THE DEATH OF GENERAL WOLFE (1759).

All-conqu'ring, cruel Death, more hard than rocks,
Thou shouldst have spar'd the Wolfe, and took the Fox.

Anon.

[From *The New Foundling Hospital for Wit* (1784). By "the Fox" is meant Henry Fox, afterward first Lord Holland, who, as Paymaster of the Forces, made himself very unpopular by his accumulations of private property at the public expense. He was the subject of some very severe lines by Gray. General Wolfe, the hero of Quebec, where he fell so nobly in the hour of victory, was born in 1726.]

---o---

XVI.

ON THE FREQUENT DEFEATS OF THE FRENCH ARMY (1759).

The toast of each Briton in war's dread alarms,
O'er bottle or bowl, is " Success to our arms."
Attack'd, put to flight, and soon forc'd from each trench,
" Success to our legs" is the toast of the French!

Anon.

[This seems to have been occasioned by the victories of the English arms in Canada, and the naval successes of Admiral Hawke; victories and successes all the more agreeable as coming after a series of very grave disasters.]

XVII.

ON WILLIAM PITT, EARL OF CHATHAM.

No letters more full or expressive can be
Than the once so respectable W. P.;
The first stands for wisdom, war, wonder, and wit,
The last points to peerage, and pension, and Pitt.

Anon.

[This appeared in Owen's *Weekly Chronicle* for 1761, when Pitt's wife was created a peeress in her own right. The following was written when Pitt himself became a peer,—that is to say, in 1766.]

—o—

XVIII.

ON THE SAME.

Says great William Pitt, with his usual emotion,
"The peers are no more than a drop in the ocean."
The city adores him; how charming the thing!
To pull down the peers, and to humble the King;
But, summon'd to court, he reflects on his words,
And, to balance the State, takes a seat with the lords.

Anon.

[From *The New Foundling Hospital for Wit* (1784). It is somewhat curious that the wife of another "Great Commoner" —Mr. Disraeli—should have been made a peeress in her own right several years before Mr. Disraeli himself became Lord Beaconsfield. The parallel between the two premiers is, so far, complete.]

XIX.

ON THE MARQUIS OF ROCKINGHAM.

The truth to declare—if one may without shocking 'em—
The nation's asleep, and the minister Rockingham.

Anon.

[Charles Watson Wentworth, Marquis of Rockingham, took office in 1765, but was compelled to give way in the following year to Pitt, who had been called to the front by the state of affairs in America. In 1782 Rockingham again came into power, but died shortly after. He was essentially a weak and timid minister.]

---o---

XX.

ON THE ROYAL MARRIAGE ACT (1772).

Quoth Dick to Tom, "This Act appears
    Absurd, as I'm alive;
To take the crown at eighteen years—
    The wife at twenty-five.

"The myst'ry how shall we explain?
    For sure, as well 't was said,
Thus early, if they're fit to reign,
    They must be fit to wed."

Quoth Tom to Dick, "Thou art a fool,
    And little know'st of life—
Alas! 't is easier to rule
    A kingdom than a wife!"

Anon.

[The Royal Marriage Act of 1772 was one by which the descendants of George II. (other than the issue of princesses married into foreign families) were incapacitated from marrying under the age of twenty-five without the consent of the sovereign. It originated in the King's disapproval of the unions contracted by his brothers the Dukes of Gloucester and of Cumberland.]

XXI.

On the Proposal for a Tax on Burials:

Addressed to George III. (1782).

Tax'd to the bone thy loving subjects see!
But still supposed, when dead, from taxes free.
Now to complete, great George, thy glorious reign,
Excis'd to death, we're then excis'd again.

Anon.

—o—

XXII.

On Pitt the Younger being Pelted by the Mob on Lord Mayor's Day (1787).

The City feast inverted here we find,
For Pitt had his des[s]ert before he din'd!

Anon.

—o—

XXIII.

On Pitt's Creation of Paper Money in War Time.

Of Augustus and Rome the poets still warble,
That he found it of brick and left it of marble.
So of Pitt and of England they say without vapour,
That he found it of gold, and he left it of paper.

Anon.

[From *Spirit of the Public Journals for* 1806.]

XXIV.
ON HAWKINS BROWNE'S ASSERTION THAT PITT HAD FOUND ENGLAND OF WOOD AND LEFT IT OF MARBLE.

" From wood to marble," Hawkins cried,
" Great Pitt transformed us, ere he died ! "
" Indeed ? " exclaimed a country gaper,
" Sure he must mean to marble paper."

Anon.

[Pitt died in 1806, leaving to England the legacy of his example and his policy. He is now recognized to have been a great peace, as well as a great war, minister.]

---o---

XXV.
ON THE SAME.

Browne says that Pitt, so wise and good,
Could marble make from worthless wood;
And who can doubt that saying bold,
Since he to paper changed our gold?

Anon.

[Isaac Hawkins Browne (1706-1760), wrote a Latin poem on *The Immortality of the Soul*, an English poem on *Design and Beauty*, and some clever imitations of the peculiarities of then living poets.]

---o---

XXVI.
ON THE DUTIES UPON CLARET.

Bold and erect the Caledonian stood,
Old was his mutton, and his claret good :
" Let him drink port," the English statesman cried :
He drank the poison, and his spirit died.

John Home (1724-1808).

[From Lockhart's *Life of Sir Walter Scott* (1832–7). It was occasioned by the enforcement of high duties upon claret, which had previously been imported into Scotland under the wine duties applicable to " Southampton Port." The " English statesman " was Pitt.]

———o———

XXVII.

ON PITT'S DRINKING HABITS.

In vino veritas, they say;
   Yet lying is so much a custom
Of certain folks, the safest way
   Is, drunk or sober, not to trust 'em.

The faltering tongue which, t' other day,
   Prov'd Billy's dire disaster,
Was so accustom'd to betray,
   That it betray'd its master.

Anon.

[From *The Morning Chronicle* (1793). Pitt's addiction to intemperance has, apparently, been much exaggerated. Port was prescribed for him when young as a remedy for constitutional debility, and he grew accustomed to the use of it as a stimulant. Lord Stanhope, however, denies that he ever yielded to such excesses as the satirists hint at.]

———o———

XXVIII.

ON THE SAME.

When Billy found he scarce could stand,
" Help, help ! " he cried, and stretch'd his hand,
   To faithful Henry calling :
Quoth Hal, " My friend, I 'm sorry for 't ;
'T is not my practice to support
   A minister that 's falling."

Richard Porson (1759–1808).

["Henry" is Dundas, afterwards Viscount Melville, who was Pitt's confidential friend and colleague. The above is one out of a hundred epigrams said to have been written by Porson in one night.]

—o—

XXIX.

ON THE SAME.

"Who's up?" inquir'd Burke of a friend at the door,
"Oh, no one," says Paddy, "tho' Pitt's on the floor."

Richard Porson (1759–1808).

[Another of the epigrammatic century referred to. Here is a third :—

"How well our friends," saith Hal, "have stood their ground!"
"Have they?" quoth Will; "I thought they all turned round."]

—o—

XXX.

ON PITT AND FOX.

On Folly ev'ry fool his talent tries;
It needs some toil to imitate the wise.
Though few like Fox can speak—like Pitt can think,
Yet all like Fox can game—like Pitt can drink.

Anon.

[Charles James Fox, in some respects one of the greatest Englishmen that ever lived—a fine orator, a generous statesman, an excellent scholar and no mean versifier—had a passion for play as unfortunate as Pitt's devotion to the table. Yet even here there was the excuse of early training in the vice. See No. XLV.]

XXXI.

EPITAPH FOR WILLIAM PITT.

With death doom'd to grapple,
Beneath this cold slab, he
Who lied in the Chapel,
Now lies in the Abbey.

Lord Byron (1788–1824).

["The Chapel": the House of Commons. "The Abbey": Westminster.]

---o---

XXXII.

ON CANNING'S DESERTION OF THE WHIGS (1793).

The turning of coats so common is grown,
That no one would think to attack it;
But no case until now was so flagrantly known
Of a school-boy turning his jacket.

Richard Fitzpatrick (1747–1813).

[From Lord Dalling and Bulwer's *Historical Characters*. Canning was born in 1770, and was only twenty-three, therefore, when, surrendering his youthful principles, he joined the Tory party.]

---o---

XXXIII.

EPITAPH FOR CANNING.

I was destroy'd by Wellington and Grey.
They both succeeded. Each has had his day.
Both tried to govern, each in his own way;
And both repent of it, as well they may.

John Hookham Frere (1769–1846).

[This is the third of three attempts in this direction, the other two being longer. See vol. ii. of the *Works*, ed. W. E. Frere (1874). Canning died in 1827, four months after the formation of his ministry, in which the Duke of Wellington and Lord Grey refused to serve. The latter statesman attacked Canning just before his death, in a speech of unusual severity. Frere was Canning's friend, political adherent, and literary collaborateur.]

---o---

XXXIV.

ON MINISTERS SAYING THAT THE SUSPENSION OF THE HABEAS CORPUS ACT HAD RAISED THE STOCKS.

" See," cry our ministerial blocks,
" See how our measures raise the stocks!"
Aye, " stocks and stones" they might have said,
For deeds like these would raise the dead.

Anon.

[The Habeas Corpus Act was suspended in 1794, and its operation not renewed until 1801.]

---o---

XXXV.

ON EDMUND BURKE (1795).

Oft have we wonder'd that on Irish ground
No poisonous reptile has e'er yet been found;
Reveal'd the secret stands of Nature's work,
She sav'd her venom to create a Burke.

Anon.

[This is attributed to Warren Hastings, of whom Burke was the great opponent. Burke, it will be remembered, was a native of Ireland.]

XXXVI.

On Bank-Notes being made a Legal Tender (1797).

The privilege hard money to demand,
  It seems but fair the public should surrender;
For I confess I ne'er could understand
  Why cash called hard should be a legal tender!

Anon.

---o---

XXXVII.

On the Victory of the Nile (1798).

Our ships at the Nile have created such terror,
" Ex Nilo fit nil" proves a logical error.

Anon.

[The victory of the Nile enabled Pitt to revive the coalition of the Continental Powers against France.]

---o---

XXXVIII.

On the Same.

Frenchmen, no more with Britons vie,—
  Nelson destroys your naval band,
Sees your designs with half an eye,
  And fights and beats you with one hand.

Anon.

[From Kett's *Flowers of Wit* (1814). It was written, of course, after Nelson's loss of an eye and an arm.]

XXXIX.

ON THE PARIS LOAN UPON ENGLAND (1798).

The Paris cits, a patriotic band,
Advance their cash on British freehold land.
But let the speculating rogues beware—
They've bought the skin, but who's to kill the bear?

John Hookham Frere (1769–1846).

[From *The Anti-Jacobin* for January 1, 1798. It was elicited by the threatened invasion of England by a French army, which was to have been called the "Army of England." With a view to the necessity of feeding and clothing this force a loan was started, to be raised by anticipation on the security of English land. "We are told," said *The Anti-Jacobin*, "that the merchants of Paris are eagerly offering to advance, on such a security, the money which is to defray the expenses of the Expedition against this country."]

XL.

ON THE UNION BETWEEN GREAT BRITAIN AND IRELAND (1801).

Why should we explain that the times are so bad,
   Pursuing a querulous strain?
When Erin gives up all the rights that she had,
   What right has she left to complain?

Anon.

[Said to have been written "by a Dublin Barrister."]

Historical and Political. 19

XLI.

ON THE ADDINGTON CABINET (1801).

If blocks can from danger deliver,
  Two places are safe from the French;
The first is the mouth of the river,
  The second the Treasury Bench.

Anon.

[Addington, says Mr. Green, was "as dull and bigoted as George III. himself," whilst "hardly a single member of his ministry could be regarded as rising even to the second rank of political eminence." The epigram is attributed to Canning, and was suggested by the fact that blocks had just been sunk in the Thames as a means of protection against the enemy.]

---o---

XLII.

ON SIR JAMES MACKINTOSH (1801).

Though thou 'rt like Judas, an apostate black,
In the resemblance thou dost one thing lack;
When he had gotten his ill-purchas'd pelf,
He went away, and wisely hang'd himself:
This thou may do at last, yet much I doubt
If thou hast any bowels to gush out!

Charles Lamb (1775–1834).

[The gentle Elia is hardly recognizable in these lines, which are recorded in the *Final Memorials* by Talfourd (1848). They were occasioned by Mackintosh accepting from Addington the Recordership of Bombay. Apropos of them, Lamb wrote to his friend Manning: "I will close my letter with an epigram on Sir J. Mackintosh, the *Vindiciæ Gallicæ* man, who has got a place at last—one of the last I did for the *Albion*."]

XLIII.

FIRE AND SMOKE:

Written on the Column erected at Boulogne to commemorate Napoleon's attempt to invade England (1804).

  When ambition achieves its desire,
   How Fortune must laugh at the joke;
  He rose in a pillar of fire,
   To set in a pillar of smoke.
    John Philpot Curran (1750–1817).

———o———

XLIV.

ON THE SAME.

Says Boney to Johnny, "I'm coming to Dover;"
 Says Johnny to Boney, "You're better at home;"
Says Boney to Johnny, "I mean to come over;"
 Says Johnny to Boney, "You'll be over-come."
       Anon.

———o———

XLV.

ON THE STAMP DUTY ON RECEIPTS (1806).

 "I would," says Fox, "a tax devise,
  That shall not fall on me;"
 "Then tax receipts," Lord North replies,
  "For those you never see."
   Richard Brinsley Sheridan (1751–1816).

Historical and Political. 21

[Fox was at one time chronically impecunious—the result of his gaming propensities. He died in the year that the duty was imposed.]

—o—

XLVI.

ON THE LEADERS OF THE WALCHEREN EXPEDITION (1809).

The Earl of Chatham, with his sword drawn,
Stood waiting for Sir Richard Strahan ;
Sir Richard, longing to be at 'em,
Stood waiting for the Earl of Chatham.
Anon.

[The story of the unfortunate Walcheren Expedition is well known. Sent against Antwerp in July, 1809, it " returned home baffled, after losing half its numbers in the marshes of Walcheren "—the result of incapacity in its leaders and mismanagement at home.]

—o—

XLVII.

ON THE PRINCE REGENT'S ABSENCE FROM THE CEREMONY OF LAYING THE FIRST STONE OF VAUXHALL BRIDGE (1811).

An arch wag has declar'd, that he truly can say
Why the Prince did not lay the first stone t' other day :
The Restrictions prevented—the reason is clear;
The Regent can't meddle in making a *pier.*
Theodore Hook (1788–1841).

[This appeared in *The Morning Chronicle* of May 11, 1811.]

XLVIII.

ON THE DISAPPOINTMENTS OF THE WHIG FRIENDS OF THE REGENT (1811).

Ye politicians, tell me, pray,
  Why thus with woe and care rent?
This is the worst that you can say,—
Some wind has blown the w[h]ig away,
  And left the *Hair Apparent.*

Charles Lamb (1775–1834).

[This was written when George IV., then Prince of Wales, became Prince Regent, and when his Whig adherents hoped to realize their expectations in the way of place and power. The Prince, however, signalized his own accession to virtual sovereignty by discarding and discountenancing his old associates.]

XLIX.

ON NAPOLEON'S RETREAT FROM RUSSIA (1812).

Of all hard-nam'd gen'rals that caus'd much distraction,
  And poor Boney's hopes so ill-naturedly cross'd,
The hardest of all, and the keenest in action,
  That Russia produces is General Frost.

Anon.

[Napoleon's defeats in Russia were chiefly those in which his battles were against the elements. There are, indeed, few more pathetic stories than that of the return march of the French army through the Russian snows, as told in the Comte de Ségur's well-known work.]

L.

Lord Wellington and the Ministers (1813).

So gently in peace Alcibiades smil'd,
  While in battle he shone forth so terribly grand,
That the emblem they grav'd on his seal was a child,
  With a thunderbolt plac'd in its innocent hand.

Oh, Wellington! long as such Ministers wield
  Your magnificent arm, the same emblem will do;
For, while they're in the Council and you in the Field,
  We've the babies in them, and the thunder in you!

Thomas Moore (1779–1852).

[The ministry here satirized was that headed by Lord Liverpool from 1812 to 1825.]

—o—

LI.

On the Duke of Wellington being nearly Choked by the Wing of a Partridge.

Strange that the Duke, whose life was charm'd
  'Gainst injury by ball and cartridge,
Nor by th' Imperial Eagle harm'd,
  Should be endanger'd by a partridge!

'T would surely every one astony,
  As soon as ever it was known,
That the great Conqueror of Boney
  Himself was conquer'd by a bone!

Anon.

[The expression, "great Conqueror of Boney," may remind some readers of Tennyson's description of the Duke as " great World-Victor's Victor."]

LII.

The Congress at Vienna (1814).

In cutting, and dealing, and playing their cards,
Revoking and shuffling for tricks and rewards,
The kings have been changed into knaves, and the rest
Of the honours have either been lost or suppress'd.

Anon.

[The reference is to the Congress which assembled at Vienna to discuss the state of Europe after the abdication of Napoleon and his retreat to Elba. No sooner had its members got together, than they began to quarrel among themselves, until surprised by the sudden reappearance of Napoleon in France.]

LIII.

On the Gasmakers (1814).

Our morals as well as appearance must show
What praise to your labours and science we owe.
Our streets and our manners you've equally brighten'd,
Our city's less wick-ed, and much more enlighten'd.

Anon.

[The application of gas to the lighting of London was a social event of very great importance.]

Historical and Political. 25

LIV.
ON HEARING THAT NAPOLEON'S SPURS HAD BEEN DISCOVERED IN HIS CARRIAGE AFTER THE BATTLE OF WATERLOO (1815).

These Napoleon left behind,
Flying swifter than the wind,
Needless to him when buckled on,
Wanting no spur but Wellington.
Thomas, Lord Erskine (1748–1823).

[Napoleon's flight from Waterloo was marked, it is well known, by great precipitancy.]

―o―

LV.
ON THE DEATH OF QUEEN CHARLOTTE (1818).

The death of the queen has caus'd great perturbation ;
We must mourn by command, thro'out the whole nation.
The theatres clos'd, the poor actors, forlorn,
Must starve : other subjects can eat while they mourn.
What follows is plain ;―'t is believed in all corners,
The mourners are actors, the actors all mourners.
Charles Mathews (1776–1835).

―o―

LVI.
TO MR. HOBHOUSE, ON HIS ELECTION FOR WESTMINSTER (1820).

Would you get to the House through the true gate,
 Much quicker than ever Whig Charley went,
Let Parliament send you to Newgate―
 And Newgate will send you to Parliament.
Lord Byron (1788–1824).

[Mr. John Cam Hobhouse, afterwards Lord Broughton, and a life-long friend of Byron's, was a Radical in political opinion, and published a pamphlet of so "advanced" a character that he was sent to Newgate by the House of Commons. His imprisonment, however, rendered him so popular that, on his release, he was elected member for Westminster amidst much enthusiasm. By "Whig Charley" is meant Fox.]

―o―

LVII.

ON THE BRAZIERS PRESENTING AN ADDRESS TO QUEEN CAROLINE (1821).

The braziers, it seems, are preparing to pass
An address, and present it themselves all in brass :
A superfluous pageant, for, by the Lord Harry,
They'll find where they're going much more than they carry.

Lord Byron (1788–1824).

[From Moore's *Diary*. This action of the braziers was in conformity with the wide-spread popular sympathy accorded to the Queen in the midst of the accusations brought against her.]

―o―

LVIII.

ON QUEEN CAROLINE'S TRIAL (1821).

When Gifford commenced his attack on the Queen,
Loud rattled the thunder, red lightnings were seen ;
When Copley summ'd up all he proved had been done,
'T was almost a total eclipse of the sun.
In the whole of the case we may clearly remark,
Accusation in thunder and proof in the dark.

Anon.

[A thunderstorm is said to have raged during the speeches of counsel against the Queen. Gifford, afterwards Lord Gifford, and Chief Justice, was Attorney-General. Copley, afterwards Lord Lyndhurst, was Solicitor-General.]

LIX.

ON JOHN WILLIAM WARD (AFTERWARDS LORD DUDLEY).

Ward has no heart, they say ; but I deny it ;—
He has a heart, and gets his speeches by it.

Samuel Rogers (1763–1855).

[This has been ascribed to Byron, but was really written by Rogers, "with some little assistance from Richard Sharp." See Rogers' *Table Talk* (1856). It is said to have been composed in revenge for an article on Rogers's *Columbus* which Ward had contributed to the *Quarterly* (vol. ix.). Lord Dudley (b. 1781) died in 1833. The fol'owing epigram is an amusing pendant to the above, and not so well known.]

LX.

LORD DUDLEY, ON HIMSELF.

"In vain my affections the ladies are seeking :
If I give up my heart, there's an end of my speaking."

Henry Luttrell (1770–1851).

[From Moore's *Diary*, under date November 24, 1828. See the epigram above.]

LXI.

ON LORD CASTLEREAGH'S SUICIDE (1822).

Oh, Castlereagh ! thou art a patriot now ;
Cato died for his country, so didst thou :
He perish'd rather than see Rome enslaved,
Thou cutt'st thy throat that Britain may be saved.

Lord Byron (1788-1824).

[Castlereagh, then Lord Londonderry, committed suicide in 1822. He was a Tory of the Tories : hence the virulence with which he was assailed by Byron in this and the two following epigrams. Hence, too, the famous epigram by Moore (*see* No. LXIV.).]

LXII.

ON THE SAME.

So Castlereagh has cut his throat !—the worst
Of this is, that his own was not the first.

Lord Byron.

LXIII.

ON THE SAME.

So *He* has cut his throat at last !—He ! who ?
The man who cut his country's long ago.

Lord Byron.

[This is strongly worded ; yet it must be confessed that the obstinate blindness of Castlereagh and his coadjutors to the signs of the times was productive of enormous evil, and somewhat excused, if it did not justify, the popular excesses of 1815-20. Lord Castlereagh's suicide prepared the way for Canning's accession to power, and rendered possible the series of reforms which followed.]

LXIV.

WHAT'S MY THOUGHT LIKE?

Why is a pump like Viscount Castlereagh?
—Because it is a slender thing of wood,
That up and down its awkward arm doth sway,
And coolly spout, and spout, and spout away,
In one weak, washy, everlasting flood!

Thomas Moore (1779-1852).

—o—

LXV.

ON MACADAM, THE ROAD-MAKER.

" My essay on Roads," quoth MacAdam, " lies here,
The result of a life's lucubration ;
But does not the title-page look rather bare ?
I long for a Latin quotation."

A Delphin edition of Virgil stood nigh,
To second his classic desire ;
When the Road-maker hit on the Shepherd's reply,
" Miror magis," *I rather ad[d]-mire.*

James Smith (1775-1839).

[John Loudon MacAdam was born in 1756, and originated his well-known system of road-making in Ayrshire, Scotland, where he was an Inspector of Roads. In 1819 he was appointed to superintend the causeways in the Bristol district, and, in 1825, General Surveyor of the Metropolitan Roads. It was in reward for his exertions to make the London thoroughfares efficient that he received the grant from Government referred to in the following epigram. He died in 1836.]

LXVI.
ON THE SAME.

The Parliament Grant to MacAdam, we find,
  Is a matter of little surprise ;
A work of invention may easily blind,
  That's made to throw dust in our eyes.
Anon.

[From *The Morning Chronicle* (1825).]

LXVII.
ON THE PRINCE REGENT'S ILLNESS.

The Regent, Sir, is taken ill,
And all depends on Halford's skill.
" Pray what," inquired the sage physician,
" Has brought him to this sad condition ? "
When Bloomfield ventured to pronounce,
" A little too much Cherry Bounce,"
The Regent, hearing what was said,
Raised from the couch his aching head,
And cried, " No, Halford, 't is not so !
Cure us, O Doctor,—Curaçoa ! "
Henry Luttrell (1770–1851).

[From *The Life and Letters of the Rev. R. H. Barham*, vol. i. (1870). Sir Henry Halford was the Court physician of the day.]

LXVIII.
THE PRINCE'S RETICULE.

What news to-day ?—" Oh, worse and worse—
Mac is the Prince's Privy Purse ! "—
The Prince's Purse ! No, no, you fool,
You mean—the Prince's *Ridicule.*
Thomas Moore (1779–1852).

[By "Mac" is meant Colonel Macmahon. The kind of bag called reticule had only recently been introduced into "society."]

---o---

LXIX.

WINDSOR POETICS.

Composed on the Occasion of His Royal Highness the Prince Regent being seen Standing between the Coffins of Henry VIII. and Charles I. in the Royal Vault at Windsor.

Famed for contemptuous breach of sacred ties,
By headless Charles see heartless Henry lies;
Between them stands another sceptr'd thing—
It moves, it reigns—in all but name, a king:
Charles to his people, Henry to his wife,
—In turn the double tyrant starts to life:
Justice and death have mix'd their dust in vain,
Each royal vampire wakes to life again!
Ah, what can tombs avail!—since these disgorge
The blood and dust of both—to mould a George.

Lord Byron (1788–1824).

---o---

LXX.

ON GEORGE IV.'S DEATH (1830).

How monarchs die is easily explain'd,
  For thus upon their tombs it might be chisell'd;
As long as George the Fourth could reign, he reign'd,
  And then—he mizzled!

Anon.

LXXI.

ON THE FOUR GEORGES.

George the First was always reckon'd
Vile—but viler George the Second;
And what mortal ever heard
Any good of George the Third?
When from earth the Fourth descended,
God be praised, the Georges ended.
Walter Savage Landor (1775–1864).

[Mark the sinister neatness of the penultimate line. Landor, it is well known—it is, indeed, obvious from the above—did not greatly love the house of Guelph; yet it is doubtful if this epigram, pungent as it is, is so mordant as the series of "quasi-epigrams" which Thackeray wrote upon the Georges. For example, he said of George I. that—

" He hated arts, and despised literature,
But he liked train-oil in his salads,
And gave an enlighten'd patronage to bad oysters."

He made George II. say of himself:

"In most things I did as my father had done,
I was false to my wife, and I hated my son;
My spending was small, and my avarice much,
My kingdom was English, my heart was High-Dutch."

George III. was made to say:

"I through a decent reputable life
Was constant to plain food, and a plain wife.
Ireland I risk'd, and lost America;
But din'd on legs of mutton every day."

Finally, this was proposed as portion of a mock epitaph on George IV.—

" He never acted well by man or woman,
And was as false to his mistress as to his wife.
He deserted his friends and his principles;

> He was so ignorant that he could scarcely spell,
>   But he had some skill in cutting out coats,
>   And an undeniable taste for cookery."

All these "quasi-epigrams," as Thackeray himself called them, appeared in *Punch*.]

---o---

LXXII.
On Dennis Collins throwing a Stone at William IV.

When at the head of our most gracious king
Disloyal Collins did his pebble fling,
"Why choose," with tears the injur'd monarch said,
"So hard a stone to break so soft a head?"

Anon.

---o---

LXXIII.
On the Same.

Talk no more of the lucky escape of the head
  From a flint so unluckily thrown;—
I think very diff'rent, with thousands indeed,—
  'T was a lucky escape for the stone.

Anon.

---o---

LXXIV.
Brag and Grab.

The initials of Brougham, Russell, Althorp, and Grey,
If rightly disposed, the word Brag will display;
Transpose them, and Grab will appear to the view;
Which hints at what many assert to be true,—
That they, like all statesmen, still follow the plan,
First to Brag what they'll do, and then Grab all they can.

Anon.

[Of the four statesmen thus stigmatized, Lord Althorp, afterwards Earl Spencer, died in 1845; Earl Grey in the same year; and Lord Brougham in 1868.]

LXXV.
ON LORD BROUGHAM.

"I wonder if Brougham thinks as much as he talks?"
　　Said a punster, perusing a trial;
"I vow, since his Lordship was made Baron Vaux,
　　He's been *Vaux* [vox] et præterea nihil."

Anon.

[From *Punch*.]

LXXVI.
ON LORD (THEN MR.) BROUGHAM SAYING THAT HIS EPITAPH SHOULD RECORD HIS ENMITY TO PITT.

　　Brougham writes his epitaph—to wit,
　　"Here lies the enemy of Pitt."
　　If we're to take him *à la lettre*,
　　The sooner 't is inscribed the better.

Rt. Hon. George Canning (1770–1827).

LXXVII.
THE ORATOR'S EPITAPH.

Here, reader, turn your weeping eyes,
　　My fate a moral teaches;
The ark in which my body lies
　　Would not contain one-half my speeches.

Henry, Lord Brougham (1779–1868).

LXXVIII.

ON THE DUKE OF BUCKINGHAM'S MODERATE REFORM BILL (1831).

For Buckingham to hope to pit
His bill against Lord Grey's is idle!
Reform, when offered bit by bit,
Is but intended for a bridle.

Anon.

---o---

LXXIX.

ON A RACING POLITICIAN.

Let Lyndhurst stride till hoarse and tired;
True sportsmen love Lord George's prate:
His speech recalls the "four-mile course,"
His arguments the "feather-weight."

Anon.

[Lord George Bentinck was an ardent patron of the Turf.]

---o---

LXXX.

ON LORD VERULAM KNOCKING DOWN LADY SALISBURY WHILST WALTZING.

Conservatives of Hatfield House
Were surely "harum-scarum;"
What could reforming Whigs do worse
Than knocking down Old Sarum?

Joseph Jekyll.

[This was written in 1834, and is said to have been the first literary use made of the word "Conservative" as the modern equivalent for "Tory." The accident in question happened during a ball at Hatfield House. The Marchioness of Salisbury was then advanced in years. Sarum is, of course, the Latin name for Salisbury.]

LXXXI.

THE QUEEN AND THE WHIGS (1839).

"The Queen's with us," the Whigs insulting say,
"For when she found us in she let us stay."
It may be so, but give me leave to doubt
How long she'll keep you, when she finds you out!

Anon.

[When the Queen came to the throne she found Lord Melbourne in power, and it was not until 1841 that there was a change of ministry.]

LXXXII.

ON THE ATTEMPTS ON THE QUEEN'S LIFE.

Three traitors—Oxford, Francis, Bean—
  Have miss'd their wicked aim;
And may all shots against the Queen
  In future do the same!

For why—I mean no turn of wit,
  But seriously insist—
That if her Majesty were hit,
  No one would be so miss'd.

Thomas Hood (1798–1845).

[From *Hood's Own*. Oxford made his attempt against the Queen in 1840; Francis and Bean theirs in 1842.]

Historical and Political.

LXXXIII.
ON THE PONTE-FRACT M.P.

You ask me why Ponte-fract borough should sully
Its fame, by returning to Parliament Gully;
The etymological cause, I suppose, is
His breaking the bridges of so many noses.

James Smith (1775-1839).

[Gully had been a prize-fighter previous to his election to the House of Commons.]

LXXXIV.
ON PEEL AND THE INCOME-TAX (1842).

A Reflection on New Year's Eve.

"Those Evening Bells—those Evening Bells!"
  How sweet they used to be, and dear!
When full of all that Hope foretells,
  Their voice proclaim'd the new-born Year!

But ah! much sadder now I feel,
  To hear that old melodious chime,
Recalling only how a Peel
  Has tax'd the comings-in of Time!

Thomas Hood (1798-1845).

[From *Hood's Own*. It was in 1842 that Sir Robert Peel brought in his bill for the imposition of an income-tax.]

LXXXV.

On the Anti-Corn-Law Bill (1846).

No wonder Tory landlords flout
Fix'd duty; for 'tis plain
With them the Anti-Corn-Law Bill
Must go against the grain!

Anon.

[The repeal of the corn duties, though virtually achieved in 1846, did not completely take effect until three years after.]

———o———

LXXXVI.

On the Defeat of the Peel Ministry on the Irish Coercion Bill (1846).

'Tis said that Peel,
The State to heal,
Without the least aversion
Resign'd his place:
'Tis not the case,—
He went out on Coercion.

Anon.

[In spite of the epigrammatist, it must be urged that Peel resigned, not on account of the single defeat sustained on the Coercion Bill, but because he felt that he was no longer at the head of a united party.]

———o———

LXXXVII.

On Sir Robert Peel.

The Tories vow the Whigs are black as night,
And boast that they alone are bless'd with light.
Peel's politics to both sides so incline,
He may be called the equinoctial line.

Anon.

LXXXVIII.
ON SIR FRANCIS HEAD'S DEFENCE OF LOUIS NAPOLEON (1851).

There was a little Bart.,
And he took the little part
Of the man with the bullets of lead, lead, lead;
He wrote to the *Times*
In defence of the crimes
Disgraceful to the heart and to the Head, Head, Head.

Anon.

[From *Punch*, which was always strongly inimical to the Third Napoleon. It was the bitterness of its attacks upon the Emperor that eventually deprived it of the services of Thackeray.]

---o---

LXXXIX.
ON THE CZAR NICHOLAS.

Czar Nicholas is so devout, they say,
His Majesty does nothing else than prey.

Anon.

[From *Punch*.]

---o---

XC.
ON THE SAME.

Czar Nicholas cried, as he look'd in the glass,
"Ha, ha! why am I like a beautiful lass?"
"Well, why?" cried the Empress. "Because," replied he,
"So many fine fellows are dying for me!"

Anon.

[From *Punch;* written at the time of the **Crimean War**.]

XCI.

ON THE LAYING OF THE ATLANTIC CABLE (1858).

    John Bull and Brother Jonathan
      Each other ought to greet;
      They've always been extravagant,
      But now " make both ends meet."
                              Anon.

[This refers to the first, and abortive, laying of the Cable, which was only finally and effectually secured in 1866.]

XCII.

ON THE INSURRECTION IN POLAND (1863).

'T was the Russian's conscription, the papers declare,
   Made the nation fling off his control;
So it is not the pole that has stirred up the bear,
   But the Bear who has stirred up the Pole.
                                Anon.

[The reference is to the last insurrection that took place in Poland—the revolt which was completely crushed in 1864.]

XCIII.

ON BISHOP WILBERFORCE AND THE OXFORD ELECTION (1865).

When the versatile Bishop of Oxford's famed city
Cast his eye on the chairman of Hardy's committee,
Says Samuel, from Samson a metaphor taking,
" They plough with my heifer—that is my Archdeacon."

But when Samuel himself leaves his friends in the lurch,
To vote with the foes of the State and the Church,
He proves beyond doubt, and the spectacle shocks one,
That Dissenters can plough with Episcopal oxen.
Anon.

[In the election for Oxford, in 1865, Dr. Wilberforce gave his vote to Mr. Gladstone, whilst the Archdeacon of Oxford was chairman of Mr. Hardy's committee. In the last line of the epigram there is, of course, a play on the word " Oxon."]

---o---

XCIV.

ON LORD PALMERSTON AND LORD DERBY BEING ATTACKED SIMULTANEOUSLY BY GOUT (1865).

The Premier in, the Premier out,
Are both laid up with pedal gout,
  And no place can they go to;
Hence it ensues, that though of old
Their differences were manifold,
  They now agree *in toto.*
Anon.

---o---

XCV.

THE TWO ORATORS.

When Palmerston begins to speak,
  He moves the House—as facts can prove.
Let Urquhart rise with accents weak,
  The House itself begins to move.
Anon.

[From *Punch*. Urquhart was a strong Russophobist and the persistent opponent of Lord Palmerston.]

XCVI.

A Suggestion.

Having finished his *Iliad*,
And ceased to be busy,
Lord Derby should try
And translate his Odd-Dizzy.

Charles Shirley Brooks (1815–1874).

[From *Punch* (1865). Mr. Disraeli, as it happened, was not "translated" till twelve years after this epigram was written.]

---o---

XCVII.

On Mr. Jacob Bright's Defeat at the General Election (1874).

And thou extruded! Sadder this, and sadder!
We thought our John would be our Jacob's ladder.

Charles Shirley Brooks.

[From *Punch*. "Our John": Mr. John Bright, brother of the defeated candidate, who was expected to profit by his relative's prestige and influence.]

---o---

XCVIII.

Cerberus.

My dog, who picks up everything one teaches,
Has got "three heads," like Mr. Gladstone's speeches,
But, as might naturally be expected,
His are considerably more connected.

Henry James Byron.

XCIX.

THE TWO POLITICAL PARTIES.

Whig and Tory scratch and bite
　Just as hungry dogs, we see :
Toss a bone 'twixt two, they fight;
　Throw a couple, they agree.

Allan Ramsay (1686–1758).

C.

ON THE SAME.

"Do this," cries one side of St. Stephen's great hall ;
"Do just the reverse," the minority bawl :
As each has obtain'd or desires to obtain,
Or envies the station he wish'd for in vain.
And what is the end of this mighty tongue-war?
—Nothing's done for the State till the State is done for !

Samuel Bishop (1731–1795).

CI.

ON THE SAME.

To the same sounds our parties two
　The sense by each applied owe :
The Whig exclaims " Reform-I-do,"
　The Tory " Reformido."

Henry Luttrell (1770–1851).

[From Moore's *Diary*.]

CII.
On the Whigs' Tenacity in Office.

The Whigs resemble nails. How so, my master?
Because, like nails, when beat, they hold the faster.

Anon.

CIII.
On Modern Statesmen.

Midas, they say, possess'd the art, of old,
Of turning whatso'er he touch'd to gold.
This modern statesmen can reverse with ease;
Touch them with gold, they'll turn to what you please.

Anon.

CIV.
On hearing a Debate in the House of Commons.

To wonder now at Balaam's ass were weak;
Is there a night that asses do not speak?

Anon.

CV.
On a certain Lord delivering his Speeches from his Seat in consequence of an Attack of Gout.

In asserting that Z. is with villainy rife,
  I very much doubt if the Whigs misreport him;
Since two members attach'd to his person thro' life
  Have, on recent occasions, refused to support him.

Anon.

CVI.
On a certain Lord's Arguments.

Yes, in debate, we must admit,
   His argument is quite profound;
His reasoning's deep, for deuce a bit
   Can anybody see the ground!

Anon.

CVII.
On Mr. (afterwards Sir John) Leach going over to the Tories.

The Leach you've just bought should first have been tried,
   To examine its nature and powers;
You can hardly expect it will stick to your side,
   Having fall'n so lately from ours.

Anon.

CVIII.
On a Shallow Speaker.

Vane's speeches to an hour-glass
   Do some resemblance show;
Because the longer time they run
   The shallower they grow.

Anon.

CIX.
On a certain M.P.'s Ponderous Speeches.

Though Sir Edward has made many speeches of late,
   The House would most willingly spare them;
For it finds they possess such remarkable weight,
   That it's really a trouble to bear them!

Anon.

CX.

On a Member of Parliament who gained his Seat by losing his Character.

His degradation is complete,
   His name with loss of honour branding;
When he resolv'd to win his seat
   He literally lost his standing.

Anon.

BOOK II.

On Books and Authors.

CXI.

On Homer's Birthplace.

Seven cities warr'd for Homer, being dead,
Who, living, had no roof to shroud his head.

Thomas Heywood (about 1596–1640).

[From *The Hierarchie of the Blessed Angells* (1635). See the following.]

CXII.

On the Same.

Seven wealthy towns contend for Homer dead,
Through which the living Homer begg'd his bread.

Thomas Seward (d. 1790).

[The number of cities which claimed the honour of being Homer's birthplace was rather seventeen than seven. The latest favourite in the race is Smyrna.]

CXIII.
ON PHILEMON HOLLAND'S TRANSLATION OF SUETONIUS.

Philemon with translations so doth fill us,
He will not let Suetonius be Tranquillus.
Anon.

[Philemon Holland (1551–1636) published translations of works by Suetonius, Livy, Pliny, Plutarch, and Zenophon. He also translated Camden's *Britannia* into English.]

---o---

CXIV.
ON PLAYWRIGHT.

Playwright, convict of public wrongs to men,
Takes private beatings, and begins again.
Two kinds of valour he doth show at once:
Active in 's brain, and passive in his bones.
Ben Jonson (1574–1637).

[The playwright here referred to is John Marston, author of *The Malcontent* and other plays. Jonson, says Drummond, "had many quarrels with Marston, beat him, and took his pistol from him."]

---o---

CXV.
ON JOHN LILBURN.

Is John departed, and is Lilburn gone?
Farewell to both, to Lilburn and to John.
Yet, being dead, take this advice from me,
Let them not both in one grave buried be:
Lay John here, and Lilburn thereabout,
For if they both should meet, they would fall out.
Anon.

On Books and Authors. 49

[This epitaph was probably founded on the saying current during Lilburn's life, that "if there was no one living but he, Lilburn would be against John, and John against Lilburn." Lilburn, who was of a very quarrelsome disposition, was a noted pamphleteer on the Puritan side, and, born in 1618, died in 1657.]

---o---

CXVI.

ON COWLEY AND KILLIGREW.

Had Cowley ne'er spoke, Killigrew ne'er writ,
Combin'd in one, they'd made a matchless wit.
Sir John Denham (1615–1668).

[Cowley, the poet and dramatist (1618–1667) wrote wittily, but talked indifferently; Killigrew, the dramatist (1611–1682), wrote indifferently, but talked wittily. His *Works* appeared in one volume in 1664; *The Parson's Wedding* is the best known of them (1663). Cowley's plays include *Naufragium Joculare* (1638), *Love's Riddle* (1638), *The Guardian* (1650), and *The Cutler of Coleman Street* (1663); his best known poems are *The Mistress*, *The Chronicle*, *The Wish*, and the *Ode on Wit*.]

---o---

CXVII.

TO DRYDEN, ON HIS CONVERSION TO ROMAN CATHOLICISM.

Traitor to God, and Rebel to thy pen,
Priest-ridden poet, perjured Son of Ben,
If ever thou prove honest, then the Nation
May modestly believe Transubstantiation.
Thomas Brown (d. 1704).

[Dryden has been too long regarded as a mere apostate, who changed his religion according to circumstances and convenience.

Professor Morley, on the other hand, has already shown that the *Hind and the Panther*, published in 1687, is the logical conclusion of the *Religio Laici*, published in 1682. In the latter, written when the author was still an Anglo-Catholic, there are distinct evidences of the writer's bias towards the repose upon authority offered by the Church of Rome. In the former, the argument for Roman Catholicism is openly put forward. It is too often forgotten that, as Cicero said, change of mind is not necessarily inconsistency. We may regret the poet's action in this matter, but there is no ground for accusing him of interested motives. By "Ben" is meant, of course, Ben Jonson.]

—o—

CXVIII.

ON THE ERECTION OF A STATUE TO THE POET BUTLER IN WESTMINSTER ABBEY.

Whilst Butler, needy wretch! was yet alive,
No gen'rous patron would a dinner give:
See him, when starved to death, and turn'd to dust,
Presented with a monumental bust!
The poet's fate is here in emblem shown,—
He ask'd for bread, and he receiv'd a stone.

Samuel Wesley (circa 1692–1739).

[The monument here referred to was erected in 1721, about forty years after the death of Butler.]

—o—

CXIX.

ON FLATMAN, THE POET, PAINTER, AND LAWYER.

Should Flatman for his client strain the laws,
The Painter gives some colour to the cause:
Should critics censure what the Poet writ,
The Pleader quits him at the bar of wit.

William Oldys (1696–1761).

[From Horace Walpole's *Works* (1798). Thomas Flatman (1635–1688) was the author of some poetic trifles, one of which, *On Marriage*, has been reprinted by Mr. Locker, in his *Lyra Elegantiarum*.]

---o---

CXX.

ON SIR RICHARD BLACKMORE.

Full oft doth Mat. with Topaz dine,
Eateth baked meats, drinketh Greek wine;
But Topaz his own werke rehearseth;
And Mat. mote praise what Topaz verseth.
Now sure as priest did e'er shrive sinner,
Full hardly earneth Mat. his dinner.

Matthew Prior (1664–1721).

[Prior describes this as "in Chaucer's style." It was probably suggested by an epigram by Lucilius. Topaz is said to be intended for Sir Richard Blackmore, physician and poet (1650–1729), author of *King Arthur*, *King Alfred*, and many other works, all now unread; of whom Cowper said that he wrote "more absurdities in verse than any writer of our country."]

---o---

CXXI.

ON THE SAME.

'T was on his carriage the sublime
Sir Richard Blackmore used to rhyme,
 And (if the wits don't do him wrong),
'Twixt death and epics pass'd his time,
 Scribbling and killing all day long.

Thomas Moore (1779–1852).

CXXII.

OCCASIONED BY SEEING SOME SHEETS OF DR. BENTLEY'S
EDITION OF MILTON'S "PARADISE LOST."

Did Milton's prose, O Charles, thy death defend?
A furious foe unconscious proves a friend.
On Milton's verse does Bentley comment? know
A weak officious friend becomes a foe.
While he but sought his author's fame to further,
The murderous critic has aveng'd thy murder.
Alexander Pope (1688–1744).

[By "Milton's prose" the poet here means *Defensio pro populo Anglicano* (1649) and *Defensio Secunda* (1654). Pope has another reference to Bentley in *The Dunciad* (iv. 212), where he describes him as a

"mighty scholiast, whose unweary'd pains
Made Horace dull, and humbled Milton's strains."]

———o———

CXXIII.

ON THEOBALD, POET AND CRITIC.

'T is generous, Tibbald! in thee and thy brothers
To help us thus to read the works of others:
Never for this can just returns be shown;
For who will help us e'er to read thy own?
Anon.

[Lewis Theobald (1688–1744) was a favourite butt of the wits of his time, and, as every schoolboy knows, was made by Pope the hero of *The Dunciad*, in revenge for his criticisms on the poet's edition of Shakespeare (1725). In 1733 Theobald brought out his own edition of the great dramatist's works, and Pope then thought fit to depose him from his pride of place, and put Colley Cibber in his stead. As a matter of fact—weak as he was as a playwright—Theobald was an excellent translator, and his Shakespearian emendations are full of ingenuity and skill. The above epigram is taken from a collection *In Praise and Laud of the Gentlemen of the Dunciad.* The spelling of Theobald's name, as given above, is in accordance with the popular pronunciation of it.]

—o—

CXXIV.

ON JAMES MOORE-SMYTHE.

Here lies what had nor birth, nor shape, nor fame;
No gentleman! no man! no-thing! no name!
For Jamie ne'er grew James; and what they call
More, shrunk to Smith—and Smith's no name at all.
Yet die thou canst not, phantom, oddly fated:
For how can no-thing be annihilated?

Alexander Pope (1688-1744).

[James Moore-Smythe, son of Arthur Moore, was the author of a comedy called *The Rival Modes*, in which, according to Pope, he plagiarized the lines addressed by the latter to Martha Blount on her birthday. Moore is bitterly castigated in *The Dunciad* (ii. 33-50).]

—o—

CXXV.

ON THE TOASTS OF THE KIT-CAT CLUB (1716).

Whence deathless Kit-Cat took its name,
  Few critics can unriddle;
Some say from Pastry-cook it came,
  And some from Cat and Fiddle.

> From no trim beaux its name it boasts,
>   Grey statesmen or green wits;
> But from this Pell-Mell pack of Toasts
>   Of old "Cats" and young "Kits."
>
> *Alexander Pope* (1688–1744).

[The Kit-Cat was a famous literary club, of which Addison, Steele, and many other celebrated men were members. In reality, it received its name from Christopher Katt, a well-known pastry-cook of the time. To be "toasted" by it was regarded as an honour. Lady Mary Wortley Montagu has told us how, on one occasion, she, as a child, was made the subject of a toast. It was the custom of the members to make verses on the toasts, and have them engraved upon the glasses. Several examples of these verses will be found in Book XI.]

—o—

CXXVI.

ON CARTHY'S TRANSLATION OF HORACE.

> "This I may boast, which few e'er could,
>   Half of my book at least is good."
>
> *Jonathan Swift* (1667–1745).

[This alludes to the fact that, in Carthy's edition of Horace, the Latin original was printed on one side, and the English translation on the other. Carthy was a schoolmaster in Dublin]

—o—

CXXVII.

ON THE SAME.

> "I must confess that I was somewhat warm,
>   I broke his teeth, but where's the mighty harm?
>   My work, he said, could ne'er afford him meat,
>   And teeth are useless where there's nought to eat!"
>
> *Jonathan Swift.*

["Carthy knocked some teeth from his news-boy, for saying he could not live by the profits of Carthy's works, as they did not sell."]

—o—

CXXVIII.

ON ONE DELACOURT'S COMPLIMENTING CARTHY ON HIS POETRY.

Carthy, you say, writes well—his genius true,
You pawn your word for him—he'll vouch for you.
So two poor knaves, who find their credit fail,
To cheat the world, become each other's bail.

Jonathan Swift (1667–1745).

[Delacourt was author of *The Prospect of Poetry* and other poems. George Buchanan (1506–1582) has a Latin epigram very similar to this.]

—o—

CXXIX.

ON THE AUTHOR OF "THE BRITISH BEAUTIES."

When one good line did much my wonder raise
In Broadhurst's works, I stood resolv'd to praise:
And had, but that the modest author cries,
"Praise undeserved is satire in disguise."

Anon.

[From *A Collection of Epigrams* (1727). The fourth line of this epigram occurs in a poem by Broadhurst, called *The British Beauties*, for which see *The Garland* (1723). It is misquoted by Pope (to whom it is often attributed) in his *Imitation of Horace* (I. ii.), where it runs,—

"Praise undeserved is scandal in disguise."]

CXXX.

ON PERRAULT'S "PARALLEL BETWEEN THE ANCIENTS AND THE MODERNS."

Perrault, the Frenchman, needs would prove
The Ancients knew not how to love;
Yet spite of all that he has said,
'T is sure they woo'd, they won, and wed.
The case beyond dispute is clear:
Or else how came the Moderns here?
Anon.

[From *The London Medley* (1731). The relative merits of ancient and of modern writers much exercised the minds of authors in the time of Anne; among others, of Sir William Temple, who wrote a treatise on the subject, which was attacked by William Wotton. Swift also took part in the controversy (see Book XI.). Charles Perrault was born in 1628 and died in 1703.]

—·o—

CXXXI.

THE DIFFERENCE BETWEEN THE ANCIENTS AND THE MODERNS.

Some for the ancients zealously declare,
Others our modern wits are fools aver;
A third affirms that they are much the same,
And differ only as to time and name:
Yet sure one more distinction may be told,
Those once were new, these never shall be old.
Anon.

[From *Elegant Extracts* (1805).]

CXXXII.

ON DR. FREIND'S EPIGRAMS.

Freind! for your epitaphs I'm griev'd,
Where still so much is said ;
One half will never be believ'd,
The other never read.
Alexander Pope (1688–1744).

["Pope," says Lord Campbell, " was in the habit of spending his winter evenings in the library of [Lord Chief Justice] Murray's house in Lincoln's Inn Fields ; and on one occasion the rising lawyer being called away to a consultation, put into the poet's hand a volume of Latin epitaphs by Dr. Freind, just published, saying, 'they had been much read and admired.' Pope, who, like other great men, felt jealous of a supposed rival, was alarmed lest his own fame in epitaph-writing, on which he particularly valued himself, should be dimmed, and on Murray's return showed him the above epigram." Dr. Freind was Head Master of Westminster School, Prebendary of Westminster, and Canon of Christ Church. See the following lines, written on his appointment to the former post.]

—o—

CXXXIII.

ON DR. FREIND'S APPOINTMENT TO THE HEAD MASTERSHIP OF WESTMINSTER.

Ye sons of Westminster, who still retain
Your ancient dread of Busby's awful reign ;
Forget at length your fears—your panic end—
The monarch of this place is now a *Freind*.
Anon.

[From Nichols' *Literary Anecdotes.* See note above.]

CXXXIV.
On Colley Cibber's Appointment as Laureate to George II.

Tell, if you can, which did the worse,
  Caligula or Grafton's Grace?
This made a Consul of a horse,
  And this a Laureate of an ass.

Alexander Pope (1688–1744).

[Colley Cibber (1671–1757) succeeded the Rev. Laurence Eusden as poet laureate in 1730. So far from his being "an ass," his comedies, which include *The Careless Husband* and *The Non-Juror*, are among the wittiest we have, whilst his autobiographical *Apology* is full of entertainment. The only mistake he made was in trying to write poetry, for which he had no capacity whatever.]

CXXXV.
On the Same.

Augustus still survives in Maro's strain,
And Spenser's verse prolongs Eliza's reign:
Great George's acts let tuneful Cibber sing,
For Nature form'd the poet for the King.

Samuel Johnson (1709–1784).

CXXXVI.
On the Same.

In merry old England it once was the rule
The king had his poet and also his fool;
But now we're so frugal, I'd have you to know it,
That one man now serves both for fool and for poet.

Anon.

CXXXVII.

On Stephen Duck and Colley Cibber.

Behold, ambitious of the British bays,
Cibber and Duck contend in rival lays.
But gentle Colley, should thy verse prevail,
Thou hast no fence, alas! against his flail:
Therefore thy claim resign; allow his right,
For Duck can thresh, you know, as well as write.

Alexander Pope (1688–1744).

[Stephen Duck (d. 1756), the author of *The Thrasher's Labour, The Shunamite*, and other poems, was originally a thresher—a circumstance which drew down upon him a number of epigrams. He afterwards took orders, and, by favour of the Queen, obtained a chaplaincy in the army—a piece of royal patronage which Swift satirized in the following lines. Duck's *Poems* were collected in 1736.]

—o—

CXXXVIII.

On Stephen Duck, the Thresher and Favourite Poet (1730).

The thresher Duck could o'er the queen prevail;
The proverb says, "No fence against a flail."
From threshing corn he turns to thresh his brains;
For which her Majesty allows him grains:
Though 't is confest, that those who ever saw
His poems think them all not worth a straw.
Thrice happy Duck, employ'd in threshing stubble,
Thy toil is lessen'd, and thy profits double.

Jonathan Swift (1667–1745).

CXXXIX.

ON POPE'S TRANSLATION OF HOMER.

Pope came off clean with Homer; but, they say,
Broome went before, and kindly swept the way.
John Henley (1692-1756).

[William Broome (1689-1745) was employed by Pope to translate from the original the second, sixth, eighth, eleventh, twelfth, sixteenth, eighteenth and twenty-third books of *The Odyssey*. Pope refers to the fact—not very gratefully—in *The Dunciad*, where he says:—

" Hibernian politics, O Swift, thy doom,
And mine, translating ten whole years with Broome."

Broome was himself a "poet," and published a volume of verse in 1727.]

---o---

CXL.

ON THE REFERENCE TO "ONE PRIOR," IN BURNET'S "HISTORY."

" One Prior——" and is this, this all the fame
The poet from th' historian can claim?
No: Prior's verse posterity shall quote
When 't is forgot " one Burnet " ever wrote.
Anon.

[From *Elegant Extracts* (1805). Bishop Burnet's *History of his Own Times* appeared in 1724. Macaulay refers to " his boastfulness, his undissembled vanity, his propensity to plunder, his provoking indiscretion, his unabashed audacity." For a reference to Prior, see the " Notices of the Epigrammatists."]

CXLI.

ON PRIOR'S "SOLOMON."

Wise Solomon, with all his rambling doubts,
Might talk two hours, I guess, or thereabouts;
And yet, quoth he, " my elders, to their shame,
Kept silence all, nor answer did they frame."
Dear me! what else but silence should they keep?
He, to be sure, had talk'd them all asleep.
John Byrom (1691–1763).

[From *Poems* (1773). Prior's *Solomon on the Vanity of the World* is a poem in three books, the first of which treats of Knowledge, the second of Pleasure, the third of Power. It is a tedious work, but its tediousness proceeds, as Dr. Johnson pointed out, " not from the uniformity of the subject—for it is sufficiently diversified—but from the continued tenor of the narration, in which Solomon relates the successive vicissitudes of his mind, without the intervention of any other speaker, or the mention of any other agent, unless it be Abra."]

—o—

CXLII.

IN SUMMARY OF LORD LYTTELTON'S "ADVICE TO A LADY" (1731).

" Be plain in dress, and sober in your diet;
In short, my deary, kiss me! and be quiet."
Lady Mary Wortley Montagu (1690–1762).

[The poem referred to is that beginning—

" The counsels of a friend, Belinda, hear."

Lyttelton (1709–1773) is best known by his *Dialogues of the Dead* and *Persian Letters*.]

CXLIII.

ON SIR JOHN HILL, PHYSICIAN AND DRAMATIST.

For physic and farces his equal there scarce is :
His farces are physic, his physic a farce is.
David Garrick (1716–1779).

[Sir John Hill (1716–1775) was the author of *The Vegetable System* and other solid works, in addition to the farces here satirized. He appears to have been unlucky in his relations with literary men, who lampooned him almost as unmercifully as they did Sir Richard Blackmore. Christopher Smart actually made him the subject of a mock epic called *The Hilliad*.]

CXLIV.

ON THE SAME.

Thou essence of dock, and valerian, and sage,
At once the disgrace and the pest of your age ;
The worst that we wish thee, for all thy sad crimes,
Is to take thine own physic, and read thine own rhymes.
Anon.

[This was the combined production of a whole body of wits.]

CXLV.

ON THE ABOVE.

The wish should be in form revers'd,
   To suit the Doctor's crimes,
For if he take his physic first,
   He'll never read his rhymes.
Anon.

CXLVI.

ON SIR JOHN HILL CENSURING GARRICK'S PRONUNCIATION OF "U" FOR "I."

If 't is true, as you say, that I've injur'd a letter,
I'll change my note soon, and, I hope, for the better.
May the just rights of letters, as well as of men,
Hereafter be fix'd by the tongue and the pen.
Most devoutly I wish they may both have their due,
And that "*I*" may be never mistaken for "*U*."

David Garrick (1716–1779).

CXLVII.

TO GOLDSMITH, ON KELLY, AT ONE TIME A STAY-MAKER.

If Kelly finds fault with the shape of your muse,
And thinks that too loosely it plays,
He surely, dear Doctor, will never refuse
To make it a new pair of stays!

Anon.

[Hugh Kelly (1739-1777) was the author of *False Delicacy*, *A Word to the Wise*, *The School for Wives*, and many other plays. He is referred to by Goldsmith in *Retaliation*.]

CXLVIII.

ON OLIVER GOLDSMITH.

Here lies Nolly Goldsmith, for shortness called Noll,
Who wrote like an angel, but talked like poor Poll.

David Garrick.

[This was written by Garrick one day in 1774 at the St. James's Coffee House, as his contribution to a series of mock epitaphs on Goldsmith which it had been agreed the company should write. Goldsmith's reply was in the form of his *Retaliation*,—a poem full of humorous satire, not only on Garrick, but on the whole company who were wont to assemble in the Coffee House, including Burke, Cumberland, Reynolds, and others. The lines on Garrick begin :

> " Here lies David Garrick, describe me who can :
> An abridgment of all that is pleasant in man.
> As an actor, confessed without rival to shine,
> As a wit, if not first, in the very first line. . . .
> On the stage he was natural, simple, affecting ;
> 'T was only that when he was off he was acting.
> With no reason on earth to go out of his way,
> He turned and he varied full ten times a day. . . .
> Of praise a mere glutton, he swallowed what came ;
> And the puff of a dunce he mistook it for fame ;
> Till his relish grown callous, almost to disease,
> Who peppered the highest was surest to please."]

―――o―――

CXLIX.

ON DR. GOLDSMITH'S CHARACTERISTICAL COOKERY.

Are these the choice dishes the Doctor has sent us?
Is this the great poet whose works so content us?
This Goldsmith's fine feast, who has written fine books?
Heaven sends us good meat—but the devil sends cooks.

David Garrick (1716–1779).

[From Davies' *Life of Garrick;* composed " in humorous revenge " for the description given of the actor in *Retaliation.*]

CL.

To O'Keefe, the Dramatist.

They say, O'Keefe,
Thou art a thief,
  That half thy works are stol'n, and more;
I say, O'Keefe,
Thou art no thief—
  Such stuff was never writ before.
                                    Anon.

[Attributed to John Wolcot (Peter Pindar). John O'Keefe (1747–1833) wrote *Wild Oats, The Agreeable Surprise,* and other plays, published in 1798.]

—o—

CLI.

On Dr. Samuel Parr.

To half of Busby's skill in mood and tense,
Add Bentley's pedantry without his sense;
Of Warburton take all the spleen you find,
And leave his genius and his wit behind;
Squeeze Churchill's rancour from the verse it flows in,
And knead it stiff with Johnson's heavy prosing;
Add all the piety of St. Voltaire,
Mix the gross compound—*Fiat* Dr. Parr.
                                    Anon.

[From Crabb Robinson's *Diary*, vol. ii. (1869). Robinson there writes (Dec. 14, 1831): " I was employed in the afternoon looking over Mr. Rooper's MS. letters belonging to Malone. Some anonymous verses against Dr. Parr were pungent. The concluding lines are not bad as an epigram, though very unjust." Parr was born in 1747, and died in 1825.]

CLII.

ON ANDREWS' "MYSTERIES OF THE CASTLE."

Andrews, 't is said, a comedy has writ,
Replete with novelty, replete with wit;
If wit it has, to both I will agree,
For wit from Andrews must be novelty.
Anon.

[The *Mysteries of the Castle* was a so-called comedy by Miles Peter Andrews, produced in 1795. It was an extraordinary production, and created a sensation—of disgust. The author, Andrews, was a member of parliament, and, as the *Biographia Dramatica* described him, "a dealer in gunpowder, but his works in their effect by no means resemble so active a composition." Among his better known productions are *The Election* and *Better Late than Never*. He died in 1814.]

—o—

CLIII.

ON LAUDER, MACPHERSON, CHATTERTON, AND IRELAND (1796).

Four Forgers, born in one prolific age,
Much critical acumen did engage.
The first was soon by doughty Douglas scar'd,
Though Johnson would have screen'd him, had he dar'd:
The next had all the cunning of a Scot;
The third invention, genius—what not?
Fraud, now exhausted, only could dispense
To her fourth son their threefold impudence.
William Mason (1725–1797).

[The forgeries of Macpherson, Chatterton, and Ireland are well known. Lauder (1710–1771) was the author of an essay, published in 1751, in which he endeavoured to prove that

Milton was largely indebted to classical authors in his *Paradise Lost*. Dr. Johnson took part in the controversy, and wrote a preface to the essay, the general allegations in which were, however, successfully disposed of by Dr. Douglas, afterwards Bishop of Salisbury. Lauder was also guilty of an attempt to convict Milton of "forgery against King Charles I." (1754)—an attempt which failed as thoroughly as its predecessor. Mason's epigram is evidently formed upon Dryden's upon Milton (which see).]

———o———

CLIV.

ON MRS. COWLEY'S "FALL OF SPARTA."

When in your mimic scenes I view'd
Of Sparta's sons the fate severe;
I caught the Spartan fortitude,
And saw their woes without a tear.

Anon.

[Mrs. Hannah Cowley (1749–1809) is less famous as the author of *The Fall of Sparta* than as the author of *The Belle's Stratagem* (1780), *A Bold Stroke for a Husband*, and other plays.]

———o———

CLV.

ON ELPHINSTON'S TRANSLATION OF MARTIAL'S EPIGRAMS.

O thou whom Poetry abhors,
Whom Prose has turnèd out of doors
Heardst thou that groan?—proceed no further;
'T was laurell'd Martial roaring murder.

Robert Burns (1759–1796).

[" I was sitting," wrote Burns to Clarinda (Mrs. Maclehose), "in a merchant's shop of my acquaintance, waiting somebody.

He put Elphinston into my hand, and asked my opinion of it. I begged leave to write it on a blank leaf, which I did." Elphinston (1721-1809) published, besides the translation of Martial, a poem on *Education* and a *Grammar of the English Language.*]

―o―

CLVI.
ON DR. TRAPP'S TRANSLATION OF VIRGIL.

Mind but thy preaching, Trapp; translate no further;
Is it not written, "Thou shalt do no murder?"
Anon.

[From the *Poetical Farrago* (1794). Dr. Trapp's translation of Virgil was in blank verse, and appeared in 1717. The same writer (1679-1747) translated *Paradise Lost* into Latin.]

―o―

CLVII.
ON A BAD TRANSLATION.

His work now done, he'll publish it, no doubt,
For sure I am that murder will come out.
Anon.

―o―

CLVIII.
ON PAINE'S "AGE OF REASON."

In systems as much out of sense as of season,
Tom Paine names this age as the true age of reason;
But if right I can judge, or if right I can see,
It is Treason he means, and he's right to a T.
Anon.

[Thomas Paine (1737-1809) published *The Age of Reason* in 1792.]

CLIX.

ON WILLIAM COBBETT.

In digging up your bones, Tom Paine,
  Will. Cobbett has done well:
You 'll visit him on earth again,
  He 'll visit you in hell.

Lord Byron (1788–1724).

[William Cobbett, editor of *The Political Register*, and perhaps the most powerful political writer of his day, was born in 1762, and died in 1835. After Paine's death, which occurred in America, Cobbett had his bones dug up and taken to England, where they were not received with the rapture and reverence no doubt anticipated.]

CLX.

ON THE RIGHTS OF MINORITIES.

Sturdy Tom Paine, biographers relate,
Once with his friends engaged in warm debate.
Said they, "Minorities are always right;"
Said he, "The truth is just the opposite."
Finding them stubborn, "Frankly, now," asked he,
"In this opinion do ye all agree;
All, every one, without exception?" When
They thus affirmed unanimously,—"Then,
Correct," said he, "my sentiment must be,
For I myself am the minority."

Richard Garnett.

CLXI.

ON THE EARL OF CARLISLE.

Carlisle subscribes a thousand pounds
  Out of his rich domains;
And for a sixpence circles round
  The produce of his brains:
'T is thus the difference you may hit
Between his fortune and his wit.

Lord Byron (1788–1824).

[This was occasioned by the Earl's publication of a pamphlet in favour of small theatres, which appeared on the same day as the announcement of a large subscription by the Earl towards some public purpose. Lord Carlisle was Lord Byron's cousin, and was much disliked by him. The poet, however, became ashamed of his attacks upon his relative, and made the *amende honorable* in *Childe Harold*, Canto III. stanza xxix.]

———o———

CLXII.

ON LORD CARLISLE'S LINES AGAINST LADY HOLLAND'S ACCEPTANCE OF NAPOLEON'S SNUFF-BOX.

Lady, accept the gift a hero wore,
  In spite of all this elegiac stuff,
Nor let seven stanzas written by a bore
  Prevent your Ladyship from taking snuff.

Lord Byron.

[The stanzas referred to begin—
  "Lady, reject the gift—'t is stained with gore."]

CLXIII.

ON THE SAME.

For this her snuff-box to resign !
A pleasant thought enough.
Alas ! my Lord, for verse like thine
Who 'd give a pinch of snuff?
Henry Vassall, Lord Holland (1773-1840).

———o———

CLXIV.

ON LORD BYRON.

"He flatter'd in youth, he lampoon'd in his prime,"
Quoth Memory's bard of our poet :
But the fault was not his,—'t was a deed done by Time,—
My very next stanza shall show it.

Whoever has sported on Tempe's green lawn
Has found out the truth of the matter ;
'T is plain that, by law mythologic, a Faun
In process of time grows a Satyr.
James Smith (1775-1839).

["Memory's Bard" : Samuel Rogers, who published *The Pleasures of Memory* in 1792.]

———o———

CLXV.

ON SHELLEY'S "PROMETHEUS UNBOUND."

Shelley styles his new poem "Prometheus Unbound,"
And 't is like to remain so while time circles round ;
For surely an age would be spent in the finding
A reader so weak as to pay for the binding !
Theodore Edward Hook (1788-1841).

[Shelley's *Prometheus Unbound*, a lyrical drama in four acts, was published in 1819. "Grand as it is," says Stedman, "it is classical only in some of its personages, and in the mythical germ of its conception—a sublime poem, full of absorbing beauty, but antique neither in spirit nor in form."]

---o---

CLXVI.

ON SCOTT'S "FIELD OF WATERLOO."

On Waterloo's ensanguined plain
Lie tens of thousands of the slain;
But none by sabre or by shot
Fell half so flat as Walter Scott.
Thomas, Lord Erskine (1750–1823).

[Scott's poem, *The Field of Waterloo*, was published in 1815, with the following preface, which to a certain extent disarms hostile criticism :—" It may be some apology for the imperfections of this poem, that it was composed hastily, and during a short tour upon the Continent, where the author's labours were liable to frequent interruption; but its best apology is, that it was written for the purpose of assisting the Waterloo subscription." The above epigram is taken from Campbell's *Lives of the Lord Chancellors*. Moore writes in his *Diary* (1815) :—" I have read *Walter*-loo. The battle murdered many, and *he* has murdered the battle : 't is sad stuff."]

---o---

CLXVII.

ON SOUTHEY AS POET LAUREATE.

Our Laureate Bob defrauds the King;—
He takes his cash and will not sing.
Yet on he goes, I know not why,
Singing for us who do not buy.
Henry Vassall, Lord Holland (1773–1840).

[See Moore's *Diary*, under date September 4, 1825:—
"Lord H. full of an epigram he had just written on Southey, which we all twisted and turned into various shapes, he as happy as a boy during the operation." Moore suggests the following as a variation on the concluding couplet:

"And yet for us, who will not buy,
  Goes singing on eternally."

Southey was appointed Poet Laureate in 1813. His Laureate poems, so far from being few, are numerous—too numerous for his fame as a poet, which rests now solely on half a dozen lyrics.]

---o---

CLXVIII.

ON THOMAS MOORE.

When Limerick once, in idle whim,
  Moore, as her member, gaily courted,
The boys, for fun's sake, ask'd of him
  To state what party he supported.

When thus to them the answer ran,—
  At least 'tis thus I've heard the story,—
"I'm of no party as a man,
  But as a poet *am-a-tory.*"

Anon.

["This," says Moore in his *Diary*, "must have been written as far back as the project set on foot for making me member for Limerick." The poet was, of course, a Whig.]

---o---

CLXIX.

ON MOORE'S DUEL WITH LORD JEFFREY.

When Anacreon would fight, as the poets have said,
  A reverse he display'd in his vapour,
For while all his poems were loaded with lead,
  His pistols were loaded with paper.

> For excuses, Anacreon old custom may thank,
> Such a salvo he should not abuse,
> For the cartridge, by rule, is always made blank,
> That is firèd away at *Reviews*.
>
> *Theodore Edward Hook* (1788–1841).

[From Barham's *Life of Hook*. Moore is here called "Anacreon" in allusion to his translations from that poet. The duel was owing to an article in the *Edinburgh Review*, which Moore thought proper to resent by challenging the editor. The combatants were, however, arrested on the ground, and conveyed to Bow Street; where the pistols were found to contain merely a charge of powder, the balls having in some way disappeared! Byron alludes to the circumstance in *English Bards and Scotch Reviewers* :—

> "When Little's leadless pistol met his eye,
> And Bow-Street myrmidons stood laughing by."

It is pleasant to reflect that, after this encounter, the poet and the critic were good friends.]

---o---

CLXX.

ON MOORE'S LAST OPERATIC FARCE, OR FARCICAL OPERA.

> Good plays are scarce,
> So Moore writes farce;
> The poet's fame grows brittle—
> We knew before
> That Little's Moore,
> But now 't is Moore that's little.
>
> *Lord Byron* (1788–1824).

[Written in 1811, but not published till 1830. "Thomas

Little" was the name assumed by Moore in the publication of a volume of erotic poetry in 1801. It was adopted in allusion to the poet's diminutive stature.]

---o---

CLXXI.
ON MOORE'S "LALLA ROOKH."

Lalla Rookh
Is a naughty book,
By Tommy Moore,
Who has written four,
Each warmer
Than the former;
So the most recent
Is the least decent.
Sneyd.

["Young ladies," says Rogers in his *Table Talk*, "read Moore's *Lalla Rookh* without (I presume) being aware of the grossness of 'The Veiled Prophet.'" The poem appeared originally in 1817. "The Veiled Prophet of Khorassan" is the title of one of the four tales in verse included in it. Sneyd, whose Christian name is not recorded, was a man of fashion of the time.]

---o---

CLXXII.
ON LORD JEFFREY SUFFERING FROM A SORE THROAT.

That throat so vex'd by cackle and by cup,
Where wine descends, and endless words come up,—
Much injur'd organ! constant is thy toil;
Spits turn to do thee harm, and coppers boil:
Passion and punch, and toasted cheese and paste,
And all that's said and swallow'd lay thee waste!
Sydney Smith (1771–1845).

[Lord Jeffrey was born in 1773 and died in 1850, having edited *The Edinburgh Review* from 1803 to 1829. See his *Life* by Cockburn (1852).]

---o---

CLXXIII.

ON SEEING MR. (AFTERWARDS LORD) JEFFREY RIDING ON A DONKEY.

Witty as Horatius Flaccus,
As great a Jacobin as Gracchus,
Short, though not as fat, as Bacchus,
Riding on a little Jackass.
Sydney Smith (1771–1845).

[See the *Life of Sydney Smith*, by Lady Holland (1855).]

---o---

CLXXIV.

ON A CRITICISM BY LORD JEFFREY.

What thanks do we owe, what respects and regards,
To Jeffrey, the old nursery-maid of us bards,
Who, resolv'd to the last his vocation to keep,
First whipp'd us all round and now puts us to sleep.
Thomas Moore (1779–1852).

[Moore quotes in his *Diary* the following lines by Jeffrey (1844) :—"The tuneful quartos of Southey are already little better than lumber ; and the rich melodies of Keats and Shelley, and the fantastical emphasis of Wordsworth, and the plebeian pathos of Crabbe, are melting fast from the field of our vision. Even the splendid strains of Moore are fading into dimness and distance," etc.]

CLXXV.

ON THE WORKS OF THE LAKE POETS.

They came from the Lakes—an appropriate quarter
For poems diluted with plenty of water.
Rev. Henry Townshend.

[The title of Lake Poets was given to Wordsworth, Southey, and Coleridge (it is believed, by Lord Jeffrey), in allusion to the residence of those writers by or near the lakes of Cumberland and Westmoreland.]

CLXXVI.

ON SAMUEL ROGERS.

So well deserv'd is Rogers' fame,
That friends, who hear him most, advise
The egotist to change his name
To Argus, with his hundred "I"s!
Anon.

[Rogers was a fluent and cultured conversationalist, and his *Table Talk* (1856) ranks next to Coleridge's in point of interest.]

CLXXVII.

ON ROGERS'S "ITALY."

Of Rogers's "Italy," Luttrell relates,
'T would sure have been dish'd if 't were not for the plates!
Marguerite, Countess Blessington (1789-1849).

[*Italy* appeared in 1822, beautifully illustrated; hence the above lines, which are a mere versification of a *mot* by Luttrell.]

CLXXVIII.

ROGERS TO MOORE,

On hearing that Lord Lauderdale had "Human Life" by Heart.

"I'm told, dear Moore, your lays are sung
  (Can it be true, you lucky man?)
By moonlight, in the Persian tongue,
  Along the streets of Ispahan.

"'T is hard; but one reflection cures,
  At once, a jealous poet's smart :
The Persians have translated yours,
  But Lauderdale has mine by heart."

Henry Luttrell (1770–1851).

[*Human Life* was published in 1819. It is quite true that *Lalla Rookh* was translated into Persian.]

———o———

CLXXIX.

ON READING A DIARY LATELY PUBLISHED.

That flesh is grass is now as clear as day,
  To any but the merest purblind pup;
Death cuts it down, and then, to make her hay,
  My Lady Bury comes and rakes it up.

Thomas Hood (1798–1845).

[Lady Charlotte Bury's *Diary, illustrative of the Times of George IV.,* appeared in 1838.]

CLXXX.

ON THE SAME.

When I resign this world so briary,
  To have across the Styx my ferrying;
Oh, may I die without a Diary!
And be interr'd without a Bury-ing!

Thomas Hood (1798–1845).

———o———

CLXXXI.

ON THE SAME.

The poor dear dead have been laid out in vain;
Turn'd into cash, they are laid out again!

Thomas Hood.

———o———

CLXXXII.

ON "WHO WROTE EIKON BASILIKE?"

"Who Wrote Eikon Basilike?"
"I," said the Master of Trinity,
"I, with my little divinity,
Wrote 'Who Wrote Eikon Basilike?'"

Richard Whately (1787–1863).

[The Master of Trinity referred to was Dr. Christopher Wordsworth, father of the present Bishops of Lincoln and St. Andrews.]

CLXXXIII.

ON SAMUEL WARREN,

Author of " Ten Thousand a Year," " Now and Then," and other Novels.

Samuel Warren, though able, yet vainest of men,
Could he guide with discretion his tongue and his pen,
His course would be clear for—" Ten Thousand a Year,"
But limited else to a brief—" Now and Then."

Sir George Rose.

[Some amusing stories are told of Warren's vanity. He was born in 1807, and died in 1877, his best work being, perhaps, that which is not mentioned by Sir George—*Passages from the Diary of a Late Physician* (1837). *Ten Thousand a Year* appeared in 1841, *Now and Then* in 1847.]

---o---

CLXXXIV.

ON MR. FROUDE AND CANON KINGSLEY.

Froude informs the Scottish youth
Parsons have small regard for truth ;
The Reverend Canon Kingsley cries
That History is a pack of lies.
What cause for judgments so malign ?
  A brief reflection solves the mystery :
Froude believes Kingsley a divine,
  And Kingsley goes to Froude for history.

Anon.

[Written, of course, before the death of Canon Kingsley in 1875. It is attributed to a well-known and highly esteemed Professor. The allusion in the first two lines is to Mr Froude's address to the students of St. Andrews.]

CLXXXV.

ON HARRISON AINSWORTH.

Says Ainsworth to Colburn—
" A plan in my pate is
To give my romance as
A supplement, gratis."

Says Colburn to Ainsworth—
" 'T will do very nicely,
For that will be charging
Its value precisely."
Anon.

[From *Punch*. William Harrison Ainsworth was born in 1805, and has published over thirty romances. Colburn was the publisher of the magazine in which so many of Ainsworth's novels originally appeared.]

———o———

CLXXXVI.

AGAINST WRITERS WHO CARP AT OTHER MEN'S BOOKS.

The readers and the hearers like my books,
But yet some writers cannot them digest:
Yet what care I? for, when I make a feast,
I would my guests should praise it, not my cooks.
Sir John Haryngton (1561–1612).

———o———

CLXXXVII.
ON A CERTAIN THUSCUS.

Thuscus writes fair, without blur or blot,
The rascal'st rhymes were ever read, God wot.
No marvel: many with a swan's quill write,
That can but with a goose's quill endite.

Thomas Freeman (circa 1591–1614).

[Freeman is here supposed to allude to one John Davies of Hereford, more famous in his day as a writing-master than as a poet.]

---o---

CLXXXVIII.
TO A BAD AUTHOR.

Half your book is to an Index grown;
You give your book contents, your readers none.

Pyne (circa 1616).

---o---

CLXXXIX.
ON A CERTAIN PHILO.

While faster than his costive brain indites,
Philo's quick hand in flowing letters writes;
His case appears to me like honest Teague's,
When he was run away with by his legs.
Phœbus, give Philo o'er himself command;
Quicken his senses or restrain his hand;
Let him be kept from paper, pen, and ink;
So he may cease to write, and learn to think.

Matthew Prior (1664–1721).

CXC.

ON A FINE LIBRARY.

With eyes of wonder the gay shelves behold,
Poets, all rags alive, now clad in gold.
In life and death one common fate they share,
And on their backs still all their riches wear.

Anon.

[From *A Collection of Epigrams* (1727).]

---o---

CXCI.

ON A CERTAIN POET.

Thy verses are eternal, O my friend,
For he that reads them reads them to no end.

Anon.

[From *A Collection of Epigrams* (1727).]

---o---

CXCII.

ON ONE SCRIBBLETONIUS.

Scribbletonius, thy volumes, whene'er we peruse,
  This idea they always instil;—
That you pilfer'd, felonious, the brains of a goose,
  When you robb'd the poor bird of a quill.

Anon.

[From *An Asylum for Fugitive Pieces* (1785).]

CXCIII.

TO GIBBS, CONCERNING HIS POEMS.

You ask me if I think your poems good;
If I could praise your poems, Gibbs,—I would.

Egerton Webbe.

[From the *London Journal*, to which Webbe contributed several similar parodies on Martial's epigrams. See Leigh Hunt's *Autobiography*.]

CXCIV.

ON A BAD POEM.

Your poem must eternal be,—
Dear Sir, it cannot fail;
For 't is incomprehensible,
And wants both head and tale.

Samuel Taylor Coleridge (1772–1834).

CXCV.

ON A SQUINTING POETESS.

To no one Muse does she her glance confine,
But has an eye, at once, to all the Nine!

Thomas Moore (1779–1852).

CXCVI.
ON ONE WHO WOULD FAIN WRITE AN EPIGRAM.

Fired with the thirst of Fame, thus honest Sam:
" I will arise and write an epigram."
An epic, Sam, more glorious still would be,
And much more easily achieved by thee.

Richard Garnett.

CXCVII.
ON DIDACTICS IN POETRY.

Parnassus' peaks still catch the sun;
But why—O lyric brother!—
Why build a Pulpit on the one,
A Platform on the other?

Austin Dobson.

[From "A Note on Some Foreign Forms of Verse" in *Latter-Day Lyrics* (1878). It is perhaps hardly necessary to remind the reader that Mount Parnassus is twi-peaked.]

CXCVIII.
ON MODEST MOORE.

Moore always smiles whenever he recites;
He smiles, you think, approving what he writes?
And yet in this no vanity is shown:
A modest man may like what's not his own.

Anon.

[From *Elegant Extracts* (1805).]

CXCIX.

ON A PLAGIARIST.

A Duke once declared, and most solemnly too,
That whatever he liked with his own he would do.
But the son of a Duke has gone farther, and shown
He will do what he likes with what isn't his own.

Anon.

[From *Punch*.]

CC.

ON SOME VERSES CALLED TRIFLES.

Paul, I have read your book, and, though you write ill,
I needs must praise your most judicious title !

Anon.

BOOK III.

The Church and the Clergy—Universities and Scholars.

THE CHURCH AND THE CLERGY.

CCI.
A Court Audience.

Old South, a witty Churchman reckon'd,
Was preaching once to Charles the Second,
But much too serious for a Court,
Who at all preaching made a sport.
He soon perceiv'd his audience nod,
Deaf to the zealous man of God.
The Doctor stopp'd; began to call,
"Pray wake the Earl of Lauderdale:
My lord! why 'tis a monstrous thing!
You snore so loud, you'll wake the king!"

Richard Graves (1715–1804).

[An old story versified. Robert South (1633–1716) was one of the most famous of our old preachers. See his *Sermons* (1823, 1843, 1850).]

CCII.

ON DR. SHERLOCK THE ELDER.

The same allegiance to two kings he pays,
Swears the same faith to both, and both betrays.
No wonder if to swear he's always free,
Who has two Gods to swear by more than we.

Thomas Brown (d. 1704).

[This alludes to Sherlock's desertion of the cause of James II. for that of William III., and to his views on the subject of the Trinity, the unity of which he to some extent denied, with the result of intensifying the separate individuality of the Three Persons. Sherlock the younger emulated his father's conduct, preaching a revolutionary sermon on the Sunday immediately following upon the battle of Preston. Hence the following epigram.]

—o—

CCIII.

ON BOTH DOCTORS SHERLOCK.

As Sherlock the elder with his jure divine
Did not comply 'till the Battle of Boyne,
So Sherlock the younger still made it a question
Which side he would take 'till the Battle of Preston.

Anon.

[Dr. William Sherlock (1641–1707) published his *Vindication of the Doctrine of the Trinity* in 1690, and it was replied to by South in some *Animadversions* published in 1693, and in his *Tritheism charged on Dr. Sherlock's New Notion of the Trinity* (1695). The younger Sherlock was Bishop of London (1678–1761).]

CCIV.

ON BISHOP BURNET.

If heaven is pleased when sinners cease to sin,
If hell is pleased when sinners enter in,
If men are pleased at parting with a knave,
Then all are pleased—for Burnet's in his grave.

Anon.

[Burnet died in 1715. Dryden described him in *The Hind and the Panther* as

"A theologue more by need than genial bent,
By breeding sharp, by nature confident;
Interest in all his actions was discern'd—
More learn'd than honest, more a wit than learn'd."

See Book II., No. CXL.]

—o—

CCV.

ON A PICTURE OF JUDAS, PAINTED TO RESEMBLE BISHOP KENNET.

To say the picture does to him belong,
Kennet does Judas and the painter wrong.
False is the image, the resemblance faint;
Judas compar'd to Kennet was a saint.

Anon.

[See Nichols' *Literary Anecdotes*. Bishop Kennet (1660-1728), at that time Dean of Peterborough, offended the Tory and Church party by the support he accorded to the Whigs, and one London clergyman actually had an altar-piece placed in his church in which Judas was so represented as greatly to resemble the unfortunate prelate. Besides the above, Bishop Atterbury is said to have written a Latin epigram on the same subject, the English version of which runs :—

> "Think not that here *thou* art represented;
> Thou 'rt not like Judas, for *he* repented."]

---o---

CCVI.
ON BISHOP ATTERBURY'S BURYING THE DUKE OF BUCKINGHAMSHIRE (1720).

"I have no hope," the Duke he says, and dies;
"In sure and certain hope," the prelate cries :
Of these two learned peers, I prithee say, man,
Who is the lying knave, the priest or layman?
The Duke he stands an infidel confest;
"He's our dear brother," quoth the lordly priest.
The Duke, tho' knave, still "brother dear" he cries;
And who can say, the reverend prelate lies?

Matthew Prior (1664-1721).

[John Sheffield, Duke of Buckinghamshire, died in 1720. Johnson wrote of him : "His religion he may be supposed to have learned from Hobbes, and his morality was such as naturally proceeds from loose opinions."]

---o---

CCVII.
ON BISHOP ATTERBURY'S SERMONS.

When Willis of Ephraim heard Rochester preach,
  Thus Bentley said to him, "I prithee, dear brother,
How lik'st thou this sermon? 't is out of my reach."
  "His is one way," said Willis, "and ours is another:
I care not for carping, but this I can tell,
  We preach very sadly, if he preaches well."

Matthew Prior.

[This is another result of Prior's enmity to Atterbury, who is meant, of course, by "Rochester;" Willis was Bishop of Gloucester.]

---o---

CCVIII.

ON BISHOP ATTERBURY.

Meek Francis lies here, friend : without stop or stay,
As you value your peace, make the best of your way.
Though at present arrested by Death's caitiff paw,
If he stirs, he may still have recourse to the law.
And in the King's Bench should a verdict be found,
That by livery and seisin his grave is his ground,
He will claim to himself what is strictly his due,
And an action for trespass will straightway ensue,
That you without right on his premises tread,
On a simple surmise that the owner is dead.

Matthew Prior (1664–1721).

[The Bishop appears to have taken very kindly this severe reflection on his fondness for litigation. Writing to Pope in 1721, he says : " I had not strength enough to attend Mr. Prior to his grave, else would I have done it, to have shew'd his friends that I had forgot and forgiven what he wrote on me." The lines themselves may, Dodd thinks, have been suggested by an epigram on Hipponax the satirist by Leonidas of Tarentum.]

---o---

CCIX.

ON ARCHBISHOP POTTER.

Alack, and well-a-day,
Potter himself is turned to clay.

Anon.

[John Potter, Archbishop of Canterbury from 1737 to 1747, was the author of *Antiquities of Greece*, a *Discourse on Church Government*, and other works (1753). He died in 1747]

CCX.

LINES WRITTEN IN EVELYN'S BOOK ON COINS.

Tom Wood of Chiswick, deep divine,
To Painter Kent gave all this coin:
'T is the first coin, I 'm bold to say,
That ever churchman gave to lay.

Alexander Pope (1688–1744).

[The book referred to is Evelyn's *Numismata: a Discourse of Medals*.]

CCXI.

TO MR. THOMAS STERNHOLD, ON THE KING'S OFFERING.

From ancient custom 't is (they say)
  Our most religious King
Does annually upon Twelfth Day
  Unto the altar bring
Gold, myrrh, and frankincense—I mean
  They do devolve by right,
Unto the royal chapel's dean,
  A certain perquisite.
Now, what I 'd know is this,—pray tell,
  In your opinion, sir,
Which to the dean does sweetest smell,
  Gold, frankincense, or myrrh?

John Hopkins (b. about 1525).

[From *The Honeysuckle* (1734). Thomas Sternhold (d. 1549) is celebrated as the co-translator with Hopkins of the Psalms of David into English metre. Campbell says of these two writers, that "mistaking vulgarity for simplicity, they turned into bathos what they found sublime."]

CCXII.

ON SEEING A WORTHY PRELATE GO OUT OF CHURCH IN TIME OF DIVINE SERVICE, TO WAIT ON THE DUKE OF DORSET ON HIS COMING TO TOWN.

Lord Pam in the church (could you think it?) kneel'd down.
When told that the Duke was just come to town—
His station despising, unaw'd by the place,
He flies from his God to attend on his Grace.
To the Court it was fitter to pay his devotion,
Since God had no hand in his Lordship's promotion.
Jonathan Swift (1667–1745).

["Lord Pam" was Josiah Harte, Bishop of Kilmore, and afterwards Archbishop of Tuam.]

CCXIII.

ON ONE TOPHET.

Thus Tophet look'd; so grinn'd the brawling fiend,
Whilst frighted prelates bow'd and call'd him friend.
Our mother-church, with half-averted sight,
Blush'd as she bless'd her grisly proselyte;
Hosannas rung through hell's tremendous borders,
And Satan's self had thoughts of taking orders.
Thomas Gray (1716–1771).

[The cleric here characterized was the Rev. Henry Etough, of Pembroke Hall, Cambridge, of whom an account is given in *The Gentleman's Magazine*, vol. 56. He is there described as "an ecclesiastical phenomenon and a most eccentric dangerous character." Originally a Scotch presbyterian, he obtained admission to the Church of England, and was preferred by Walpole. "Odd was his figure," says his biographer, "and mean and nasty his apparel."]

---o---

CCXIV.

ON DR. SECKER, ARCHBISHOP OF CANTERBURY (1758).

The bench hath oft 'posed us, and set us a-scoffing,
By signing "Will. London," "John Sarum," "John Roffen";
But *this* head of the Church no expounder will want,
For his Grace signs his own proper name—Thomas *Cant*.

Horace Walpole, Earl of Orford (1717-1797).

["Cant." is, of course, an abbreviation of Cantuaria, the Latin name of the diocese of Canterbury. Dr. Moore was the first of Dr. Secker's successors who altered the signature to that now adopted, viz. "Cantuar." Thomas Secker was Archbishop of Canterbury from 1758 to 1768. His *Life* was written by Bishop Porteous.]

---o---

CCXV.

ON BISHOP BARRINGTON OF SALISBURY, AND BARRINGTON THE PICKPOCKET.

Two of a name—both great in their way—
 At Court lately well did bestir 'em;
The one was transported to Botany Bay,
 The other translated to Durham.

Anon.

The Church and the Clergy.

[Bishop Barrington was appointed to Durham in 1791, about the same time that his namesake was sentenced for stealing a snuff-box at a levée. The latter was the author of the well-known lines,—

> True patriots all—for, be it understood,
> We left our country for our country's good—

which formed part of an address delivered at the opening of the Sydney Theatre.]

CCXVI.

ON AN INN, WITH THE SIGN OF BISHOP BLAIZE, BEING PULLED DOWN, TO MAKE WAY FOR THAT OF BISHOP WATSON OF LLANDAFF.

> "Two trades can ne'er agree"—
> No proverb e'er was juster—
> For Bishop Blaize pull'd down we see
> To put up Bishop Bluster.
>
> *Anon.*

[From *The Mirror*. Richard Watson, Bishop of Llandaff (1737-1816), was the author of an *Apology for the Bible*.]

CCXVII.

ON DEANS JACKSON AND WETHERALL.

> As Cyril and Nathan were walking by Queen's,
> Said Nathan to Cyril, "We're both of us Deans,
> And both of us Bishops may be:"
> Said Cyril to Nathan, "I certainly shall
> Stay here to look after my little *canal*,
> And *you* may look after the *see*."
>
> *Anon.*

[By "Cyril" is meant Cyril Jackson, Dean of Christchurch, who had promoted and purchased shares in the Oxford Canal, and was known to have declined the offer of a bishopric. "Nathan" was Nathan Wetherall, Master of University College, and Dean of Hereford.]

---o---

CCXVIII.

On Dr. Dent.

If on penitence bent, you want to keep Lent,
Just go to the Foundling, and hear Dr. Dent,
And I'll be damn'd for you, if you don't repent.

Anon.

[From Moore's *Diary*, under date September 1818. Moore calls it "an admirable epigram."]

---o---

CCXIX.

On the Appointment of Cardinal Wiseman by Pope Pius to the Titular Archbishopric of Westminster.

Pius with Wiseman tries
  Our English Church to ban;
O Pius, man unwise!
  O impious Wiseman!

Dr. Robert Scott.

[This was originally written in Latin—

Cum sapiente Pius nostras juravit in aras;
Impius heu! sapiens, desipiensque Pius!—

from which it was translated into English by the author.]

CCXX.

ON THE PROSECUTION OF BISHOP HAMPDEN FOR HERESY (1848).

As once the Pope with fury full,
   When Luther laid his heavy knocks on,
At the Reformer loosed a Bull;—
   So these at Hampden set an Ox-on.

Anon.

[From *Punch.* Dr. Renn Dickson Hampden, Bishop of Hereford (1793-1868), was accused of heresy by the High Church party, headed by the Bishop of Oxford. His most important work was on *The Philosophical Evidences of Christianity* (1827).]

CCXXI.

ON ARCHDEACON HALE AND THE CHURCHYARD CONTROVERSY.

The intramural churchyard's reeking pale
   Breathes health around it, says a reverend party;
But though the spot may keep a parson Hale,
   Can people who in-hale its fumes be hearty?

Anon.

[From *Punch.*]

CCXXII.

ON A PART OF ST. MARY'S CHURCH AT OXFORD BEING CONVERTED INTO A LAW SCHOOL.

Yes, yes, you may rail at the Pope as you please,
But trust me, that miracles never will cease.

See here—an event that no mortal suspected!
See Law and Divinity closely connected!
Which proves the old proverb, long reckon'd so odd,
That the nearer the church the farther from God.
Anon.

CCXXIII.
NE SUTOR ULTRA CREPIDAM.

A cobbler and a curate once disputed,
　Before a judge about the King's injunctions;
Wherein the curate being still confuted,
　One said 't were good if they two changèd functions.
"Nay," quoth the judge, " I thereto should be loth,
But an you will, we'll make them cobblers both."
Henry Parrot (about 1613).

CCXXIV.
ON PARSON BEANS.

Old Parson Beans hunts six days of the week,
And on the seventh has his notes to seek:
Six days a week he holloas so much breath away,
That on the seventh he can nor preach nor pray.
Robert Herrick (1591–1674).

CCXXV.
ON MARRIAGES IN HEAVEN.

Cries Sylvia to a reverend Dean,
　"What reason can be given,
Since marriage is a holy thing,
　That there is none in heaven?"

"There are no women," he replies.
She quick returns the jest:—
"Women there are, but I'm afraid
They cannot find a priest."
Robert Dodsley (1703–1764).

[So Butler, in his *Hudibras*, part III. canto i. :—
"Quoth she, there are no bargains driv'n,
Nor marriages clapp'd up in heav'n;
And that's the reason, as some guess,
There is no heav'n in marriages."]

—o—

CCXXVI.
ON A CERTAIN QUACK.

Paulus, the famous quack, renown'd afar,
For killing more than pestilence or war,
Of late, in orders, is a curate made,
And buries people—not to change his trade.
Anon.
[From *A Collection of Epigrams* (1727).]

—o—

CCXXVII.
DIALOGUE BETWEEN AN OLD INCUMBENT AND THE PERSON PROMISED THE NEXT PRESENTATION.

"I'm glad to see you well."—"O faithless breath!
What! glad to see me well, and wish my death?"—
"No more," replies the youth, "Sir, this misgiving;
I wish not for your death, but for your living."
Anon.
[From *A Collection of Epigrams* (1727).]

CCXXVIII.

ON A CERTAIN PREACHER.

The preacher Maurus cries, "All evil is vain,"
Unless 't is like his godliness, for gain;
Of most vain things he may the folly own,
But wit's a vanity he has not known.

Anon.

[From *A Collection of Epigrams* (1727).]

---o---

CCXXIX.

WRITTEN ON A WINDOW AT CHESTER.

The church and clergy here, no doubt,
　Are very near akin;
Both weather-beaten are without,
　And empty both within.

Jonathan Swift (1667–1745).

---o---

CCXXX.

ON A CERTAIN PARSON.

By purchase a man's property is known:
Scarf's sermons and his livings are his own.

Anon.

[From *Epigrams in Distich* (1740).]

The Church and the Clergy.

CCXXXI.

The Peers and the Ploughboy.

John Trott was desir'd by two witty peers,
To tell them the reason why asses had ears?
"An 't please you," quoth John, "I'm not given to letters,
Nor dare I pretend to know more than my betters;
Howe'er, from this time I shall ne'er see your graces,
As I hope to be sav'd! without thinking of asses."

Oliver Goldsmith (1728–1774).

[A very similar witticism is said to have been uttered by Spratt, Bishop of Rochester, whilst chaplain to the Duke of Buckingham.]

—o—

CCXXXII.

On a Dull Preacher.

Though a railroad, learnèd Rector,
  Passes near your parish spire,
Think not, Sir, your Sunday lecture
  E'er will overwhelmed expire.

Put not then your hopes in weepers;
  Solid work my road secures;
Preach whate'er you will—my "sleepers"
  Never will awaken yours.

James Smith (1775–1839).

[These were the last lines ever written by the author of *Rejected Addresses*.]

CCXXXIII.
ON HEARING A LADY PRAISE A CERTAIN REV. DOCTOR'S EYES.

I cannot praise the Doctor's eyes;
I never saw his glance divine;
He always shuts them when he prays,
And when he preaches he shuts mine.

George Outram (1805–1856).

CCXXXIV.
ON A BAD SERMON, FROM THE TEXT "WATCH AND PRAY."

When each points out a different way,
What mediums shall we keep?
The text invites to watch and pray,
The priest himself, to sleep.

T. Russell.

CCXXXV.
ON THE ATHANASIAN CREED.

Creed of St. Athanasius? No, indeed.
Call it, good priests, the Anathemasian Creed.

Charles Shirley Brooks (1815–1874).

[From *Punch*.]

CCXXXVI.

"Ἄλλος ἄλλο λέγει.

And which is right? who knows? Do you?
  For me, I'm sore perplex'd;
The last one proved his doctrine true:—
  And so, too, will the next!

Samuel Waddington.

---o---

CCXXXVII.

ON DIVISION OF LABOUR.

A parson, of too free a life,
  Was yet renown'd for noble preaching,
And many grieved to see such strife
  Between his living and his teaching.

His flock at last rebellious grew:
  "My friends," he said, "the simple fact is,
Nor you nor I can both things do:—
  But I can preach—and you can practise."

Anon.

---o---

CCXXXVIII.

ON PARSONS VERSUS DOCTORS.

How D.D. swaggers—M.D. rolls!
  I dub them both a brace of noddies:
Old D.D. takes the cure of souls,
  And M.D. takes the cure of bodies.

Between them both what treatment rare
  Our souls and bodies must endure!
One takes the cure without the care,
  T'other the care without the cure.

Anon.

CCXXXIX.

ON THE LONG SERMON OF A CERTAIN BISHOP.

When he holds forth, his reverence doth appear
  So lengthily his subject to pursue,
That listeners, out of patience, often fear
  He has indeed eternity in view.

Anon.

CCXL.

ON A RECENT ROBBERY.

They came and stole my garments,
  My stockings, all my store,
But they could not steal my sermons,
  For they were stolen before.

Rev. Henry Townshend.

CCXLI.

ON A PARSON COMPLAINING HE HAD LOST HIS PORTMANTEAU.

"I've lost my portmanteau;"
  I pity your grief.
"All my sermons are in it;"
  I pity the thief.

Anon.

CCXLII.
LENT AND BORROWED.

To the Church I once went,
  But I grieved and I sorrow'd;
For the season was Lent,
  And the sermon was borrow'd.

Anon.

CCXLIII.
ON THE PARSON OF A COUNTRY PARISH.

Come let us rejoice, merry hearts, at his fall;
For egad, had he lived, he'd have buried us all!

Anon.

UNIVERSITIES AND SCHOLARS.

CCXLIV.
ON DR. TADLOW.

Ten thousand tailors, with their length of line,
Strove, though in vain, his compass to confine;
At length, bewailing their exhausted store,
Their packthread ceas'd, and parchment was no more.

Dr. Abel Evans (about 1699).

[From Nichols' *Select Collection of Poems* (1780). Dr. Tadlow was an Oxford Fellow, and remarkable for his obesity, which drew down upon him countless epigrams. Of these the following is one of the best.]

CCXLV.
ON THE SAME.

When Tadlow walks the streets, the paviours cry
"God bless you, sir!" and lay their rammers by.

Anon.

[This is probably by Evans also. Compare it with the following.]

———o———

CCXLVI.
ON A VERY FAT MAN.

The paviours bless his steps where'er they come:
Chairmen dismay'd fly the approaching doom.

Anon.

[From *Epigrams in Distich* (1740).]

———o———

CCXLVII.
ON DR. EVANS,

Bursar of St. John's College, Oxford, Cutting Down a Row of Trees.

Indulgent Nature on each kind bestows
A secret instinct to discern its foes:
The goose, a silly bird, avoids the fox;
Lambs fly from wolves; and sailors steer from rocks.
Evans the gallows as his fate foresees,
And bears the like antipathy to trees.

Anon.

[For a reference to Dr. Evans, see "Notices of the Epigrammatists." The above epigram has been frequently applied to others than Dr. Evans, for whom, however, it was certainly intended originally.]

CCXLVIII.
ON A REGIMENT BEING SENT TO OXFORD, AND A PRESENT OF BOOKS TO CAMBRIDGE, BY GEORGE I. (1715).

The King, observing with judicious eyes,
The state of both his universities,
To Oxford sent a troop of horse; and why?
That learnèd body wanted loyalty:
To Cambridge books he sent, as well discerning
How much that loyal body wanted learning.

Dr. Joseph Trapp (1679–1747).

[From Nichols' *Literary Anecdotes*.]

—o—

CCXLIX.
EXTEMPORE REPLY TO THE ABOVE.

The King to Oxford sent a troop of horse,
For Tories own no argument but force;
With equal skill to Cambridge books he sent,
For Whigs admit no force but argument.

Sir William Browne.

[Dr. Johnson called this one of the happiest extemporaneous productions he had ever met with.]

—o—

CCL.
ON DR. JOWETT, FELLOW OF ST. JOHN'S, CAMBRIDGE.

A little garden little Jowett made,
And fenced it with a little palisade;
A little taste hath little Dr. Jowett;
This little garden doth a little show it.

Richard Porson (1759–1808).

[There is a longer version of this *jeu d'esprit:*—

> A little garden little Jowett made,
> And fenced it with a little palisade ;
> Because this garden made a little talk,
> He changed it to a little gravel walk :
> And now, if more you'd know of little Jowett,
> A little time, it will a little show it.

See the *Life of Richard Porson*, by J. Selby Watson (1861).]

CCLI.
ON A FELLOW OF TRINITY COLLEGE.

Here lies a Doctor of Divinity,
Who was a Fellow too of Trinity;
He knew as much about Divinity
As other Fellows do of Trinity.

Richard Porson (1759–1808).

CCLII.
ON FOOTMAN TOM AND DR. TOE.

'Twixt Footman Tom and Dr. Toe
  A rivalship befell,
Which should become the fav'rite beau,
  And bear away the belle.

The footman won the lady's heart ;
  And who can wonder ? No man:
The whole prevail'd against the part—
  'T was Foot-man versus Toe-man.

Reginald Heber (1783–1826).

["There are, doubtless," says the author of the *Life of R. D. Barham*, "many Oxford men yet living [1870] who can remember 'Doctor Toe,' as from a peculiarity of his gait he was nicknamed, the Dean of Brasenose, and the hero of Reginald Heber's *Whippiad*. Jilted in love, deserted by his affianced bride, who ran off with her father's footman, the unfortunate Doctor formed the subject of a number of University squibs."]

—o—

CCLIII.
ON THE SAME.

Dear lady, think it no reproach—
It show'd you lov'd the more,
To take poor Thomas in the coach,
Who rode behind before.
Anon.

[Another version of this runs—

Dear lady, think it no reproach,—
It show'd a generous mind,
To take poor Thomas in the coach,
Who rode before behind.]

—o—

CCLIV.
ON A MR. SHEEPSHANKS WRITING "SATYRS" FOR "SATIRES."

The satyrs of old were satyrs of note,
With the head of a man, and the shanks of a goat;
But the satyrs of Jesus these satyrs surpass,
With the shanks of a sheep and the head of an ass.
Anon.

[Sheepshanks was a tutor of Jesus College, Cambridge, and the epigram was written by a University wit (circa 1814).]

CCLV.

ON AN EXAMINER NAMED SHELFORD, FAMOUS FOR
"PLUCKING" CANDIDATES.

I've seen a man pluck geese on Shelford fen,
And now I've seen a Shelford goose pluck men.

Anon.

[Shelford Fen is near Cambridge, in the University of which Shelford (of Corpus) was public examiner in 1821.]

———o———

CCLVI.

ON OXFORD FEES FOR DEGREES.

When Alma Mater her kind heart enlarges,
Charges her graduates, graduates her charges,
What safer rule could guide the accountant's pen
Than that of doubling fees for Dublin men?

Henry Longueville Mansel (1820–1871).

[This was written at a time when Oxford degrees were much sought after by the graduates of Trinity College, Dublin, who were charged double the usual fees.]

———o———

CCLVII.

ON A PROPOSAL TO LOWER THE CHARGES FOR DEGREES
OBTAINED BY ACCUMULATION.

Oxford, beware of over-cheap degrees,
Nor lower too much accumulators' fees;
Lest unlike Goldsmith's "land to ills a prey,"
"Men" should "accumulate," and "wealth" "decay."

Henry Longueville Mansel.

["Accumulation" is the process by which two degrees are taken, the one immediately after the other. The allusion to Goldsmith's lines refers to a passage in *The Traveller*.]

CCLVIII.

ON GIVING DEGREES FOR THESES.

When Rusticus from Watercresses
Comes to Oxford with his theses,
Is 't safe the hood to give away
To an A double S for a double S A?

Henry Longueville Mansel (1820–1871).

CCLIX.

ON A DISTINGUISHED OFFICER DECLINING THE OXFORD HONORARY DEGREE OF D.C.L., ON ACCOUNT OF THE HEAVY FEES THEN DEMANDED.

"Oxford, no doubt you wish me well,
 But, prithee let me be;
I can't, alas! be D.C.L.,
 Because of L. S. D."

Henry Longueville Mansel.

CCLX.

THE COURTIER AND THE SCHOLAR.

A haughty courtier, meeting in the streets
A scholar, him thus insolently greets:
"Base men to take the wall I ne'er permit;"
The scholar said, "I do," and gave him it.

Anon.

[From *Elegant Extracts* (1805).]

CCLXI.

PROPOSED VALENTINE FOR A GREEK PROFESSOR OF GREAT LEARNING BUT ROUGH MANNERS.

Thou great descendant of the critic line,
　True lineal child of Bentley, Brunck, and Porson,
Forgive my sending you this Valentine—
　It is but coupling Valentine with Orson.

Anon.

CCLXII.

BY A STUDENT, ON BEING PUT OUT OF COMMONS FOR MISSING CHAPEL.

"To fast and pray we are by Scripture taught:
Oh, could I do but either as I ought!
In both, alas! I err; my frailty such—
I pray too little, and I fast too much."

Anon.

CCLXIII.

ON THE MARRIAGE OF A FELLOW OF ALL SOULS' COLLEGE.

Silvio, so strangely love his mind controls,
Has, for one single body, left All Souls.
Anon.

—o—

CCLXIV.

ON THE UNIVERSITIES.

No wonder that Oxford and Cambridge profound
In learning and science so greatly abound;
Since some carry thither a little each day,
And we meet with so few who bring any away.
Anon.

BOOK IV.

On Medicine and Doctors—Law and Lawyers.

MEDICINE AND DOCTORS.

CCLXV.
ON A DISPUTE BETWEEN DR. RADCLIFFE AND SIR GODFREY KNELLER.

Sir Godfrey and Radcliffe had one common way
Into one common garden—and each had a key.
Quoth Kneller,—" I'll certainly stop up that door,
If ever I find it unlock'd any more."
"Your threats," replies Radcliffe, " disturb not my ease,
And so you don't paint it, e'en do what you please."
"You're smart," rejoins Kneller, " but say what you will,—
I'll take anything from you—but potion or pill."

Anon.

[The Dr. Radcliffe here referred to is the Radcliffe satirized by Prior in the following well-known epigram. He was born in 1650 and died in 1714. He founded the Radcliffe Library at Oxford. Sir Godfrey Kneller, the painter, died in 1723.]

CCLXVI.

THE REMEDY WORSE THAN THE DISEASE.

I sent for Radcliffe : was so ill
    That other doctors gave me over ;
He felt my pulse, prescrib'd a pill,
    And I was likely to recover.

But when the wit began to wheeze,
    And wine had warm'd the politician,
Cur'd yesterday of my disease,
    I died last night of my physician.

Matthew Prior (1664–1721).

---o---

CCLXVII.

ON THE DEATH OF POPE.

Dunces, rejoice ; forgive all censures past,
The greatest dunce has kill'd your foe at last.

Dr. Burton.

[This epigram has often been attributed to Pope, who is said to have made it on his death-bed, and to have requested that it should be added to future editions of *The Dunciad*. There seems no doubt, however, that it was directed by Burton against the doctor (Thompson) who was associated with him in attendance on the poet during his last illness, and of whose treatment he disapproved. See Archbishop Hering's *Letters to William Duncombe* (1777), where the following is given in answer to the above.]

CCLXVIII.

ON THE ABOVE.

As both physic and verse to Phœbus belong,
So the College oft dabble in potion and song;
Hence, Burton, resolv'd his emetics shall hit,
When his recipe fails, gives a puke to his wit.

Anon.

CCLXIX.

ON DR. MEAD.

Mead's not dead, then, you say; only sleeping a little—
Why, egad! sir, you've hit it off there in a tittle.
Yet, friend, his awaking I very much doubt,
Pluto knows who he's got, and will ne'er let him out.

Anon.

[From Hackett's *Select Epigrams* (1757). Mead was a celebrated physician during the reigns of George I. and II.]

CCLXX.

ON THE MALVERN WATERS.

Those waters, so famed by the great Dr. Wall,
Consist in containing just nothing at all.

Anon.

[Dr. Wall was a well-known practitioner who, in the eighteenth century, wrote a treatise in description of the Malvern Waters.]

CCLXXI.
On George the Fourth's Physicians.

The king employ'd three doctors daily,
Willis, Heberden, and Baillie;
All exceeding clever men,
Baillie, Willis, Heberden;
But doubtful which most sure to kill is,
Baillie, Heberden, or Willis.
Anon.

---o---

CCLXXII.
On Dr. Lettsom, by Himself.

When people's ill, they comes to I,
I physics, bleeds, and sweats 'em;
Sometimes they live, sometimes they die.
What's that to I? I lets 'em.
John Coakley Lettsom (1744-1815).

---o---

CCLXXIII.
Sent to a Patient, with the Present of a Couple of Ducks.

I've dispatch'd, my dear madam, this scrap of a letter,
To say that Miss ——— is very much better.
A Regular Doctor no longer she lacks,
And therefore I've sent her a couple of Quacks.
Dr. Edward Jenner (1749-1823).

CCLXXIV.

Impromptu Reply.

Yes! 't was politic, truly, my very good friend,
Thus a " couple of Quacks " to your patient to send ;
Since there's nothing so likely as " Quacks," it is plain,
To make work for a " Regular Doctor " again!

Anon.

CCLXXV.

What Jenner said in Elysium when he heard of the Opposition to his having a Statue in Trafalgar Square.

England's ingratitude still blots
The scutcheon of the brave and free;
I saved you from a million spots,
And now you grudge one spot to me.

Anon.

[From *Punch*. The allusion, of course, is to Jenner's discovery of vaccination.]

CCLXXVI.

On Doctor Cheyne, the Vegetarian.

Tell me from whom, fat-headed Scot,
Thou didst thy system learn ;
From Hippocrates thou hadst it not,
Nor Celsus, nor Pitcairn.

Suppose we own that milk is good,
  And say the same of grass;
The one for babes is only food,
  The other for an ass.

Doctor! our new prescription try
  (A friend's advice forgive);
Eat grass, reduce thyself, and die;—
  Thy patients then may live.
Dr. Wynter.

CCLXXVII.

REPLY TO THE ABOVE.

My system, Doctor, is my own,
  No tutor I pretend;—
My blunders hurt myself alone,
  But yours your dearest friend.

Were you to milk and straw confin'd,
  Thrice happy might you be;
Perhaps you might regain your mind,
  And from your wit get free.

I can't your kind prescription try,
  But heartily forgive;
'T is nat'ral you should bid me die,
  That you yourself may live.
Dr. Cheyne.

CCLXXVIII.
To Doctor Empiric.

When men a dangerous disease did 'scape,
Of old, they gave a cock to Esculape :
Let me give two, that doubly am got free—
From my disease's danger, and from thee.

Ben Jonson (1574–1637).

CCLXXIX.
On a Doctor who Died from Using his own Recipe.

Cade, who had slain ten thousand men
With that small instrument, a pen,
Being sick, unluckily he tried
The point upon himself, and died.

Anon.

[From *A Collection of Epigrams* (1727).]

CCLXXX.
On a Famous Physician being called out of Church.

Whilst holy pray'rs to heav'n were made,
One soon was heard and answer'd too ;
"Save us from sudden death," was said,
And straight from church Sir John withdrew.

Anon.

[From *A Collection of Epigrams* (1727). It is apparently directed against Sir John Hill (see page 62).]

CCLXXXI.
A Doctor's Motto.

A doctor, who, for want of skill,
Did sometimes cure—and sometimes kill;
Contriv'd at length, by many a puff,
And many a bottle fill'd with stuff,
To raise his fortune, and his pride;
And in a coach, forsooth! must ride.
His family coat long since worn out,
What arms to take, was all the doubt.
A friend, consulted on the case,
Thus answer'd with a sly grimace:
"Take some device in your own way,
Neither too solemn nor too gay;
Three Ducks, suppose; white, grey, or black;
And let your motto be, Quack! quack!"

Richard Graves (1715–1804).

CCLXXXII.
The Consultation.

Three doctors, met in consultation,
Proceed with great deliberation;
The case was desperate, all agreed,
But what of that? they must be fee'd.

They write then (as 't was fit they shou'd)
But for their own, not patients' good.
Consulting wisely (don't mistake, sir)
Not what to give, but what to take, sir.

Richard Graves.

CCLXXXIII.

THE WORM-DOCTOR.

Vagus, advanced on high, proclaims his skill,
By cakes of wondrous force the worms to kill:
A scornful ear the wiser sort impart,
And laugh at Vagus's pretended art.
But well can Vagus what he boasts perform,
For man (as Job has told us) is a worm.

Josiah Relph (1712–1743).

CCLXXXIV.

ON A QUACK.

This quack to Charon would his penny pay:
The grateful ferryman was heard to say—
"Return, my friend! and live for ages more,
Or I must haul my useless boat ashore."

William Wadd.

[From *Nugæ Canoræ* (1827).]

CCLXXXV.

AUDI ALTERAM PARTEM.

When quacks, as quacks may by good luck, to be sure,
Blunder out at haphazard a desperate cure,
In the prints of the day, with due pomp and parade,
Case, patient, and doctor are amply display'd.

All this is quite just—and no mortal can blame it ;
If they save a man's life, they've a right to proclaim it :
But there's reason to think they might save more lives still,
Did they publish a list of the numbers they kill !

Samuel Bishop (1731-1795).

———o———

CCLXXXVI.

TO A FRIEND WHO RECOMMENDED ASS'S MILK.

And, doctor, do you really think
That ass's milk I ought to drink?
'T would quite remove my cough, you say,
And drive my old complaints away.
It cured yourself—I grant it true ;
But then—'t was mother's milk to you !

John Wolcot (1738-1819).

[Attributed to Wolcot in *Flowers of Anecdote* (1829). It does not figure in his *Works*.]

———o———

CCLXXXVII.

ON DOCTORS AND THE UNDERTAKERS.

At Highgate, by salubrious air,
  Had thriven butchers, bakers ;
But since a doctor settled there,
  None thrive but undertakers.

Anon.

CCLXXXVIII.

ON A PETIT-MAÎTRE PHYSICIAN.

When Pennington for female ills indites,
Studying alone not what, but how, he writes,
The ladies, as his graceful form they scan,
Cry, with ill-omen'd rapture—" Killing man!"

Anon.

CCLXXXIX.

THE DOCTOR'S SECURITY.

Quoth Doctor Squill of Ponder's End,
" Of all the patients I attend,
  Whate'er their aches or ills,
None ever will my fame attack."
" None ever can," retorted Jack,
  " For dead men tell no tales."

Anon.

CCXC.

ON A VALIANT DOCTOR.

From no man yet you've run away!
  Doctor, that may be true;
You've kill'd so many in your day,
  Men mostly fly from you.

Anon.

THE LAW AND LAWYERS.

CCXCI.
ON LORD ELDON.

The Chancellor, so says Lord Coke,
His title from *cancello* took;
And every cause before him tried,
It was his duty to decide.

Lord Eldon, hesitating ever,
Takes it from *chanceler*, to waver;
And thinks, as this may bear him out,
His bounden duty is to doubt.
Anon.

[This originally appeared in *The Morning Chronicle.* It is preserved in *The Spirit of the London Journals* (1814).]

—o—

CCXCII.
ON THE SAME.

Eldon was ask'd by one of note,
  Why merit he did not promote;
" For this good reason," answer'd he,
" That merit ne'er promoted me."
Anon.

[John Scott, Lord Eldon, was born in 1751 and died in 1838. He was made Lord Chancellor in 1801.]

CCXCIII.
On Eldon's Meanness.
Inquest Extraordinary.

Found dead, a rat—no case could sure be harder;
Verdict—Confined a week in Eldon's larder.

Anon.

CCXCIV.
On Sir Charles Wetherell's Uncleanly Habits.
Inquest Extraordinary.

Died, Sir Charles Wetherell's laundress, honest Sue;
Verdict—Ennui, so little work to do.

Anon.

[Sir Charles Wetherell was a Chancery lawyer, and Recorder of Bristol (1770–1846). His carelessness and untidiness of attire is amusingly satirized by Moore in some verses called "The Reform Bill," printed in his *Prose and Verse, hitherto inedited* (1878).]

CCXCV.
On the Same.
Another Inquest Extraordinary.

Died from fatigue, three laundresses together all;
Verdict—Had tried to wash a shirt marked Wetherell.

Anon.

CCXCVI.

ON GARROW, THE BARRISTER, CROSS-QUESTIONING AN OLD WOMAN, TO PROVE THAT A TENDER HAD BEEN MADE FOR CERTAIN PREMISES.

> Garrow, forbear! That tough old jade
> Can never prove a tender *made!*
>
> *Joseph Jekyll.*

---o---

CCXCVII.

ON CRAVEN STREET, STRAND.

In Craven Street, Strand, ten attorneys find place,
And ten dark coal-barges are moored at the base:
Fly, Honesty, fly, to some safer retreat;
There's *craft* in the river and *craft* in the street.

James Smith (1775–1839).

[The following reply to the above was first printed in Barham's *Life of Hook* (1849).]

---o---

CCXCVIII.

REPLY TO THE ABOVE.

Why should Honesty seek any safer retreat
   From the lawyers or barges, odd-rot-'em?
For the lawyers are *just* at the top of the street,
   And the barges are *just* at the bottom!

Sir George Rose.

CCXCIX.

ON THE LONG SPEECHES AND SCARLET ROBES OF SERJEANTS-AT-LAW.

The Serjeants are a grateful race:
Their dress and language show it;
Their purple robes from Tyre we trace,
Their arguments go to it.

Joseph Jekyll.

CCC.

ON A LAWYER DESIRING ONE OF THE TRIBE TO LOOK WITH RESPECT ON A GIBBET.

The lawyers may revere that tree
Where thieves so oft have strung,
Since, by the law's most wise decree,
Her thieves are never hung.

Robert Fergusson (1750-1774).

CCCI.

ON A LAWYER.

How comes it that Quibus should pass for a wit?
He sold what he spoke, and bought what he writ.

Anon.

[From *A Collection of Epigrams* (1727).]

CCCII.

On Another.

Entomb'd within this vault a lawyer lies,
Whom fame assureth us was just and wise.
An able advocate and honest, too :—
That's wondrous strange, indeed—if it be true !
Anon.

[From *Elegant Extracts* (1805).]

----o----

CCCIII.

On Another.

God works a wonder now and then—
Here lies a lawyer, an honest man.
Anon.

----o----

CCCIV.

On Meum and Tuum.

The law decides questions of *Meum* and *Tuum*,
By kindly arranging to make the thing *Suum*.
Anon.

----o----

CCCV.

On a Statue of a Slave in Clement's Inn.

In vain, poor sable son of woe,
  Thou seek'st a tender ear;
In vain thy tears with anguish flow,
  For mercy dwells not here.

From cannibals thou fliest in vain;
 Lawyers less quarters give;
The first won't eat you till you're slain,
 The last will do't alive.

Anon.

CCCVI.
On Lawyers and their Clients.

Two lawyers, when a knotty case was o'er,
Shook hands and were as good friends as before.
"Say," cried the losing client, "how come you
To be such friends who were such foes just now?"
"Thou fool," one answers, "lawyers, tho' so keen,
Like shears, ne'er cut themselves, but what's between."

Anon.

CCCVII.
A Change of Tenant.

The house a lawyer once enjoy'd
 Now to a smith doth pass:
How naturally the iron age
 Succeeds the age of brass!

Anon.

BOOK V.

On Celebrities, and Others.

CCCVIII.
On the Offering made by King James I. at a Grave Comedy called "The Marriage of Arts."

At Christ Church " Marriage," play'd before the King,
Lest these learn'd mates should want an offering,
The King himself did offer—what, I pray?
He offer'd, twice or thrice, to go away.
Anon.

[From *A Collection of Epigrams* (1727). This epigram hits off very happily the King's proverbial stinginess.]

CCCIX.
On Lord Burlington's House at Chiswick.

Possess'd of one great hall for state,
Without one room to sleep or eat;
How well you build, let flatt'ry tell,
And all mankind how ill you dwell.
John, Lord Hervey (1696–1743).

[From *The New Foundling Hospital for Wit* (1784). The Lord Burlington referred to is the architect—Richard Doyle, third Earl of Burlington (1695–1753).]

CCCX.

ON THE DUKE OF MARLBOROUGH'S HOUSE AT WOODSTOCK.

"See, sir, here's the grand approach,
This way is for his Grace's coach:
Here lies the bridge, and here's the clock,
Observe the lion and the cock,
The spacious court, the colonnade,
And mark how wide the hall is made!
The chimneys are so well design'd,
They never smoke in any wind.
The gallery's contrived for walking,
The windows to retire and talk in;
The council chamber for debate,
And all the rest are rooms of state."
"Thanks, sir," cried I, "'t is very fine,
But where d'ye sleep, or where d'ye dine?
I find, by all you have been telling,
That 't is a house, but not a dwelling."

Alexander Pope (1688–1744).

[This has been attributed to several authors, including Swift and Byrom. The "house at Woodstock" was Blenheim, built by Vanbrugh.]

CCCXI.

ON A HIGH BRIDGE BUILT OVER A SMALL STREAM AT BLENHEIM.

> The lofty arch his high ambition shows,
> The stream an emblem of his bounty flows.
>
> *Dr. Abel Evans* (about 1699).

[Marlborough was as notoriously mean as he was notoriously ambitious.]

CCCXII.

ON THE QUEEN'S GROTTO AT RICHMOND, ADORNED BY BUSTS.

> Lewis the living genius fed,
> And rais'd the scientific head :
> Our Queen, more frugal of her meat,
> Raises those heads which cannot eat.
>
> *Anon.*

[From *Elegant Extracts* (1805). The Queen was Caroline, consort of George II.]

CCCXIII.

ON SIR JOHN VANBRUGH.

> Under this stone, reader, survey
> Dead Sir John Vanbrugh's house of clay.
> Lie heavy on him, earth ! for he
> Laid many heavy loads on thee.
>
> *Dr. Abel Evans* (about 1699).

[From Nichols' *Select Collection of Poems* (1780). "The heaviness of Vanbrugh's style of architecture was the subject of the constant ridicule of Horace Walpole and others." Vanbrugh is now best remembered as a dramatist. *The Relapse* was produced in 1679, and *The Provoked Wife* in the same year. Their author died in 1726. The above epigram (the last couplet of which alone is generally quoted) has its antitype in the following lines from the Greek :—

"Hail, mother Earth! lie light on him
   Whose tombstone here we see;
Æsigenes, his form was slim,
   And slight his weight on thee."]

—o—

CCCXIV.

ON VOLTAIRE RIDICULING MILTON'S ALLEGORY OF SIN AND DEATH.

You are so witty, profligate, and thin,
At once we think thee Milton, Death, and Sin.
            Edward Young (1684–1765).

[Said to have been made extempore.]

—o—

CCCXV.

ON THE FIRST DUKE OF DORSET AND HIS SON.

Folly and sense, in Dorset's race,
   Alternately do run;
As Carey one day told his Grace,
   Praising his eldest son.

But Carey must allow for once
Exception to the rule,
For Middlesex is but a dunce,
Though Dorset be a fool.
Sir Charles Hanbury Williams (1709–1759).

—o—

CCCXVI.

ON DR. THOMAS SHERIDAN.

Beneath this marble stone there lies
Poor Tom, more merry much than wise;
Who only liv'd for two great ends,
To spend his cash and lose his friends:
His darling wife of him bereft,
Is only griev'd—there's nothing left.
Jonathan Swift (1667–1745).

[Dr. Thomas Sheridan was the grandfather of the famous politician and playwright, whose improvidence he rivalled. The above epitaph is taken, not from Swift's *Works*, in which it is not included, but from Watkins' *Memoir of the Public and Private Life of R. B. Sheridan* (1817).]

—o—

CCCXVII.

ON FOOTE, THE ACTOR AND DRAMATIST.

Foote, from his earthly stage, alas! is hurl'd;
Death took him off, who took off all the world.
Anon.

[Samuel Foote (1722–1777) was famous for his powers of mimicry. His best-known plays are *The Lyar* (1762), *The*

Mayor of Garratt (1764), *The Lame Lover* (1770), and *The Nabob* (1772). " Foote," says Davies, the biographer of Garrick, "saw the follies of mankind with a quick and a discerning eye; his discrimination of character was quick and exact; his humour pleasant, his ridicule keen, his satire pungent, and his wit brilliant and exuberant."]

———o———

CCCXVIII.

ON QUICK, THE ACTOR.

The great debt of Nature he paid, as all must,
And came, like a gentleman, down with his dust.

Anon.

[John Quick was born in 1748 and died in 1831.]

———o———

CCCXIX.

ON QUIN, MACKLIN, AND RICH.

"Your servant, sir," says surly Quin;
"Sir, I am yours," replies Macklin.
"Why you 're the very Jew you play,
  Your face performs the task well."
"And you are Sir John Brute, they say,
  And an accomplished Maskwell."
Says Rich, who heard the sneering elves,
  And knew their horrid hearts,
"Acting too much your very selves,
  You overdo your parts."

William Hogarth (1697-1764).

[From Nichols' *Collection of Poems* (1780). Charles Macklin (1690-1797) was famous for his representation of Shylock, which is said to have earned for him the praise of Pope in the form of a celebrated distich. Sir John Brute and Maskwell figure in *The Provoked Wife* and *The Double Dealer* respectively, and were favourite characters with Quin, whose Brute is pungently celebrated in *The Rosciad*. Rich was manager of Lincoln's Inn Fields Theatre, and afterwards patentee of Covent Garden.]

―o―

CCCXX.

On Quin, the Actor.

Pope Quin, who damns all churches but his own,
Complains that heresy infects the town;
That Whitfield Garrick has misled the age,
And taints the sound religion of the stage.
Schism, he cries, has turned the nation's brain,
But eyes will open, and to church again!—
Thou great infallible, forbear to roar,
Thy bulls and errors are revered no more :
When doctrines meet with general approbation,
It is not heresy, but reformation.
        David Garrick (1716–1779).

[James Quin was born in 1793, and died in 1766. The two latter lines alone are generally quoted.]

―o―

CCCXXI.

On the Same.

Says epicure Quin—"Should the devil in hell
  In fishing for men take delight,
His hook bait with ven'son, I love it so well,
  Indeed I am sure I should bite."
        David Garrick.

CCCXXII.

ON FARREN, THE ACTOR.

If Farren, cleverest of men,
   Should go to right-about,
What part of town will he be then?
   Why, " Farren-done-without ! "
Anon.

[William Farren, the famous comedian, died in 1861.]

CCCXXIII.

ON A RELIGIOUS DISPUTE AT BATH.

On Reason, Faith, and mystery high,
   Two wits harangue the table;
Bentley believes, he knows not why,—
   Nash swears 't is all a fable.

Peace, coxcombs, peace, and both agree;
   Nash, kiss thy empty brother;
Religion laughs at foes like thee,
   And dreads a friend like t' other.
Anon.

[From *The Foundling Hospital for Wit* (1743). The Bentley here referred to was the son of the great classical scholar; Nash, the famous beau of that name.]

CCCXXIV.

ON THE PICTURE OF BEAU NASH STANDING BETWEEN BUSTS OF NEWTON AND POPE.

This picture, placed these busts between,
    Gives satire its full strength;
Wisdom and wit are seldom seen,
    But folly at full length.

Jane Brereton (1685–1740).

[Lord Chesterfield's comment on the above was as follows :—

Immortal Newton never spoke
    More truth than here you'll find;
Nor Pope himself ere penn'd a joke
    Severer on mankind.

In some collections this stanza is prefixed to Mrs. Brereton's (for which, see her *Poems*, published in 1744), and the two together are attributed to Chesterfield. There is no question, however, that the original epigram was Mrs. Brereton's, and the comment, only, Chesterfield's.]

—o—

CCCXXV.

ON NASH, THE ARCHITECT, WHO INTRODUCED THE USE OF ROMAN CEMENT IN LONDON HOUSES.

Augustus at Rome was for building renown'd,
And marble he left what but brick he had found;
But is not our Nash, too, a very great master?
He found London brick, and he leaves it all plaster.

Anon.

[John Nash, architect, was born in 1752, and died in 1835.]

CCCXXVI.

ON COLONELS SIBTHORP, PERCIVAL, AND VERNER,

The first of whom was remarkable for his Length of Beard, whilst the others had none.

>Three colonels, in three distant counties born,
>Lincoln, Armagh, and Sligo did adorn.
>The first in matchless impudence surpass'd,
>The next in bigotry, in both the last.
>The force of nature could no further go—
>To beard the first she shaved the other two.
>
>*Daniel O'Connell* (1775–1847).

[A parody on Dryden's celebrated tribute to Milton, for which see Book XI..]

CCCXXVII.

ON LORD KENMARE AND O'CONNELL HESITATING TO FIGHT A DUEL WITH SIR C. SAXTON, THE ONE ON ACCOUNT OF HIS SICK DAUGHTER, THE OTHER THROUGH THE INTERFERENCE OF HIS WIFE.

>These heroes of Erin, abhorrent of slaughter,
>   Improve on the Jewish command;
>One honours his wife, and the other his daughter,
>   That their days may be long in the land.
>
>*Thomas Moore* (1779–1852).

[This is but an old story versified. It is said, however, to have given great umbrage to O'Connell. See Moore's *Memoirs* (1853).]

CCCXXVIII.

ON THE DUKE OF CUMBERLAND.

Said His Highness to Ned, with that grim face of his,
  "Why refuse us the Veto, dear Catholic Neddy?"
"Because, Sir," said Ned, looking full in his phiz,
  "You're forbidding enough, in all conscience, already!"

Thomas Moore.

["Ned" was Edward Byrne, head of the Irish Catholic Delegates.]

CCCXXIX.

ON JOHN WILSON CROKER.

They say his wit's refined. Thus is explain'd
The mystery—his wit is strain'd.

Anon.

[Croker (1780–1857), who sat to Lord Beaconsfield for his portrait as Rigby in *Coningsby*, is now best known for his edition of Boswell's *Life of Johnson*. He was a very voluminous writer, contributing largely to the *Quarterly Review*.]

CCCXXX.

ON THE DEATH OF SOYER, THE COOK.

Soyer is gone! Then be it said,
Indeed, indeed, great Pan is dead.

Anon.

[From *The Mirror*.]

CCCXXXI.

ON LORD ELLENBOROUGH'S PERICRANIUM.

Let none, because of its abundant locks,
   Deceive themselves by thinking for a minute
That dandy Ellenborough's " knowledge-box "
   Has anything worth larceny within it.
Anon.

———o———

CCCXXXII.

ON THE SAME.

" I'm very glad," to Ellenborough said
   His brother exquisite Macassar Draper,
" That 't is the outer product of your head,
   And not the inner, you commit to paper!"
Anon.

———o———

CCCXXXIII.

ON IDA PFEIFFER.

Through regions by wild men and cannibals haunted,
Old Dame Ida Pfeiffer goes lone and undaunted;
But, bless you, the risk's not so great as it's reckon'd,
She's too plain for the first, and too tough for the second.
James Hannay (1827–1873).

[Ida Pfeiffer, the celebrated traveller, was born in 1795, and died in 1858. Her adventures, in which she manifested great intrepidity, were frequently of the most romantic character.]

CCCXXXIV.

On John Combe, an Usurer.

Ten in the hundred the devil allows,
But Combe will have twelve, he swears and he vows:
If any one ask, who lies in this tomb,
Oh! quoth the devil, 't is my John O'Combe.

William Shakespeare (1588–1616).

[From Boswell's edition of Malone's Shakespeare. Rowe, in his *Life* of the poet, gives a slightly different version :

Ten in the hundred lies here engrav'd,
'T is a hundred to ten his soul is not sav'd ;
If any man ask, who lies in this tomb?
Oho! quoth the Devil, 't is my John a Comb.

This, we are asked to believe, was written in the usurer's lifetime, and shown to him by Shakespeare. Malone, however, declares that his version is the correct one, and that it was written on the occasion of Combe's funeral, July 12, 1614.]

———o———

CCCXXXV.

On Randolph Peter, of Oriel, the Eater.

Whoe'er you are, tread softly, I entreat you,
For if he chance to wake, be sure he'll eat you.

Anon.

[From *Select Epitaphs* (1757).]

CCCXXXVI.

ON TWO MILLERS, NAMED BONE AND SKIN, WHO WISHED A MONOPOLY OF CORN.

Two millers thin,
Call'd Bone and Skin,
Would starve us all, or near it;
But be it known
To Skin and Bone,
That Flesh and Blood can't bear it.

John Byrom (1691–1763).

CCCXXXVII.

ON TWO ROGUES, CALLED ATKINSON.

To rob the public, two contractors come,
One deals in corn, the other cheats in rum;
Which is the greater rogue, ye wits—explain—
A rogue in spirit or a rogue in grain?

Thomas Warton (1728–1790).

[Signed T. W., in *The Gentleman's Magazine* for August, 1784.]

CCCXXXVIII.

ON THE EARL OF GALLOWAY.

What dost thou in that mansion fair?
    Flit, Galloway, and find
Some narrow, dirty, dungeon cave,
    The picture of thy mind.

Robert Burns (1759–1796).

CCCXXXIX.

ON THE SAME.

No Stewart art thou, Galloway;
   The Stewarts were all brave.
Besides, the Stewarts were but fools,
   Not one of them a knave.
         Robert Burns (1759–1796).

CCCXL.

ON THE SAME.

Bright ran thy line, O Galloway,
   Thro' many a far-famed sire;—
So ran the far-famed Roman way,
   And ended in a mire.
         Robert Burns.

CCCXLI.

ON THE SAME.

Spare me thy vengeance, Galloway,
   In quiet let me live;
I ask no kindness at thy hand,—
   For thou hast none to give.
         Robert Burns.

CCCXLII.

ON JOHN DOVE, INNKEEPER.

Here lies Johnnie Pigeon:
What was his religion?
   Whaever desires to ken,

To some other warl'
Maun follow the carl,
    For here Johnnie Pigeon had nane!

Strong ale was ablution—
Small beer persecution—
    A dram was *memento mori;*
But a full flowing bowl
Was the saving his soul,
    And port was celestial glory.

Robert Burns (1759-1796).

[The John Dove here described was owner of an inn at Mauchline, and well known to Burns.]

CCCXLIII.

ON MR. WILLIAM GRAHAM OF MORSKNOWE.

"Stop thief," Dame Nature cried to Death,
As Willy drew his latest breath;
"How shall I make a fool again?
My choicest model thou hast ta'en."

Robert Burns.

CCCXLIV.

ON ONE OF WHOM IT WAS SAID THAT THERE WAS FALSEHOOD IN HIS FACE.

That there is falsehood in his looks
I must and will deny;
They tell their master is a knave,
And sure they do not lie.

Robert Burns.

[The subject of these savage lines was a certain Dr. Babington.]

CCCXLV.
ON A CERTAIN LORD.

Through and through the inspirèd leaves,
    Ye maggots, make your windings :
But, oh ! respect his lordship's taste,
    And spare his golden bindings.

Robert Burns (1759–1796).

CCCXLVI.
ON A PENURIOUS ELDER.

Here Souter Hood in death does sleep ;
    To hell if he's gane thither,
Satan, gie him thy gear to keep ;
    He'll haud it weel thegether.

Robert Burns.

CCCXLVII.
ON JAMES GRIEVE, LAIRD OF BOGHEAD.

Here lies Boghead among the dead,
    In hopes to get salvation ;
But if such as he in heav'n may be,
    Then welcome—hail ! damnation.

Robert Burns.

CCCXLVIII.

ON A CERTAIN SQUIRE'S FUNERAL.

One Queen Artemisa, as old stories tell,
When deprived of her husband she lovèd so well,
In respect for the love and affection he show'd her,
She reduc'd him to dust, and she drank up the powder.

But Queen Netherplace, of a diff'rent complexion,
When call'd on to order the fun'ral direction,
Would have ate her dead lord, on a slender pretence,
Not to show her respect, but—to save the expense!
Robert Burns (1759–1796).

[This epigram, referring to Mr. Campbell, of Netherplace, and his wife, was printed by Burns in his first edition, and afterwards suppressed.]

CCCXLIX.

TO AN ARTIST, ENGAGED ON A PICTURE OF "JACOB'S DREAM."

Dear ———, I'll gie ye some advice,—
  Ye'll tak it no uncivil;
You shouldna paint at angels mair,
  But try and paint the devil.

To paint an Angel's kittle wark,—
  Wi' Nick there's little danger;
You'll easy draw a lang-kent face,
  But no sae weel a stranger.
Robert Burns.

[The name of the artist is omitted from the original; it is understood, however, to have been that of a well-known Edinburgh painter of Burns's time. "Kittle" means "difficult."]

———o———

CCCL.

ON JOHN ADAMS, OF SOUTHWELL,

A Carrier, who died of Drunkenness.

John Adams lies here, of the parish of Southwell,
A Carrier who carried his can to his mouth well:
He carried so much, and he carried so fast,
He could carry no more—so was carried at last;
For, the liquor he drank, being too much for one,
He could not carry off,—so he's now carri-on.

Lord Byron (1788-1824).

———o———

CCCLI.

LINES IN THE TRAVELLERS' BOOK AT ORCHOMENUS.

Fair Albion, smiling, sees her son depart
To trace the birth and nursery of art:
Noble his object, glorious is his aim;
He comes to Athens, and he writes his name.

Anon.

[These lines drew from Lord Byron the following retort.]

CCCLII.

Reply to the Above.

The modest bard, like many a bard unknown,
Rhymes on our names, but wisely hides his own;
But yet, whoe'er he be, to say no worse,
His name would bring more credit than his verse.

Lord Byron (1788–1824).

CCCLIII.

On a Livery-Stable Keeper, called Milton.

Two Miltons in separate ages were born:
　The cleverer Milton 't is clear we have got,
Though the other had talents the world to adorn,
　This lives by his *mews*, which the other could not!

Theodore Edward Hook (1788–1841).

CCCLIV.

On a Friend, named Hog, Promising him a Pair of Breeches Woven from the Fleece of his Own Flock.

Friend Hog once promised me a pair of breeches,
Wove from the fleecy flocks that swell his riches.
I trusted him, forgetting, like a fool,
That Hogs afford much cry, but little wool.

Lord Neaves (1800–1876).

BOOK VI.

On Individuals, and Types of Character.

CCCLV.
On a Good Writer.

There's none were fitter than thou to endite
If thou couldst pen as well as thou canst write.

John Heath (about 1585–1607).

[From *Two Centuries of Epigrams* (1610).]

CCCLVI.
On a Left-Handed Writing Master.

Though Nature thee of thy right hand bereft,
Right well thou writest with the hand that's left.

Francis Fuller (about 1691).

[From Nichols' *Literary Anecdotes*.]

CCCLVII.
On a Bad Writer.

You ask me, Edward, what I think
Of this new fashionable ink?
    I'll answer briefly, Ned.
Methinks it will be always blue;
At all events, when used by you,
    It never will be *red*.
James Smith (1775–1839).

CCCLVIII.
Written over a Gate.

Here lives a man who, by relation,
Depends upon predestination;
For which the learned and the wise
His understanding much despise.

But I pronounce with loyal tongue
Him in the right, them in the wrong;
For how could such a wretch succeed,
But that, alas, it was decreed?
John, Duke of Buckinghamshire (1649–1720-1).

CCCLIX.
On a Rich Man's Heir.

"I owe," says Metius, "much to Colon's care;
Once only seen, he chose me for his heir."
True, Metius; hence your fortunes take their rise;
His heir you were not, had he seen you twice.
Leonard Welsted (1689–1747).

CCCLX.

ON A CERTAIN SYLLA.

Sylla declares the world shall know
That he's my most determined foe!
I wish him wide the tale to spread;
For all that I from Sylla dread
Is, that the knave, to serve some end,
May one day swear that he's my friend.

Anon.

[From *The Poetical Register* (1801).]

CCCLXI.

ON AN ALDERMAN.

That he was born it cannot be denied,
He ate, drank, slept, talk'd politics, and died.

John Cunningham (1729-1773).

CCCLXII.

ON A USELESS MAN.

Here lies one who was born and cried,
Told threescore years and then he died.
His greatest actions that we find,
Were that he wash'd his hands and din'd.

Anon.

[From Hackett's *Select Epitaphs* (1757).]

CCCLXIII.

ON A VERY IDLE FELLOW.

Here lieth one that was born once and cried,
Liv'd several years, and then—and then—he died.

Anon.

[From *Elegant Extracts* (1805). All the three epitaphs above were probably suggested by a distich on Timocreon by Simonides.]

CCCLXIV.

ON A PARISH CLERK WITH A BAD VOICE.

Sternhold and Hopkins had great qualms,
When they translated David's Psalms,
   To make the heart full glad;
But had it been poor David's fate
To hear thee sing and them translate,
   By Jove, 't would have drove him mad.

John Wilmot, Earl of Rochester (1647–1680).

CCCLXV.

ON A BAD SINGER.

Swans sing before they die: 't were no bad thing
Did certain persons die before they sing.

Samuel Taylor Coleridge (1772–1834).

CCCLXVI.

TO A BAD FIDDLER.

Old Orpheus play'd so well, he mov'd old Nick,
While thou mov'st nothing but thy fiddle-stick.

Anon.

[From *A Collection of Epigrams* (1727).]

---o---

CCCLXVII.

ON A LADY WHOSE PLAYING LACKED EXPRESSION.

When Orpheus play'd, he touch'd the rocks and trees;
But you, my lady, only touch the keys.

Anon.

[From *Once a Week.*]

---o---

CCCLXVIII.

ON BAD DANCING TO GOOD MUSIC.

How ill the motion to the music suits!
So Orpheus fiddled, and so danced the brutes.

Eustace Budgell (1685–1736).

---o---

CCCLXIX.

ON A SABBATH-BREAKER.

Ned will not keep the Jewish Sabbath, he,
  Because the Church hath otherwise ordain'd;
Nor yet the Christian, for he does not see
  How alt'ring of the day can be maintain'd.
Thus seeming for to doubt of keeping either,
He halts 'twixt them both, and so keeps neither.

John Heath (about 1585–1607).

CCCLXX.

On Another.

Lollius, with head bent back and close shut eyes,
All service time devoutly snoring lies:
Its great dislike in *fies!* the parish speaks,
And wonders Lollius thus the Sabbath breaks.
But I think Lollius keeps the Sabbath best;
For why,—he makes it still a day of rest.

Josiah Relph (1712–1743).

CCCLXXI.

On a Coward.

Thomas is sure a most courageous man,
"A word and a blow" for ever is his plan;
And thus his friends explain the curious matter,—
He gives the first, and then receives the latter.

Anon.

CCCLXXII.

On One who Laughed at his Own Jokes.

Neddy laugh'd loud at every word he spoke;
And we laugh'd too—but not at Neddy's joke.

Anon.

[From *Epigrams in Distich* (1740)]

CCCLXXIII.
On One who Stood Well in his Own Conceit.

He standeth well in his own conceit each man tells ;
So had he need, for he standeth in no man's else.
John Heywood (1506–1565).

CCCLXXIV.
On Another.

Of all speculations the market holds forth,
  The best that I know for a lover of pelf,
Is to buy Marcus up, at the price he is worth,
  And then sell him at that which he sets on himself.
Thomas Moore (1779–1852).

CCCLXXV.
On Another.

Said vain Andrew Scalp, " My initials, I guess,
Are well known; so I sign all my poems, A.S."
Said Jerrold, " I own you 're a reticent youth,
For that 's telling only two-thirds of the truth."
Anon.

[A well-known repartee versified.]

CCCLXXVI.
On a Vain Man.

Jack his own merit sees : this gives him pride,
For he sees more than all the world beside.
Anon.

CCCLXXVII.

On One who Bragged of Knowledge.

All things you know: what all? If it be so,
Then you know this too, that you nothing know.

John Heath (about 1585–1607).

CCCLXXVIII.

On a Conceited Coxcomb.

See Clodio, happy in his own dear sense!
And hark! the world cries, "Coxcomb in th' excess."
Now let me undertake the fop's defence—
What man could ever be content with less?

John Wolcot (1738–1819).

[From *Pindariana*.]

CCCLXXIX.

On a certain Vallius.

When thunder rumbles in the skies,
Down to the cellar Vallius flies.
There, to be sure, he's safe: why so?
He thinks there is no God below.

Anon.

[From *A Collection of Epigrams* (1727).]

CCCLXXX.

On a certain Rufus.

That ignorance makes devout, if right the notion,
Troth, Rufus, thou 'rt a man of great devotion.

Anon.

[From *A Collection of Epigrams* (1727).]

---o---

CCCLXXXI.

On a certain Duke.

That he 's ne'er known to change his mind
　Is surely nothing strange;
For no one yet could ever find
　He 'd any mind to change.

Anon.

---o---

CCCLXXXII.

To Alchemists.

If all you boast of your great art be true,
Sure, willing poverty lies most in you.

Ben Jonson (1574–1637).

[" That is," says Bell, " if it be true that you can convert the baser metals into gold, how is it that you are yourselves so poor?"]

CCCLXXXIII.
On a Purse-proud Blockhead.

When I meet Tom, the purse-proud and impudent blockhead,
   In his person the poets' three ages I trace:
For the gold and the silver unite in his pocket,
   And the brazen is easily seen in his face.

Anon.

[From *The Green Book* (1845).]

CCCLXXXIV.
On One Stealing a Pound of Candles.

Light-finger'd Catch, to keep his hands in ure,
Stole anything,—of this you may be sure,
That he thinks all his own that once he handles,—
For practice' sake did steal a pound of candles;
Was taken in the act;—oh, foolish wight!
To steal such things as needs must come to light!

Anon.

[From *A Collection of Epigrams* (1727).]

CCCLXXXV.
On a Robbery.

Ridway robb'd Duncote of three hundred pound;
   Ridway was ta'en, arraign'd, condemn'd to die;
But, for this money, was a courtier found,
   Begg'd Ridway's pardon: Duncote now doth cry,
Robb'd both of money, and the law's relief,
   "The courtier is become the greater thief."

Ben Jonson (1574–1637).

CCCLXXXVI.

ON A CERTAIN BOBADIL.

Three years in London Bobadil had been,
Yet not the lions nor the tombs had seen:
I cannot tell the cause without a smile;—
The rogue had been in Newgate all the while.

Anon.

CCCLXXXVII.

ON A TURNCOAT.

Tho' George, with respect to the wrong and the right,
Is of twenty opinions 'twixt morning and night,
If you call him a turncoat, you injure the man;
He's the pink of consistency, on his own plan.
While to stick to the strongest is always his trim;
'T is not he changes side, 't is the side changes him!

Samuel Bishop (1731–1795).

CCCLXXXVIII.

TO A WEALTHY VINEGAR MERCHANT.

Let Hannibal boast of his conquering sway,
   Thy liquid achievements spread wider and quicker;
By vinegar he through the Alps made his way,
   But you through the world by the very same liquor.

James Smith (1775–1839).

CCCLXXXIX.

ON ONE WHO HAD A LARGE NOSE AND SQUINTED.

The reason why Doctor Dash squints, I suppose,
Is because his two eyes are afraid of his nose.

Anon.

[From Moore's *Diary*, where Bowles is represented as quoting it.]

---o---

CCCXC.

ON A CORONER WHO HANGED HIMSELF.

He lived and died
By suicide.

Anon.

---o---

CCCXCI.

ON A CERTAIN RADICAL.

Blogg rails against high birth. Yes, Blogg—you see
Your ears are longer than your pedigree.

James Hannay (1827–1873).

---o---

CCCXCII.

ON A VERY THIN METAPHYSICIAN.

Scarce from Privation's dreary lap,
  Thy shadowy form dawn forth we see;
A scanty shred; a tiny scrap
  Of metaphysic entity!

Thy face, in hieroglyphic style,
  Seems just mark'd out; thy waist a span:
Thou sketch! thou outline! thou profile!
Thou bas-relievo of a man!
Richard Graves (1715–1804).

CCCXCIII.

ON A HYPOCRITE.

His son he cheats; he leaves his bail i' th' lurch:
Where is the rascal gone?—he's gone to church.
Anon.

[From *Epigrams in Distich* (1740).]

CCCXCIV.

ON ANOTHER.

Joe hates a hypocrite: which shows
Self-love is not a fault of Joe's.
Anon.

CCCXCV.

ON A CERTAIN POLLIO.

Pollio, who values nothing that's within,
Buys books, like beavers,—only for their skin.
Anon.

[From *A Collection of Epigrams* (1727).]

CCCXCVI.
ON TONGUE VERSUS WIT.

Thou hast a swift running tongue: how be it,
Thy tongue is nothing so quick as thy wit.
Thou art, when wit and tongue in running contend,
At thy wit's end ere thou be at thy tale's end.

John Heywood (1506–1565).

CCCXCVII.
ON A LIGHT-WITTED PERSON.

"Nothing is lighter than a feather, Kit."
"Yes, Clim." "What light thing is that?" "Thy light wit."

John Heywood.

CCCXCVIII.
TO FOOL, OR KNAVE.

Thy praise or dispraise is to me alike;
One doth not stroke me, nor the other strike.

Ben Jonson (1574–1637).

CCCXCIX.
ON A FELLOW THAT FEARED HE SHOULD RUN MAD FOR HIS MISTRESS.

Ralph is love-sick, and thinks he shall run mad,
And lose his wits—a thing Ralph never had.
Take comfort, man, if that be all thou fearest;
A groat will pay the loss when wit's at dearest.

John Eliot (about 1658).

CD.

ON A STUPID FAMILY.

" My children ! to cope with the world and its tricks,"
(Said old Prosy, addressing his sons half a score,)
" I would have you resemble the bundle of sticks."
Well, they proved a bundle of sticks, and no more.

Thomas Dibdin (1771–1841.)

CDI.

ON A FOOLISH PERSON.

Jack, eating rotten cheese, did say,
" Like Samson, I my thousands slay."
" I vow," quoth Roger, " so you do,
And with the self-same weapon too."

Anon.

[From *A Collection of Epigrams* (1727).]

CDII.

ON ANOTHER.

You beat your pate, and fancy wit will come :
Knock as you please, there's nobody at home.

Alexander Pope (1688–1744).

CDIII.

On Another.

Rant is, they say, indicted for a wit,
  To which he pleads "Not Guilty," and is quit.

Thomas Jordan (about 1671–84).

[From Nichols' *Collection of Poems* (1781).]

CDIV.

On a Sycophant.

Of great connections with great men,
  Ned keeps up a perpetual pother;
"My Lord knows what, knows who, knows when;
  My Lord says this, thinks that, does t'other."

My Lord had formerly his Fool,
  We know it, for 't is on recòrd;
But now, by Ned's inverted rule,
  The Fool, it seems, must have his Lord!

Samuel Bishop (1731–1795).

CDV.

On a certain Dilemma.

My head and my purse had a quarrel of late,
And referr'd it to me to decide the debate;
Not great was the diff'rence—it seems this was it—
"Had purse the most money, or head the most wit?"
"I know not," cried I, "which at present is worst;
But surely the head had the vacuum first."

Anon.

[From *The Poetical Farrago* (1794).]

CDVI.

ON A FOOLISH ATTORNEY.

"What with briefs and attending the court, self and clerk,
  I'm at my wits' end," muttered Drone, the attorney.
"I fear 't is a medical case," answered Shark—
  "You 're so terribly tired by so little a journey."

James Smith (1775–1839).

[See Smith's *Memoirs* (1840).]

―o―

CDVII.

ON ONE NAMED DICK.

"I cannot comprehend," says Dick,
"What 't is that makes my legs so thick."
"You cannot comprehend," says Harry,
"How great a calf they have to carry."

Horace Smith (1779–1849).

―o―

CDVIII.

IDLE IDEALISM.

In all things that round him move
  M—— but nothingness doth find;—
Why, did not Berkeley plainly prove
  Nought exists apart from Mind?

Samuel Waddington.

CDIX.

A Repartee.

"To this night's masquerade," quoth Dick,
  "By pleasure I am beckon'd,
And think 't would be a pleasant trick
  To go as Charles the Second."

Tom felt for repartee a thirst,
  And thus to Richard said:
"You 'd better go as Charles the First,
  For that requires no head."

Anon.

CDX.

An April Fool.

"This," Richard says, "is April-day,
  And though so mighty wise you be,
A bet, whate'er you like, I'll lay,
  Ere night I make a fool of thee."

"A fool I may be, it is true,
  But, Dick," cries Tom, "ne'er be afraid;
No man can make a fool of you,
  For you 're a fool already made."

Anon.

CDXI.

On a certain Bufo.

If it be true, on Watts's plan,
"That mind 's the standard of the man;"
Though, Bufo, you are six feet three,
Why, what a pigmy you must be!

Anon.

CDXII.

ON A LAUGHING FOOL.

"I laugh," a would-be sapient cried,
　"At every one that laughs at me."
"Good lack!" a lively friend replied,
　"How very merry you must be!"

Anon.

---o---

CDXIII.

ON A CERTAIN SCRIBBLER.

Pamphlet last week, in his fantastic fits,
Was ask'd, How he liv'd? He said, By 's wits.
Pamphlet, I see, will tell lies by the clock;
How can he live upon so poor a stock?

Anon.

---o---

CDXIV.

A THOROUGHFARE.

"My head, Tom's, confused with your nonsense and
　　bother;
It goes in at one ear and out at the other."
"Of that, my friend Dick, I was ever aware;
For nonsense your head is a pure thoroughfare."

Anon.

CDXV.

ON A RADICAL REFORMER.

Tomkins will clear the land, they say,
    From every foul abuse;
So chimneys in the olden time
    Were cleansèd by a goose.

James Hannay (1827–1873).

---o---

CDXVI.

NON SUNT.

As Tom was one day in deep chat with his friend,
He gravely advised him his manners to mend;
That his morals were bad, he had heard it from many:
"They lie," replied Tom,—"for I never had any."

Anon.

---o---

CDXVII.

THE TRAVELLER AND THE GORILLA.

The gift by Nature boon supplied
This pair unequally divide:
The traveller's tale is far from small,
The monkey has no tale at all.

Richard Garnett.

CDXVIII.

ON A GENTLEMAN OF SEVENTY WHO MARRIED A LADY OF SIXTEEN.

What woes must such unequal union bring,
When hoary Winter weds the youthful Spring?
You, like Mezentius, in the nuptial bed,
Once more unite the living and the dead.
William Broome (d. 1745).

[See *The Æneid*, bk. VIII., where it is said of Mezentius :—

"The living and the dead, at his command,
Were coupled face to face and hand to hand."]

---o---

CDXIX.

ON A VENERABLE BEAU.

Still hovering round the fair at sixty-four,
Unfit to love, unable to give o'er;
A flesh-fly, that just flutters on the wing,
Awake to buzz, but not alive to sting;
Brisk where he cannot, backward where he can,—
The teazing ghost of the departed man.
David Mallet (1700–1765).

---o---

CDXX.

SUBSTITUTE FOR AN EPITAPH.

Kind reader! take your choice to cry or laugh;
Here Harold lies—but where's his Epitaph?
If such you seek, try Westminster, and view
Ten thousand just as fit for him as you.
Lord Byron (1788–1824).

CDXXI.
ON AN UNFAIR DRINKER.

"I drink to thee, Tom." "Nay, thou drinkest *from* me, John,
For when thou drinkest *to* me, drink thou leavest none."
John Heywood (1506–1565).

CDXXII.
ON A DRUNKEN SMITH.

I heard that Smug the smith, for ale and spice
Sold all his tools, and yet he kept his vice.
Sir John Haryngton (1561–1612).

CDXXIII.
ON A CLUB OF SOTS.

The jolly members of a toping club,
Like pipe-staves, are best hoop'd into a tub,
And in a close confederacy link,
For nothing else but only to hold drink.
Samuel Butler (1600–1680).

CDXXIV.
ON A CERTAIN BIBULUS.

Here, who but once in 's life did thirst, doth lie;
Perhaps the dust may make him once more dry.
Robert Heath (about 1620–50).

CDXXV.

ON A CERTAIN THRASO.

Thraso picks quarrels when he's drunk at night;
When sober in the morning dares not fight.
Thraso, to shun those ills that may ensue,
Drink not at night, or drink at morning too.

William Walsh (1663–1709).

[Martial has an epigram very similar in idea (XII. 12).]

---o---

CDXXVI.

ON AN INTEMPERATE HUSBAND.

Whence comes it that in Clara's face
The lily only has a place?
Is it that the absent rose
Is gone to paint her husband's nose?

Anon.

[From *A Collection of Epigrams* (1727).]

---o---

CDXXVII.

ON A DRUNKEN LANDLORD.

Landlord, with thee now even is the wine :
For thou hast pierc'd his hogshead and he thine.

Anon.

[From *Elegant Extracts* (1805).]

CDXXVIII.
ON AN IGNORANT SOT.

Five letters his life and his death will express:
He scarce knew A B C and he died of X S.

Anon.

CDXXIX.
ON AN ENEMY.

Lie on! while my revenge shall be
To speak the very truth of thee.

Robert Craggs, Earl Nugent (d. 1788).

CDXXX.
ON A LIAR.

See! yonder goes old Mendax, telling lies
 To that good easy man with whom he's walking.
"How know I that?" you ask, with some surprise:
 Why don't you see, my friend, the fellow's talking?

Anon.

CDXXXI.
ON ANOTHER.

Charles keeps a secret well, or I'm deceived;
For nothing Charles can say will be believed.

Anon.

CDXXXII.

ON A CERTAIN MAN'S VERACITY.

He boasts about the truth, I've heard,
  And vows he'd never break it;
Why, zounds! a man must keep his word
  When nobody will take it.

Anon.

CDXXXIII.

ON A BORROWER.

Ten guineas Tom would borrow: I give five;
'T is a good bargain, as I'm here alive.

Anon.

[From *Epigrams in Distich* (1740). Martial has a very similar epigram.]

CDXXXIV.

TO ONE WHO OWED HIM MONEY.

Money thou ow'st me: prithee fix a day
For payment promis'd, though thou never pay:
Let it be dooms-day; nay, take longer scope;
Pay when thou'rt honest, let me have some hope.

Robert Herrick (1591–1674).

CDXXXV.

On a Spendthrift.

Why walks Nick Flimsy like a malcontent?
Is it because his money all is spent?
No :—but because the ding-thrift now is poor,
And knows not where i' th' world to borrow more.

Robert Herrick (1591–1674).

CDXXXVI.

On a Rich Miser and a Ruined Spendthrift.

Gold in Gripe's pocket is, and on Strut's coat :
'T is strange that neither should be worth a groat.

Anon.

[From *Epigrams in Distich* (1740).]

CDXXXVII.

On a Spendthrift's Death.

His last great debt is paid. Poor **Tom**'s no more :
Last debt !—Tom never paid a debt before.

Anon.

CDXXXVIII.

On One who Spent his Fortune in Horse-racing.

John ran so long, and ran so fast,
No wonder he ran out at last ;
He ran in debt ; and then, to pay,
He distanced all—and ran away.

Anon.

CDXXXIX.

ON A PRODIGAL.

Sir, can you tell where young Pandorus lives,
   That was surnamèd here the Prodigal :
He that so much for his silk stockings gives,
   Till nought is left to buy him shoes withal?
Oh blame him not, to make what show he can ;
How should he else be thought a gentleman?

Henry Parrot (about 1613).

CDXL.

ON MY LORD FOPPINGTON'S PROPOSAL TO PARLIAMENT.

He thinks it might advance the nation's trade,
Were a law made, no tailor should be paid.

Anon.

[From *Epigrams in Distich* (1740).]

CDXLI.

ON A NOTED COXCOMB.

Light lay the earth on Billy's breast,
   His chicken heart so tender ;
But build a castle on his head,—
   His skull will prop it under.

Robert Burns (1759–1796).

CDXLII.
ON THE OILED AND PERFUMED RINGLETS OF A CERTAIN LORD.

Of miracles this is sans doute the most rare
I ever perceived, heard reported, or read;
A man with abundance of scents on his hair
Without the least atom of sense in his head.

Anon.

CDXLIII.
ON A FOP.

No wonder he is vain of coat or ring;
Vain of himself, he may of any thing.

Anon.

CDXLIV.
ON ONE WHO SPOKE LITTLE.

"I hardly ever ope my lips," one cries:
  "Simonides, what think you of my rule?"
"If you're a fool, I think you're very wise;
  If you are wise, I think you are a fool."

Richard Garnett.

CDXLV.
ON A DUNCE.

Young Courtly takes me for a dunce,
For all night long I spoke but once:
On better grounds I think him such—
He spoke but once, yet once too much.

Anon.

CDXLVI.

ON A PEDANT.

Lysander talks extremely well;
On any subject let him dwell,
  His tropes and figures will content ye:
He should possess, to all degrees,
The art of talk: he practises
  Full fourteen hours in four-and-twenty.

Matthew Prior (1664–1721).

—o—

CDXLVII.

ON A PERSON OF SMALL FORTUNE BUILDING A LARGE HOUSE, WITH A MAUSOLEUM FOR HIMSELF.

This house is form'd with art, and wrought with pains,
The project shows a head, the building want of brains;
But wonder not to see a pile so great,
For here two things must share a common fate,—
This tomb must hold the man, the fabric his estate.

Anon.

[From Hammond's *Miscellany of Original Poems, Translations, and Imitations, by the most eminent hands* (1720).]

—o—

CDXLVIII.

OF DISPRAISE.

All men must be blind and deaf, ere thou praise win,
For no man seëth or heareth ought to praise thee in.

John Heywood (1506–1565).

CDXLIX.

ON A BULLY.

How kind has Nature unto Bluster been,
Who gave him dreadful looks and dauntless mien,
Gave tongue to swagger, eyes to strike dismay,
And, kinder still, gave legs to run away.

Anon.

CDL.

ON THE DEATH OF AN UNDERTAKER.

Subdu'd by Death, here Death's great herald lies,
And adds a trophy to his victories:
Yet sure he was prepar'd, who, while he'd breath,
Made it his business still to look for death.

Anon.

[From *A Collection of Epigrams* (1727). Compare this with the following lines.]

CDLI.

ON AN UNDERTAKER.

Here lyeth Robin Masters. Faith, 't was hard
   To take away our honest Robin's breath.
Yet surely Robin was full well prepar'd;
   Robin was always looking out for death.

Anon.

[This is from *Select Epitaphs* (1757).]

CDLII.

ON A VERY TRIFLING FELLOW BEING KNIGHTED.

What! Darès made a knight! No; don't be frighted:
He only lost his way, and was be-nighted.

Richard Graves (1715–1804).

---o---

CDLIII.

ON A FLATTERER.

No: Varus hates a thing that's base.
   I own, indeed, he's got the knack
Of flatt'ring people to their face;
   He'd scorn to do 't behind their back.

Josiah Relph (1712–1743).

---o---

CDLIV.

ON A CENSORIOUS PERSON.

"What a sad world we live in!" Scandal cries:
I own it will be better when he dies.

Anon.

[From *Epigrams in Distich* (1740).]

---o---

CDLV.

ON A RELIGIOUS BUT CENSORIOUS LADY.

The Law and the Gospels you always have by you,
But for truth and good-nature they seldom come nigh you:
In short, my good creature, the matter of fact is,
You daily are learning what never you practise.

Anon.

CDLVI.

ON A GRACELESS PEER.

"By proxy I pray, and by proxy I vote,"
A graceless peer said to a Churchman of note;
Who answered, "My lord, then I'll venture to say,
You'll to heaven ascend in a similar way."

Anon.

CDLVII.

ON A CERTAIN GRUMUS.

Grumus ne'er saw, he says, a bearded ass;
What, then, did Grumus ne'er consult his glass?

Anon.

[From *Epigrams in Distich* (1740).]

CDLVIII.

A CASE OF CONSCIENCE.

"My friend and I did faithfully agree,
He to extol all I wrote, I all he;
Now he has writ a satire against me.
Resolve me, Phœbus, what am I to do?
Can I retort, yet to my bond be true?"
"Ay, son, abuse him well," Apollo says;
"Panegyric from thee were sore dispraise."

Richard Garnett.

CDLIX.

On a False Friend.

Thus with kind words Sir Edward cheer'd his friend:
"Dear Dick, thou on my friendship mayst depend;
I know thy fortune is but very scant,
But be assur'd I'll ne'er see Dick in want."
Dick's soon confined—his friend, no doubt, would free him;
His word he kept—in want he ne'er would see him.

Anon.

[From *Elegant Extracts* (1805).]

CDLX.

On a Miser.

Reader, beware immoderate love of pelf;
Here lies the worst of thieves—who robb'd himself.

Anon.

[From *Select Epitaphs* (1757).]

CDLXI.

On Another.

Here crumbling lies, beneath this mould,
A man whose sole delight was gold.
Content was never once his guest,
Though thrice ten thousand fill'd his chest;
For he, poor man, with all his store,
Died in great want—the want of more.

Anon.

CDLXII.

On Close-fist's Subscription.

The charity of Close-fist, give to fame:
He has at last subscrib'd—how much?—his name.

Anon.

CDLXIII.

On a Miser's Dinner.

Thanks for this miracle! it is no less
Than finding manna in the wilderness.
In midst of famine we have had relief,
And seen the wonder of a chine of beef;
Chimneys have smok'd that never smok'd before,
And we have din'd—where we shall dine no more.

John Wilmot, Earl of Rochester (1647–1680).

[Also ascribed to Swift.]

CDLXIV.

On a Miser's Feast.

His chimney smokes—it is some omen dire:
His neighbours are alarm'd, and cry out "Fire!"

Anon.

[From *Elegant Extracts* (1805).]

CDLXV.
ON A MISER'S VAULTS.

Thy cellars, friend, may justly vaults be styl'd,
Where casks on casks, on bottles bottles pil'd,
By locks and bolts so closely are confin'd;
Thy liquor's dead—and buried to mankind.
Richard Graves (1715–1804).

CDLXVI.
ON THE FUNERAL OF A RICH MISER.

What num'rous lights this wretch's corpse attend,
Who, in his lifetime, saved a candle's end!
Anon.

CDLXVII.
ON A MEAN HOST.

Last night thou didst invite me home to eat,
And show'dst me there much plate, but little meat.
Prithee, when next thou dost invite, bar state,
And give me meat,—or give me else thy plate.
Robert Herrick (1591–1674).

CDLXVIII.
ON A MEAN HOST.

"You see," said our host, as we entered his doors,
"I have furnished my house à la Louis Quatorze."
"Then I wish," said a guest, "when you ask us to eat,
You would furnish your board à la Louis Dixhuit.
The eye, can it feast when the stomach is starving?
Pray less of your gilding and more of your carving."
Egerton Warburton.

[From *Hunting Songs and Miscellaneous Verses* (1860). This is a mere versification of a remark said to have been made by Lord Alvanley, at a dinner given by Mr. Greville, of Greville Memoirs celebrity. It should be remarked, that Louis XIV. was noted for his gorgeous upholstery; Louis XVIII. for his devotion to the table.]

CDLXIX.

ON A MEAN HOSTESS.

With lace bedizen'd comes the man,
And I must dine with Lady Anne.
A silver service loads the board,
Of eatables a slender hoard.
"Your pride and not your victuals spare;
I came to dine, and not to stare."

John Hoadley.

CDLXX.

ON A MISERLY LANDLORD.

Thy nags (the leanest things alive)
So very hard thou lov'st to drive;
I heard thy anxious coachman say,
It costs thee more in whips than hay.

Matthew Prior (1674–1721).

CDLXXI.

ON A MEAGRE LIVER.

Thus to the master of an house
Which, like a church, would starve a mouse,
Which never guest had entertain'd,
Nor meat nor wine its floors had stain'd,
I said, "Well, sir, 't is vastly fine;
But where d' you drink, and where d' you dine?
If one may judge by rooms so neat,
It costs you more in mops than meat!"

Richard Graves (1715–1804).

CDLXXII.

ON A STINGY LORD.

My Lord complains that Pope, stark mad with gardens,
Has cut three trees, the value of three farthings.
"But he's my neighbour," cries the peer polite;
"And if he visit me, I'll waive the right."
What! on compulsion, and against my will,
A lord's acquaintance? Let him file his bill!

Alexander Pope (1688–1744).

["My Lord" is Lord Radnor.]

CDLXXIII.

On a certain Lord giving a Large Sum for a House.

So many thousands for a house;
For you of all the world, Lord Mouse!
A little house would best accord
With you, my very little lord!
And then exactly match'd would be
Your house and hospitality.

David Garrick (1716-1779).

CDLXXIV.

On a Stingy Fellow.

Urles had the gout, so that he could not stand;
Then from his feet it shifted to his hand:
When it was in his feet, his charity was small;
Now it is in his hand, he gives no alms at all.

Robert Herrick (1591-1674).

CDLXXV.

On Another.

The other day, says Ned to Joe,
  Near Bedlam's confines groping,
"Whene'er I hear the cries of woe,
  My hand is always open."

"I own," says Joe, "that to the poor
 You prove it ev'ry minute;
 Your hand is open, to be sure,
 But then there's nothing in it."

Anon.

CDLXXVI.
On a Stingy Fop.

Curio's rich sideboard seldom sees the light,
Clean is his kitchen, and his spits are bright;
His knives and spoons, all ranged in even rows,
No hands molest, or fingers discompose;
A curious jack, hung up to please the eye,
For ever still, whose flyers never fly;
His plates unsullied, shining on the shelf;
For Curio dresses nothing but himself.

Anon.

CDLXXVII.
On a Loving Couple.

O'Leary was as poor as Job,
 But love and poverty can please us;
He saw the Widow Bonna-robe,
 And lov'd—for she was rich as Crœsus.

Mutual the love their bosoms own;
 Sincere was he, and none could doubt her—
She lov'd him for himself alone,
 And he—he could not live without her!

Anon.

[From *Papers relating to Suffolk*, in the British Museum.]

CDLXXVIII.

On a Thief and his Friends.

Said a thief to a wit, "There's no knowing one's friends
  Until they've been tried and found steady."
Said the wit to the thief, "All yours, I presume,
  Have been tried and found guilty already."

Anon.

---o---

CDLXXIX.

On a certain Jack.

"What bringest thou from the sermon, Jack? Declare that."
"Forsooth, master" (quoth he), "your cloak and your hat."
"I can thee good thank, Jack, for thou art yet sped,
Of somewhat in thy hand, though nought in thy head."

John Heywood (1506–1565).

---o---

CDLXXX.

On Enclosing a Common.

A lord that purposed for his more avail
To compass in a common with a rail,
Was reckoning with his friends about the cost
And charge of every rail and every post.
But he that wished his greedy humour crost,
Said: "Sir, provide your posts, and, without failing,
Your neighbours roundabout will find you railing."

Sir John Haryngton (1561–1612).

CDLXXXI.

ON A PARASITE.

My Lord feeds Gnatho; he extols my Lord;
Gnatho eats well, but dearly pays his board.

Anon.

[From *Epigrams in Distich* (1740).]

CDLXXXII.

ON A GLUTTONOUS PARASITE.

Frank carves very ill, yet will palm all the meats;
He eats more than six, and drinks more than he eats.
Four pipes after dinner he constantly smokes,
And seasons his whiffs with impertinent jokes.
Yet, sighing, he says we must certainly break;
And my cruel unkindness compels him to speak;
For of late I invite him—but four times a week.

Matthew Prior (1664–1721).

CDLXXXIII.

ON ONE WHO WAS A SLAVE TO HIS PHYSICIAN.

Dacus doth daily to his doctor go,
As doubting if he be in health or no;
For when his friends salute him passing by,
And ask him how he doth in courtesy,
He will not answer thereunto precise,
Till from his doctor he hath ta'en advice.

Henry Parrot (about 1613).

CDLXXXIV.
On a certain Magistrate.

When would-be Suicides in purpose fail,
  Who could not find a morsel though they needed,—
If Peter sends them for attempts to jail,
  What would he do to them if they succeeded?

Thomas Hood (1798–1845).

CDLXXXV.
On Patrons' Promises.

A minister's answer is always so kind!
I starve, and he tells me, he'll keep me in mind.
Half his promise, God knows, would my spirits restore,—
Let him keep me, and faith, I will ask for no more.

Henry Vassal, Lord Holland (1773–1840).

[From Moore's *Diary*, under date August, 1840.]

CDLXXXVI.
On a certain Priscus.

When Priscus, rais'd from low to high estate,
  Rode through the streets in pompous jollity,
Caius, his poor familiar friend of late,
  Bespake him thus: "Sir, now you know not me."
"'T is likely, friend" (quoth Priscus), "to be so,
For at this time myself I do not know."

Sir John Davies (1570–1626).

CDLXXXVII.

ON ONE PUFFED UP.

When Jack was poor, the lad was frank and free;
   Of late he's grown brimfull of pride and pelf;
You wonder that he don't remember me;
   Why so? you see he has forgot himself.

Anon.

[From *Select Epigrams* (1757).]

CDLXXXVIII.

ON A CERTAIN ROOK.

Rook, he sells feathers, yet he still doth cry,
" Fie on this pride, this female vanity!"
Thus, though the Rook does rail against the sin,
He loves the gain that vanity brings in.

Robert Herrick (1591–1674).

CDLXXXIX.

ON A BANKRUPT TURNED PREACHER.

No more by creditors perplext,
   Or ruin'd tradesmen's angry din,
He boldly preaches from the text,
   " A stranger, and I took him in."

Anon.

CDXC.

On a Weak Young Man, who Thought he had Invented a Method of Flying to the Moon.

And will Volatio quit this world so soon,
To fly to his own native seat, the moon?
'T will stand, however, in some little stead
That he sets out with such an empty head.

Philip Doddridge (1702–1751).

CDXCI.

On Unionists.

What is a Unionist? One who has yearnings
For an equal division of unequal earnings;
Idler or bungler, or both, he is willing
To fork out his penny and pocket your shilling.

Ebenezer Elliott (1781–1849).

CDXCII.

On a Great Talker.

To hear Dash by the hour blunder forth his vile prose,
  Job himself scarcely patience could keep;
He's so dull that each moment we're ready to doze,
  Yet so noisy, we can't go to sleep.

Anon.

BOOK VII.

On Women.

CDXCIII.

ON MRS. TOFTS, A CELEBRATED OPERA SINGER.

So bright is thy beauty, so charming thy song,
As had drawn both the beasts and their Orpheus along;
But such is thy av'rice, and such is thy pride,
That the beasts must have starv'd, and the poet have died.

Alexander Pope (1688–1744).

[Katherine Tofts made her first appearance in England in 1703, retiring from the stage in 1709. The cause of her withdrawal was insanity, which led her to identify herself with the characters she played in opera. The story of her calamity was told by Steele in No. 20 of *The Tatler*, and may be read in Hogarth's *Memoirs of the Musical Drama*. See, also, Sir John Hawkins' *History of Music*.]

CDXCIV.

INSCRIPTION FOR THE COLLAR OF A LADY'S DOG.

"Pray steal me not: I'm Mrs. Dingley's,
Whose heart in this four-footed thing lies."

Jonathan Swift (1667–1745).

[Mrs. Dingley was companion to "Stella" (Esther Johnson), whom Swift married in 1716. Compare this with Pope's distich, given elsewhere.]

CDXCV.

ON A CERTAIN LORD'S PASSION FOR A SINGER.

Nerina's angel-voice delights ;
Nerina's devil-face affrights :
How whimsical her Strephon's fate,
Condemn'd at once to like and hate !
But be she cruel, be she kind,
Love ! strike her dumb, or make him blind.

David Mallet (1700 1765).

[The "Lord" was Lord Peterborough (1658-1735); the vocalist Anastasia Robinson (d. 1750), whom he privately married, and afterwards acknowledged as his wife.]

CDXCVI.

ON WOMEN'S FAULTS.

We men have many faults ;
Poor women have but two—
There's nothing good they say,
There's nothing good they do.

Anon.

[From *A Collection of Epigrams* (1727).]

CDXCVII.

ON WOMEN AND THEIR WHIMS.

When Eve brought woe to all mankind,
    Old Adam call'd her *wo*-man ;
But when she woo'd with love so kind,
    He then pronounced her *woo*-man.

But now with folly and with pride,
    Their husbands' pockets trimming,
The ladies are so full of whim,
    That people call them *whim*-men.

Anon.

CDXCVIII.

ON A WOMAN'S MIND.

What is lighter than a feather?—
Dust, my friend, in driest weather.
What's lighter than the dust, I pray?—
The wind that wafts it far away.
What is lighter than the wind?—
The lightness of a woman's mind.
And what is lighter than the last?—
Nay! now, my friend, you have me fast.

Anon.

CDXCIX.

ON ATALANTA.

When the young Greek for Atalanta sigh'd,
He might have fool'd and follow'd, till he died!
He learn'd the sex, the bribe before her roll'd,
And found, the short way to the heart, is—Gold.

George Croly (1780–1860).

[The story of Atalanta's race has been beautifully told of recent years by Mr. Morris in his *Earthly Paradise*.]

D.

ON THE COQUETRY OF WOMEN.

Womankind more joy discovers
Making fools than keeping lovers.

John Wilmot, Earl of Rochester (1647–1680).

DI.

ON THE LADIES.

Their care and pains the fair ones do bestow,
Not to please GOD above, but men below.
Who think them saints are damnably mistook;
They're only saints and angels in their look.

Thomas Brown (d. 1704).

DII.

ON THE SAME.

The ladies here their lovers' hearts
   By their devotion win;
Though all is rock and stone without,
   Yet all is soft within.

Thomas Brown.

DIII.
On Women's Conquests.

Ask not why Laura should persist
    To lure with smiles and dimples;
A woman, like a botanist,
    Delights in culling simples.

Anon.

DIV.
On Women as Unionists.

Among the men, what dire divisions rise—
For " Union " one, " No Union " t' other cries.
Shame on the sex that such dispute began—
Ladies are all for union—to a man!

Anon.

DV.
On Women and Hymen.

Whether tall men, or short men, are best,
    Or bold men, or modest and shy men,
I can't say, but I this can protest,
    All the fair are in favour of Hy-men.

Anon.

DVI.
On a Gay Widow.

Her mourning is all make-believe;
    'T is plain there's nothing in it;
With weepers she has tipp'd her sleeve,
    The while she's laughing in it.

Anon.

DVII.

On One who Married for Money.

Lucia thinks happiness consists in state;
She weds an idiot,—but she eats on plate.

Anon.

DVIII.

On Feminine Talkativeness.

How wisely Nature, ordering all below,
Forbade a beard on woman's chin to grow!
For how could she be shaved, whate'er the skill,
Whose tongue would never let her chin be still?

Anon.

DIX.

To a Lady, with a Book returned, called "The Intelligencer."

I have kept your "Intelligence," madam, so long,
That I hardly dare hope you will pardon the wrong.
Had you been but a man, no excuse I had writ,
For we're seldom severe to the faults we commit.
But "Intelligence" kept the kind ladies must gall,
Who no sooner receive it than part with it all!

Alian Ramsay (1686–1758).

DX.

ON A CERTAIN LESBIA.

When Lesbia first I saw, so heavenly fair,
With eyes so bright and with that awful air,
I thought my heart, which durst so high aspire,
Was bold as his who snatch'd celestial fire.

But soon as e'er the beauteous idiot spoke,
Forth from her coral lips such folly broke,
Like balm the trickling nonsense heal'd my wound,
And what her eyes enthrall'd her tongue unbound.

William Congreve (1670–1729).

DXI.

ON A CERTAIN CHLOE.

How apt are men to lie! how dare they say,
When Life is gone, all Learning fleets away?
Sure this glad grave holds Chloe fair and young,
Who, where she is, first learnt to hold her tongue.

Aaron Hill (1685–1750).

DXII.

ON A TALKATIVE OLD MAID.

Beneath this silent stone is laid
A noisy antiquated maid,
Who from her cradle talk'd till death,
And ne'er before was out of breath.

Whither she's gone we cannot tell;
For if she talks not, she's in Hell:
If she's in Heaven, she's there unblest,
Because she hates a place of rest.

Anon.

[From *A Collection of Epigrams* (1727).]

DXIII.

BY AN OLD GENTLEMAN WHOSE DAUGHTER IMPORTUNED HIM FOR MONEY.

"Dear Bell, to gain money, sure, silence is best,
For dumb bells are fittest to open the chest."

Anon.

DXIV.

ON MISS-REPRESENTATION.

Should women sit in Parliament,—
A thing unprecedented,—
A great part of the nation then
Would be miss-represented.

Anon.

DXV.

TO BLUE STOCKINGS.

The newspapers lately have taught us to know
How some strong-minded hens are beginning to crow.
But, dear ladies, beware;—take the word of a friend,
That, when rivalry comes, all affection must end.

We men take a pride in concealing our chains,
And would like to be thought to monopolize brains;
So I give you this maxim, my counsels to crown,
"If the stockings are blue, keep the petticoats down."

Anon.

[From *Once a Week.*]

---o---

DXVI.
ON EVENING DRESS.

When dress'd for the evening, girls, now-a-days,
   Scarce an atom of dress on them leave;
Nor blame them—for what is an Evening Dress,
   But a dress that is suited for Eve?

Anon.

---o---

DXVII.
ON A SMALL EATER.

Simplicity is best, 't is true,
   But not in every mortal's power:
If thou, O maid, canst live on dew,
   'T is proof thou art indeed a flower.

Richard Garnett.

---o---

DXVIII.
OF A FAIR SHREW.

Fair, rich, and young? how rare is her perfection,
Were it not mingled with one foul infection!
I mean, so proud a heart, so curst a tongue,
As makes her seem, nor fair, nor rich, nor young.

Sir John Haryngton (1534–1582).

DXIX.

On Women's Will.

Kind Katherine to her husband kiss'd these words,
  " Mine own sweet Will, how dearly do I love thee!"
" If true," quoth Will, " the world no such affords."
  And that it's true I durst his warrant be:
For ne'er heard I of woman, good or ill,
But always lovèd best her own sweet will.

Henry Parrot (about 1613).

DXX.

On a Beautiful Lady, with a Loud Voice.

  Lucetta's charms our hearts surprise,
    At once, with love and wonder:
  She bears Jove's lightning in her eyes,
    But in her voice his thunder.

Anon.

DXXI.

To a Stout Elderly Lady.

You ask me, your servant, to give you in rhyme
Some apt definitions of space and of time.
If your ladyship look'd at your form and your face,
You 'd gain excellent notions of time and of space.

Anon.

DXXII.

ON A LADY WHO SQUINTED.

If ancient poets Argus prize,
Who boasted of a hundred eyes,
Sure greater praise to her is due
Who looks a hundred ways with two.

Anon.

———o———

DXXIII.

ON A CERTAIN SYLVIA.

"Sylvia makes sad complaints; she's lost her lover."
"Why, nothing strange I in that news discover."
"Nay, then thou 'rt dull; for here the wonder lies:
She had a lover once—don't that surprise?"

Anon.

[From *A Collection of Epigrams* (1727).]

———o———

DXXIV.

ON AN ILL-FAVOURED WOMAN.

Your homely face, Flippanta, you disguise
With patches numerous as Argus' eyes.
I own that patching's requisite for you,
For more we're pleas'd the less your face we view:
Yet I advise, since my advice you ask,
Wear but one patch, and that one patch a mask.

Anon.

[From *Elegant Extracts* (1805).]

DXXV.

ON A CERTAIN DELIA.

View Delia's toilet, see the borrowed plumes:
Here paints and patches rang'd, there rich perfumes;
This box an eye, the next her tooth contains:—
Delia, in short, wants nothing there but brains.

Anon.

DXXVI.

ON JULIA'S CHOICE.

A fool and knave, with different views,
  For Julia's hand apply:
The knave, to mend his fortunes, sues—
  The fool, to please his eye.

Ask you how Julia will behave?
  Depend on 't for a rule,
If she's a fool, she'll wed the knave—
  If she's a knave, the fool.

Samuel Bishop (1731–1795).

DXXVII.

ON LADIES' ACCOMPLISHMENTS.

Your dressing, dancing, gadding, where's the good in?
Sweet lady, tell me—can you make a pudding?

Anon.

[From *Epigrams in Distich* (1740).]

DXXVIII.

Written on a Looking-Glass.

"I change, and so do women too;
But I reflect, which women never do."

Anon.

DXXIX.

Answer by a Lady.

If women reflected, oh scribbler, declare,
What man, faithless man, would be bless'd by the fair?

Anon.

DXXX.

An Epitaph.

A lovely young lady I mourn in my rhymes:
She was pleasant, good-natured, and civil sometimes.
Her figure was good: she had very fine eyes,
And her talk was a mixture of foolish and wise.
Her adorers were many, and one of them said,
"She waltzed rather well! It's a pity she's dead!"

George John Cayley.

DXXXI.

On Cloris and Fanny.

Cloris! if I were Persia's king,
   I'd make my graceful queen of thee;
While Fanny, wild and artless thing,
   Should but thy humble handmaid be.

There is but one objection to it—
  That, verily, I 'm much afraid
I should, in some unlucky minute,
  Forsake the mistress for the maid.
            Thomas Moore (1779–1852).

DXXXII.
To Chloe.

I could resign that eye of blue
  Howe'er its splendour used to thrill me;
And e'en that cheek of roseate hue,—
  To lose it, Chloe, scarce would kill me.

That snowy neck I ne'er should miss,
  However much I raved about it;
And sweetly as that lip can kiss,
  I think I could exist without it.

In short, so well I 've learn'd to fast,
  That, sooth my love, I know not whether
I might not bring myself at last
  To—do without you altogether.
            Thomas Moore (1779–1852).

DXXXIII.
Written in an Album.

O thou who read'st what 's written here,
Commiserate the lot severe,
  By which, compell'd, I write them.
In vain Sophia I withstand,
For Anna adds her dread command;
  I tremble—and indite them.

Blame Eve, who, feeble to withstand
One single devil, rais'd her hand,
 And gather'd our damnation;
But do not me or Adam blame,
Tempted by two, who did the same—
 His Wife—and her Relation.

Sir George Rose.

DXXXIV.

ON A CERTAIN PHRYNE.

Thy flattering picture, Phryne, 's like to thee
Only in this, that you both painted be.

John Donne (1573-1631.)

DXXXV.

ON A PAINTED GENTLEWOMAN.

Men say you 're fair; and fair ye are, 't is true;
But, hark! we praise the painter now, not you.

Robert Herrick (1591-1674).

DXXXVI.

ON A LADY WHO WAS PAINTED.

It sounds like paradox—and yet 't is true,
You 're like your picture, though it 's not like you.

Anon.

[From *Epigrams in Distich* (1740).]

DXXXVII.

ON SEEING A LADY PAINT HERSELF.

When, by some misadventure crossed,
The banker hath his fortune lost,
Credit his instant need supplies,
And for a moment blinds our eyes.

So Delia, when her beauty's flown,
Trades on a bottom not her own,
And labours to escape detection,
By putting on a false complexion.

Robert Fergusson (1750–1774).

DXXXVIII.

ON CHLOE AND HER PICTURE.

When Chloe's picture was to Chloe shown,
Adorn'd with charms and beauties not her own;
Where Reynolds, pitying nature, kindly made
Such lips, such eyes, as Chloe never had:
"Ye Gods!" she cries, in ecstasy of heart,
"How near can nature be express'd by art!
Well, it is wondrous like!—nay, let me die,
The very pouting lip—the killing eye!"
Blunt and severe, as Manly in the play,
Downright replies—" Like, Madam, do you say?
The picture bears this likeness, it is true—
The canvas painted is, and so are you."

Anon.

DXXXIX.

On a Made-up Beauty.

"What a frail thing is beauty!" says Baron Lebras,
Perceiving his mistress had one eye of glass:
    And scarcely had he spoke it,
When she, more confus'd as more angry she grew,
By a negligent rage prov'd the maxim too true:
    She dropt the eye, and broke it.

Matthew Prior (1664–1721).

DXL.

On a certain Nell.

How capricious were Nature and Art to poor Nell!
She was painting her cheeks at the time her nose fell.

Matthew Prior.

DXLI.

On Helen's Eyebrows.

Her eyebrow box one morning lost
(The best of folks are oftenest crost),
Sad Helen thus to Jenny said
(Her careless but afflicted maid),
"Put me to bed, then, wretched Jane,
Alas! when shall I rise again?
I can behold no mortal now:
For what's an eye without a brow?

Matthew Prior.

DXLII.

On Phillis's Age.

How old may Phillis be, you ask,
   Whose beauty thus all hearts engages?
To answer is no easy task:
   For she has really two ages.

Stiff in brocade, and pinch'd in stays,
   Her patches, paint, and jewels on;
All day let envy view her face,
   And Phillis is but twenty-one.

Paint, patches, jewels laid aside,
   At night astronomers agree,
The evening has the day belied;
   And Phillis is some forty-three.

Matthew Prior (1664–1721).

DXLIII.

On Hairs and Years.

Mark how the beaux, in fond amaze,
On Julia's wanton ringlets gaze,
Whose glossy meshes seem combin'd
To catch the hearts of all mankind.

Ah, false as fair those glittering snares
Had Julia no more years than hairs,
No question, were the truth but told,
Julia would be some three years old.

Anon.

[From *The Globe* (1825).]

DXLIV.
ON A CERTAIN CELIA.

Celia, we know, is sixty-five,
    Yet Celia's face is seventeen;
Thus winter in her breast doth live,
    While summer in her face is seen.

How cruel Celia's fate, who hence
    Our heart's devotion cannot try;
Too pretty for our reverence,
    Too ancient for our gallantry!

Alexander Pope (1688–1744).

DXLV.
ON AN OLD LOVE.

Upon the cabin stairs we met—the voyage nearly over;
You leant upon his arm, my pet, from Calais unto Dover!
And *he* is looking very glad, tho' I am feeling sadder,
That *I'm* not your companion-lad on that companion-ladder!

J. Ashby Sterry.

DXLVI.
A LADY ON THE PRINCESSE DRESS.

"My dress, you 'll aver, is Economy's own,
    Designed with most exquisite taste:
From zone unto hem, and from tucker to zone,
    You can't find a vestige of *waist!*"

J. Ashby Sterry.

BOOK VIII.

On Matrimony.

DXLVII.

ON A SCHOLAR, WHO MARRIED UNFORTUNATELY.

A student, at his book so plast
    That wealth he might have won,
From book to wife did fleet in haste,
    From wealth to woe to run.

Now, who hath played a feater cast,
    Since juggling first begun?
In knitting of himself so fast,
    Himself he hath undone.

Sir Thomas More (1478–1535).

[From *Tottel's Miscellany* (1557); modernized as regards the spelling only. On "At his book so plast" Warton annotates: "So pursuing his studies." The same authority describes this as "the first pointed English epigram that I remember. The humour," he says, "does not arise from the circumstances of the character. It is a general joke on an unhappy match."]

On Matrimony.

DXLVIII.
Two Wishes for Two Manners of Mouths.

" I wish thou hadst a little narrow mouth, wife,
Little and little to drop out words in strife ! "
" And I wish you, sir, a wide mouth, for the nonce,
To speak all that you ever shall speak at once ! "

John Heywood (1506–1565).

---o---

DXLIX.
Of a Sharp Tongue.

" Wife, I perceive thy tongue was made at Edgeware."
" Yes, sir, and yours made at Rayly, hard by there."

John Heywood.

---o---

DL.
On Deliverance from Ill.

" Wife, from all evil, when shalt thou delivered be ? "
" Sir, when I " (said she) " shall be delivered from thee."

John Heywood.

---o---

DLI.
On Milton's Wife.

When Milton was blind, as all the world knows,
He married a wife, whom his friend call'd a rose ;
" I am no judge of flowers, but indeed," cried the poet,
" If she be a rose, by the thorns I may know it."

Anon.

[Milton, as every schoolboy knows, was very unfortunate in his first marriage (with Mary Powell, 1643). His second marriage was more happy. See his sonnet on the subject.]

---o---

DLII.
EPITAPH INTENDED FOR HIS WIFE.

Here lies my wife ! here let her lie !
Now she's at rest, and so am I.
John Dryden (1631–1701).

[This is genuine, and is included in the poet's works. It has been frequently paraphrased. For example :

" Here lies my wife, poor Molly : let her lie,
She's found repose at last, and so have I."

This figures in *Elegant Extracts*.]

---o---

DLIII.
ON A SCHOLAR AND HIS WIFE.

To a deep scholar said his wife :
"Would that I were a book, my life,
On me you then would sometimes look ;
But I should wish to be the book
That you would mostly wish to see ;
Then say what volume should I be?"
"An almanac," said he, "my dear;
You know we change them every year."
Anon.

[A similar story is told of the poet Dryden in Kett's *Flowers of Wit* (1814). From *Literary Anecdotes* (1852).]

DLIV.

WHY WIVES CAN MAKE NO WILLS.

Men dying make their wills, why cannot wives?
Because wives have their wills during their lives.

R. Hugman (about 1628).

---o---

DLV.

ON JOHN AND HIS WIFE.

When Nell, given o'er by the doctor, was dying,
And John at the chimney stood decently crying;
"'T is in vain," said the woman, "to make such ado,
For to our long home we must all of us go!"

"True, Nell," replied John; "but, what yet is the worst
For us that remain, the best always go first:
Remember, dear wife, that I said so last year,
When you lost your white heifer, and I my brown mare!"

Matthew Prior (1664–1721).

---o---

DLVI.

ON LUBIN AND HIS WIFE.

On his death-bed poor Lubin lies;
  His spouse is in despair:
With frequent sobs, and mutual cries,
  They both express their care.

"A different cause," says Parson Sly,
"The same effect may give:
Poor Lubin fears that he shall die;
His wife, that he may live."

Matthew Prior (1664–1721).

DLVII.

ON TOM AND HIS WIFE.

As Thomas was cudgell'd one day by his wife,
He took to the street, and fled for his life:
Tom's three dearest friends came by in the squabble,
And saved him at once from the shrew and the rabble;
Then ventured to give him some sober advice—
But Tom is a person of honour so nice,
Too wise to take counsel, too proud to take warning,
That he sent to all three a challenge next morning.
Three duels he fought, thrice ventured his life,
Went home and was cudgell'd again by his wife.

Jonathan Swift (1667–1745).

DLVIII.

ON A WINDOW AT THE FOUR CROSSES IN THE WATLING-STREET ROAD, WARWICKSHIRE.

Fool, to put up four crosses at your door,
Put up your wife, she's crosser than all four.

Jonathan Swift.

DLIX.

On Marriage v. Hanging.

" Lo ! here's the bride, and there's the tree,
Take which of these best liketh thee."
" The bargain's bad on either part—
But, hangman, come—drive on the cart."

Anon.

[From *The Festoon* (1767). Compare the lines with the following passage from *The Schole Howse*, an anonymous satire published in 1542 :—

" Trewly some men there be
    That lyve alwaye in great horroure :
And say it goeth by destynye
    To hange or wed, both hath one houre :
And whether it be, I am well sure,
Hangynge is better of the twayne,
Sooner done and shorter payne."]

DLX.

On one Codrus.

Only mark how grim Codrus's visage extends !
How unlike his own self ! how estrang'd from his friends !
He wore not this face, when, eternally gay,
He revell'd all night, and he chirrup'd all day.

Honest Codrus had then his own house at his call :
'T was Bachelor, and therefore 't was Liberty Hall :
But now he has quitted possession for life,
And he lodges, poor man ! in the house of his wife !

Samuel Bishop (1731–1795).

DLXI.

ON FOOTE'S MARRIAGE WITH A MISS PATTEN.

With a Patten to wife,
Through the rough road of life
May you safely and merrily jog;
May the ring never break,
Nor the tie prove too weak,
Nor the Foote find the Patten a clog.

Anon.

[See the note to No. CCCXVII.]

DLXII.

ON A HENPECKED SQUIRE.

As father Adam first was fool'd
(A case that's still too common),
Here lies a man a woman rul'd,
The Devil rul'd the woman.

Robert Burns (1759–1796).

DLXIII.

TO A SCHOLAR.

A scholar was about to marry.
His friend said, " Ere thou dost, be wary;
So wise art thou that I foresee
A wife will make a fool of thee."

Walter Savage Landor (1775–1864).

DLXIV.

ON ONE PETER AND HIS WIFE.

Outrageous hourly with his wife is Peter;
Some do aver he has been known to beat her.
"She seems unhappy," said a friend one day:
Peter turn'd sharply: "What is that you say?
Her temper you have there misunderstood;
She dares not be unhappy if she would."

Walter Savage Landor (1775–1864).

DLXV.

ON ANOTHER PETER AND HIS WIFE.

After such years of dissension and strife,
Some wonder that Peter should weep for his wife;
But his tears on her grave are nothing surprising,—
He's laying her dust, for fear of its rising.

Thomas Hood (1798–1845).

DLXVI.

ON HERALDRY AND MARRIAGE.

Where'er a hatchment we discern
  (A truth before ne'er started),
The motto makes us surely learn
  The sex of the departed.

If 't is the husband sleeps, he deems
  Death's day a "*felix dies*"
Of unaccustom'd quiet dreams,
  And cries—"*In cœlo quies.*"

> But if the wife, she from the tomb
> Wounds, Parthian-like, "*post tergum*,"
> Hints to her spouse his future doom,
> And threatening cries—"*Resurgam.*"
>
> > *James Smith* (1775-1839).

[From Smith's *Memoirs* (1840).]

DLXVII.

ON THE UNFORTUNATE MARRIAGE OF A MISS HONEY.

> This pair in matrimony
> Go most unequal snacks:
> He gets all the Honey,
> And she gets all the whacks.
>
> > *Theodore Edward Hook* (1788-1841).

DLXVIII.

ON THE SURPLICE QUESTION.

> A very pretty public stir
> Is making, down at Exeter,
>   About the surplice fashion;
> And many bitter words and rude
> Have been bestow'd upon the feud,
>   And much unchristian passion.
>
> For me, I neither know nor care
> Whether a Parson ought to wear
>   A black dress or a white dress;
> Fill'd with a trouble of my own,—
> A wife who preaches in her gown,
>   And lectures in her nightdress!
>
> > *Thomas Hood* (1798-1845).

DLXIX.

ON HEARING OF THE MARRIAGE OF JOB WALL TO MARY BEST.

Job, wanting a partner, thought he'd be blest,
If, of all womankind, he selected the Best;
For, said he, of all evils that compass the globe,
A bad wife would most try the patience of Job.

The Best, then, he chose, and made bone of his bone,
Though 't was clear to his friends she'd be Best left alone;
For, though Best of her sex, she's the weakest of all,
If 't is true that the weakest must go to the Wall.

Hicks.

[From J. C. Young's *Journal* (1871).]

---o---

DLXX.

ON THE MARRIAGE OF A MR. LOT WITH A MISS SALTER.

Because on her way she chose to halt,
Lot's wife, in the Scriptures, was turn'd into Salt;
But though in her course she ne'er did falter,
This young Lot's wife, strange to say, was Salter.

Hicks.

[From the same.]

---o---

DLXXI.
On Wives in General.

Lord Erskine, at women presuming to rail,
Calls a wife "a tin canister tied to one's tail,"
And fair Lady Anne, while the subject he carries on,
Seems hurt at his Lordship's degrading comparison.

Yet wherefore degrading? consider'd aright,
A canister's useful, and polish'd, and bright,
And should dirt its original purity hide,
That's the fault of the puppy to whom it is tied.

Richard Brinsley Sheridan (1751–1816).

—o—

DLXXII.
Endorsement to the Deed of Separation between Lord Byron and his Wife, April, 1816.

A year ago, you swore, fond she!
"To love, to honour," and so forth:
Such was the vow you pledged to me,
And here's exactly what 't is worth.

Lord Byron (1788–1824).

—o—

DLXXIII.
On his Wedding-Day.

Here's a happy new year! but with reason,
I beg you'll permit me to say—
Wish me many returns of the season,
But as few as you please of the day.

Lord Byron.

[Written on January 2, 1820.]

DLXXIV.
ON THE SAME.

This day, of all our days, has done
　　The worst for *me* and *you* :—
'T is just *six* years since we were *one*,
　　And *five* since we were *two*.

Lord Byron (1788–1824).

[Written on January 2, 1821.]

—o—

DLXXV.
ON THE MARRIAGE OF A VERY THIN COUPLE.

St. Paul has declar'd that when persons, tho' twain,
Are in wedlock united, one flesh they remain :
But had he been by, when, like Pharaoh's kine pairing,
Dr. Douglas of Barnet espoused Miss Mainwaring,
The Apostle, no doubt, would have alter'd his tone,
And have said, "These two splinters shall now make one
　　bone."

Anon.

[From *Blackwood's Magazine* (1825).]

—o—

DLXXVI.
ON MARRIAGE-MAKING.

Though matches are all made in Heaven, they say,
　　Yet Hymen, who mischief oft hatches,
Sometimes deals with the house t' other side of the way,
　　And there they make Lucifer-matches.

Samuel Lover (1797–1868).

DLXXVII.
On Married Men.

A fellow that's single, a fine fellow's he;
But a fellow that's married's a felo-de-se.

Charles Shirley Brooks (1815–1874).

[From *Punch*.]

—o—

DLXXVIII.
On Love and Marriage.

'T is highly rational, we can't dispute,
That Love, being naked, should promote a suit:
But doth not oddity to him attach
Whose fire's so oft extinguished by a match?

Richard Garnett.

—o—

DLXXIX.
On Dress.

He who a gold-finch strives to make his wife
Makes her, perhaps, a wag-tail all her life.

Anon.

[From *A Collection of Epigrams* (1727).]

—o—

DLXXX.
To a Lady.

My heart still hovering round about you,
I thought I could not live without you;
Now we've lived three months asunder,
How I lived with you is the wonder.

Anon.

DLXXXI.

ON A VIOLENT WIFE.

A woman lately fiercely did assail
Her husband with sharp tongue, but sharper nail:
But one, that heard and saw it, to her said:
" Why do you use him thus? He is your head."
" He is my head indeed," said she, " 't is true;
Sir, I may scratch my head, and so may you."
Anon.

DLXXXII.

ON A MERCENARY MARRIAGE.

When Lovelace married Lady Jenny,
Whose beauty was the ready penny,
" I chose her," said he, " like old plate,
Not for the fashion, but the weight!"
Anon.

DLXXXIII.

ON THE ACHIEVEMENT OF A MARRIED LADY, DECEASED.

God has to me sufficiently been kind,
To take my wife, and leave me here behind.
Anon.

DLXXXIV.

ON ONE JACK AND HIS WIFE.

Brutus unmoved heard how his Portia fell;
Should Jack's wife die—he would behave as well.

Anon.

DLXXXV.

ON ONE NED AND HIS WIFE.

Cries Ned to his neighbours, as onwards they prest,
Conveying his wife to the place of long rest,
"Take, friends, I beseech you, a little more leisure;
For why should we thus make a toil of a pleasure?"

Anon.

DLXXXVI.

ON ONE PETER AND HIS WIFE.

Know we not all, the Scripture saith,
That man and wife are *one* till death?
But Peter and his scolding wife
Wage such an endless war of strife,
You'd swear, on passing Peter's door,
That man and wife at least were *four*.

Anon.

DLXXXVII.

On a Lady who Beat her Husband.

"Come hither, Sir John, my picture is here:
   What say you, my love, does it strike you?"
"I can't say it does just at present, my dear,
   But I think it soon will, it's so like you."

Anon.

DLXXXVIII.

The End of Life.

Tom praised his friend, who changed his state,
For binding fast himself and Kate
   In union so divine:
"Wedlock's the end of life," he cried;—
"Too true, alas!" said Jack, and sigh'd—
   "'T will be the end of mine."

Anon.

DLXXXIX.

Alone and Weary.

"My dear, what makes you always yawn?"
   The wife exclaim'd, her temper gone;
     "Is home so dull and dreary?"
"Not so, my love," he said, "not so;
   But man and wife are one, you know,
     And when alone I'm weary!"

Anon.

DXC.

ON HIS WIFE'S PICTURE.

How like is this picture, you'd think that it breathes!
    What life! what expression! what spirit!
It wants but a tongue. "Oh no!" said the spouse,
    "That want is its principal merit."

Anon.

DXCI.

NO WILL OF HIS OWN.

Jerry dying intestate, his relatives claim'd,
Whilst his widow most vilely his mem'ry defam'd:
"What!" cries she, "must I suffer because the old knave,
Without leaving a will, is laid snug in the grave?"
"That's no wonder," says one, "for 't is very well known,
Since he married, poor man, he'd no will of his own!"

Anon.

DXCII.

BENEVOLENT NEUTRALITY.

When man and wife at odds fall out,
    Let syntax be your tutor;
'Twixt masculine and feminine,
    What should one be but neuter?

Anon.

DXCIII.

NOT KEPT, BUT SOLD.

" My wife 's so very bad," cried Will,
  " I fear she ne'er will hold it—
She keeps her bed."—" Mine 's worse," said Phil,
  " The jade has just now sold it."

Anon.

DXCIV.

ON AN OLD WOMAN MARRYING A YOUNG LAD.

Hard is the fate of ev'ry childless wife;
The thoughts of wedlock tantalize her life.
Troth, aged bride, by thee 't was wisely done,
To choose a child and husband both in one.

Anon.

DXCV.

ON A MR. HUSBAND'S MARRIAGE.

This case is the strangest we 've known in our life,
The husband's a husband, and so is the wife.

Anon.

DXCVI.

Of all Evils the Least.

" Good morning, dear Major," quoth Lieutenant B——,
" So you 're married, I hear, to the little Miss E——;
Is it true that she scarcely comes up to your knee?"
" It is, dear Lieutenant, and this I contest,
That of all human evils the least is the best."

Anon.

DXCVII.

The Only Happy Hour.

Cries she to Will, 'midst matrimonial strife,
  " Cursed be the hour I first became your wife!"
" By all the powers," said Will, " but that's too bad!
  You've cursed the only happy hour we've had."

Anon.

DXCVIII.

Under Government.

  A place under Government
    Was all that Paddy wanted:
  He married soon a scolding wife,
    And thus his wish was granted.

Anon.

BOOK IX.
General.

DXCIX.
The World.

"What makes you think the world is round?
  Give me the reason fair!"
"Because so very few are found
  Who act upon the square."

Thomas Dibdin (1771–1841).

DC.
On the Same.

The world is like a rink, you know:
You lose your *wheel*, and come to woe!

J. Ashby Sterry.

DCI.
On John Bull.

The world is a bundle of hay;
  Mankind are the asses who pull;
Each tugs it a different way,
  And the greatest of all is John Bull.

Lord Byron (1788–1824).

DCII.
ON SCOTCH WEATHER.

Scotland! thy weather's like a modish wife;
Thy winds and rain for ever are at strife;
Like thee, the termagants their blustering try,
And, when they can no longer scold, they cry.

Aaron Hill (1685–1750).

DCIII.
ON SCOTCHMEN AND THEIR COUNTRY.

Indians assert that wheresoe'er they roam,
If slain they reach again their native home.
If every nation held this maxim right,
Not English bread would make a Scotchman fight.

Anon.

[From *A Collection of Epigrams* (1707). It was in a similar spirit of satire that Cleveland introduced into a poem of his the following couplet :—

" Had Cain been Scot, God would have changed his doom;
Not forced him wander, but compell'd him home."]

DCIV.
ON THE SAME.

I wonder'd not when I was told
The venal Scot his country sold :
I rather very much admire
How he could ever find a buyer!

Anon.

[From Nichol's *Select Collection of Poems*.]

DCV.

ON AN APPLE BEING THROWN AT COOKE, THE ACTOR, WHILST PLAYING SIR PERTINAX MACSYCOPHANT.

Some envious Scot, you say, the apple threw,
Because the character was drawn too true.
It can't be so, for all must know "right weel"
That a true Scot had only thrown the peel.

Anon.

[Cooke was born in 1786, and died in 1864. Sir Pertinax MacSycophant is a character in Macklin's *Man of the World*.]

DCVI.

ON NORTHERN LIGHTS.

To roar and bore of Northern wights
    The tendency so frail is,
That men do call those Northern Lights
    Au-ror-a Bor-ealis.

Joseph Jekyll.

[From Miss Mitford's *Letters*.]

DCVII.

ON THE BANKS AND PAPER CREDIT OF SCOTLAND.

To tell us why banks thus in Scotland obtain,
  Requires not the head of a Newton or Napier;
Without calculation the matter's quite plain—
  Where there's plenty of rags, you'll have plenty of paper.

Anon.

DCVIII.

ON EDINBURGH.

Pompous the boast, and yet a truth it speaks:
A "Modern Athens"—fit for modern Greeks.

James Hannay (1827–1873).

—o—

DCIX.

ON SCOTCH FRUGALITY.

It seems that the Scots
Turn out much better shots
At long distance, than most of the Englishmen are;
But this we all knew
That a Scotchman could do—
Make a small piece of metal go awfully far.

Charles Shirley Brooks (1815–1874).

[From *Punch*.]

—o—

DCX.

ON SCOTCHMEN AND "GOOD WORKS."

There's this to say about the Scotch,
So bother bannocks, braes, and birks;—
They can't produce a decent Watch,
For Calvinists despise good works.

Charles Shirley Brooks.

[From *Punch*.]

General. 237

DCXI.

On Irish Sense.

Behold! a proof of Irish sense;
    Here Irish wit is seen!
When nothing's left that's worth defence,
    We build a magazine.
            Jonathan Swift (1667–1745).

[This was the Dean's last composition, and was written during one of the lucid intervals of the madness that afflicted the latter years of his life. It originated in his seeing a new building in course of erection in Dublin, and being told, in reply to his inquiry, that it was a magazine.]

——o——

DCXII.

On French Taste.

The French have taste in all they do,
    Which we are quite without;
For Nature, that to them gave *goût*,
    To us gave only gout.
            Thomas, Lord Erskine (1748–1823).

[Rogers calls this "far from bad." See his *Table Talk* (1856).]

——o——

DCXIII.

Answer to the Above.

Condemn not in such haste,
    To letters four appealing;
Their "goût" is only taste,
    The English "gout" is feeling.
            Anon.

DCXIV.

ON WELSH POVERTY.

A Welshman and an Englishman disputed
   Which of their lands maintained the greatest state;
The Englishman the Welshman quite confuted,
   Yet would the Welshman naught his brags abate.
"Ten cooks," quoth he, "in Wales one wedding sees."
"True," quoth the other, "each man toasts his cheese."

Henry Parrot (about 1613).

DCXV.

WELSH RABBIT.

The way to make a Welshman thirst for bliss,
   And say his prayers daily on his knees,
Is to persuade him that most certain 't is
   The moon is made of nothing but green cheese;
And he'll desire of God no greater boon,
But place in heav'n to feed upon the moon.

John Taylor (1580–1654).

DCXVI.

ON FRENCH AND ENGLISH.

The French excel us very much in millinery;
They also bear the bell in matters culinary.
The reason's plain: French beauty and French meat
With English cannot of themselves compete.

Thus, an inferior article possessing,
Our neighbours help it by superior dressing.
They dress their dishes, and they dress their dames,
Till Art, almost, can rival Nature's claims.

Lord Neaves (1800–1876).

―o―

DCXVII.

THE SWISS AND THE FRENCHMAN.

To a Swiss, a gay Frenchman in company said,
"Your soldiers are forced, sir, to fight for their bread,
Whilst for honour alone the French rush to the field ;—
So your motives to ours, sir, must certainly yield."
"By no means," cried the other, "pray why should you boast?
Each fights for the thing he's in need of the most."

Anon.

―o―

DCXVIII.

ON A PASSAGE IN THE "SCALIGERIANA."

When you with High-Dutch Heeren dine,
Expect false Latin and stumm'd wine ;
They never taste, who always drink ;
They always talk, who never think.

Matthew Prior (1664–1721).

[The passage in question is as follows :—" Les Allemans ne ce soucient pas quel vin ils boivent, pourveu que ce soit vin, ni quel Latin ils parlent, pourveu que ce soit Latin."]

DCXIX.
ON GERMAN DRINKING.

I went to Frankfort and got drunk
With that most learn'd Professor Brunck:
I went to Wortz and got more drunken
With that more learn'd Professor Ruhnken.
    Richard Porson (1759–1808).

[This epigram is wholly imaginary, for Porson was never out of England. The lines are from *Facetiae Cantabrigienses* (1825).]

---o---

DCXX.
ON COLOGNE AND THE RHINE.

In Köln, a town of monks and bones,
And pavement fang'd with murderous stones,
And rags, and hags, and hideous wenches,
I counted two-and-seventy stenches,
All well defined, and several stinks!
Ye Nymphs that reign o'er sewers and sinks,
The river Rhine, it is well known,
Doth wash your city of Cologne;
But tell me, Nymphs! what power divine
Shall henceforth wash the river Rhine?
   Samuel Taylor Coleridge (1772–1834).

[Coleridge does not, however, represent Cologne as wholly without attraction. He writes elsewhere:

"As I am a rhymer,
And now, at least, a merry one,
Mr. Mum's Rudesheimer,
And the church of St. Geryon,
Are the two things alone
That deserve to be known
In the body-and-soul-stinking town of Cologne."]

DCXXI.
OF FRIENDSHIP.

New friends are no friends; how can that be true?
The oldest friends that are, were sometimes new.

Sir John Haryngton (1561–1612).

---o---

DCXXII.
OF TREASON.

Treason doth never prosper; what's the reason?
For if it prosper, none dare call it treason.

Sir John Haryngton.

---o---

DCXXIII.
TO THE FLATTERERS.

Thy flattering of me this followeth thereupon :
Either thou art a fool, or else I am one.
Where flattery appeareth, at least, by wise men's school,
The flatterer, or the flattered, is a fool.

John Heywood (1506–1565).

---o---

DCXXIV.
OF A MAN AND A CLOCK.

Men take man of earthly things most excellent :
But in one thing thou seem'st under that extent.
A clock after noon above thee I avow,—
A clock can go alone then; so canst not thou.

John Heywood.

DCXXV.

OF NEWGATE WINDOWS.

All Newgate windows bay windows they be;
All lookers out there stand at bay we see.
John Heywood (b. 1506, d. 1565).

DCXXVI.

IN VIRTUTEM.

Virtue we praise, but practise not her good,
  (Athenian-like) we act not what we know.
So many men do talk of Robin Hood
  Who never yet shot arrow from his bow.
Thomas Freeman (circa 1591–1614).

DCXXVII.

ON DRUNKEN COURAGE.

Who only in his cups will fight is like
A clock that must be oil'd well ere it strike.
Thomas Bancroft (about 1600).

DCXXVIII.

ON BLESSED IGNORANCE.

He is most happy sure that knoweth nought,
Because he knows not that he knoweth not.
Robert Heath (about 1620–50).

[Everybody recollects the lines by Gray:—

> "Where ignorance is bliss,
> 'T is folly to be wise."]

———o———

DCXXIX.

ON POVERTY.

He who in his pocket has no money
Should, in his mouth, be never without honey.

Anon.

[From *Epigrams in Distich* (1740).]

———o———

DCXXX.

ON READING THAT LORD EXETER'S HORSE "PROGRESS" HAD REFUSED TO RUN AGAINST MR. WORTLEY'S "SCANDAL."

Oh! surely this horse had more wit than his master,
　　In thus wisely refusing to run;
For we know by experience Scandal flies faster
　　Than any horse under the sun.

Mrs. Carey.

———o———

DCXXXI.

ON SEEING THE WORDS "DOMUS ULTIMA" INSCRIBED ON THE VAULT OF THE DUKES OF RICHMOND IN CHICHESTER CATHEDRAL.

   Did he, who thus inscrib'd the wall,
   Not read, or not believe St. Paul,
   Who says there is, where'er it stands,
   Another house not made with hands ;
   Or may we gather from these words,
   That house is not a House of Lords?

      William Clarke (1696–1771).

[From Nichols' *Literary Anecdotes* (1812).]

DCXXXII.

ALL SAINTS'.

In a church which is furnish'd with mullion and gable,
 With altar and reredos, with gargoyle and groin,
The penitents' dresses are sealskin and sable,
 The odour of sanctity's eau-de-Cologne.

But only could Lucifer, flying from Hades,
 Gaze down on this crowd with its panniers and paints,
He would say, as he look'd at the lords and the ladies,
 "Oh, where is All Sinners', if this is All Saints'?"

     Edmund Hodgson Yates.

DCXXXIII.

ON DRESS v. DINNER.

What is the reason, can you guess,
    When men are poor, and women thinner?
So much do they for dinner dress,
    There's nothing left to dress for dinner.
Anon.

DCXXXIV.

ON MONEY.

Gold is so ductile, learned chemists say,
That half an ounce will stretch a wondrous way:
The metal's base, or else the chemists err,
For now-a-days our Sovereigns won't go far!
Anon.

DCXXXV.

ON FASHION AND RIGHT.

"What's fashionable, I'll maintain
Is always right," cries sprightly Jane:
"Ah, would to Heaven," cries graver Sue,
"What's right were fashionable too."
Anon.

DCXXXVI.

ON TRUTH.

Truth, they say, lies in a well;
    A paradox, forsooth!
For if it lies, as people tell,
    How can it then be truth?

Anon.

DCXXXVII.

AN EPITAPH FOR HIMSELF.

Nobles and Heralds, by your leave,
    Here lies what once was Matthew Prior,
The son of Adam and of Eve:
    Can Bourbon or Nassau claim higher?

Matthew Prior (1664–1721).

[This, says Singer, "has its prototype in one long previously written by or for one John Carnegie," as follows:—

    Johnnie Carnegie lais heer,
        Descendit of Adam and Eve,
    Gif ony can gang hieher,
        I'se willing gie him leve.

The same lines, with only slight verbal alterations, are given in *Sharpe's London Journal*, vol. xiv., where they are stated to have been taken from a monument erected in 1703, in the New Church burying-ground of Dundee, to the memory of one "J. R."]

DCXXXVIII.

An Epitaph on Himself.

Life is a jest, and all things show it:
I thought so once, and now I know it.
John Gay (1688–1732).

—o—

DCXXXIX.

Engraved on the Collar of a Dog which he gave to His Royal Highness.

I am his Highness' dog at Kew;
Pray tell me, sir, whose dog are you?
Alexander Pope (1688–1744).

[The "Royal Highness" here referred to was Frederick, Prince of Wales, who began his lease of Kew House in 1730. "When Pope wrote this epigram," says Hackett, "I think he must have recollected a passage from Sir William Temple's 'Heads designed for an Essay on Conversation.' 'Mr. Grantam's fool's reply to a great man that asked him whose fool he was:—I am Mr. Grantam's fool: pray whose fool are you?'"]

—o—

DCXL.

On a Public-House.

On this establishment how can we speak?
Its cheese is mity, and its ale is weak.
Anon.

DCXLI.

ON THE FASHIONABLE MANIA FOR JEWELLERY AND GAMBLING.

Thoughtless that "all that's brightest fades,"
Unmindful of that Knave of Spades,
      The Sexton and his Subs,
How foolishly we play our parts—
Our wives on *diamonds* set their *hearts*,
      We set our *hearts* on *clubs*.
        Sydney Smith (1771–1845).

[Written at the time that Crockford's Club was opened.]

DCXLII.

ON A WATCH LOST IN A TAVERN.

A watch lost in a tavern! that's a crime;
Then see how men by drinking lose their time.

Henceforth, if you will keep your Watch, this do,—
Pocket your Watch, and watch your Pocket too.

        Anon.

[From *Westminster Drollery* (1671).]

DCXLIII.

ON FOREKNOWLEDGE.

If a man might know
The ill he must undergo,
And shun it so,
Then it were good to know.

But if he undergo it,
Though he know it,
What boots him know it?
He must undergo it.

Sir John Suckling (1609-1641).

DCXLIV.

THE METAMORPHOSES OF LOVE.

The little boy, to show his might and pow'r,
Turn'd Iö to a cow, Narcissus to a flow'r;
Transform'd Apollo to a homely swain,
And Jove himself into a golden rain.
These shapes were tolerable; but, by the mass,
He's metamorphos'd me into an ass!

Sir John Suckling.

DCXLV.

ON LOVE.

Love levels all,—it elevates the clown,
And often brings the fattest people down.

Henry James Byron.

DCXLVI.

ON ST. PAUL'S CATHEDRAL.

This is God's House; but 't is to be deplor'd
More come to see the House than serve its Lord.

Anon.

[From *Epigrams in Distich* (1740).]

DCXLVII.

ON THE ART-UNIONS.

That Picture-Raffles will conduce to nourish
Design, or cause good colouring to flourish,
Admits of logic-chopping and wise-sawing;
But surely Lotteries encourage Drawing?

Thomas Hood (1798–1845).

DCXLVIII.

SCIRE TUUM NIHIL EST.

To have a thing is little, if you're not allowed to show it,
And to know a thing is nothing, unless others know you
  know it.

Lord Neaves (1800–1876).

[Pascal has a *Pensée* founded on very much the same idea.]

DCXLIX.

A MERRY THOUGHT.

He cannot be complete in aught
  Who is not humorously prone—
A man without a merry thought
  Can hardly have a funny bone.

Frederick Locker.

DCL.

ON TRAVELLERS' INVENTION.

'T is stated by a captious tribe,
Travellers each other but transcribe.
This charge to truth has no pretension,
For half they write's their own invention.

Anon.

DCLI.

ON INCLOSURES.

'T is bad enough, in man or woman,
To steal a goose from off a common;
But surely he's without excuse
Who steals the common from the goose.

Anon.

DCLII.

ON A MIRROR.

A mirror has been well defined
An emblem of a thoughtful mind;
For, look upon it when you will,
You find it is reflecting still.

Anon.

BOOK X.

Miscellaneous.

DCLIII.

ON THE CASTLE OF DUBLIN (1715).

This house and inhabitants both well agree,
And resemble each other as near as can be;
One-half is decay'd, and in want of a prop,
The other new-built, but not finish'd at top.

Thomas Parnell (1679–1718).

DCLIV.

FIVE REASONS FOR DRINKING.

If all be true that I do think,
There are five reasons we should drink:
Good wine: a friend: or being dry:
Or lest we should be by-and-by:
Or any other reason why.

Henry Aldrich (1647–1710).

[It is not certain that these lines are by the Dean. They

are, however, a translation, by whomsoever executed, of the following Latin epigram from his pen :—

"Si bene commemini, causæ sunt quinque bibendi;
Hospitis adventus; præsens sitis; atque futura;
Et vini bonitas; et quælibet altera causa."]

—o—

DCLV.

WRITTEN IN A LADY'S PRAYER-BOOK.

In vain Clarinda night and day
For mercy to the Gods you pray.
What arrogance on Heaven to call
For that which you deny to all!

George Granville, Lord Lansdowne (1667–1735).

—o—

DCLVI.

ON THE INN AT INVERARY.

Whae'er he be that sojourns here,
  I pity much his case,
Unless he come to wait upon
  The Lord their God, his Grace.

There's nothing here but Highland pride,
  And Highland scab and hunger;
If Providence has sent me here,
  'T was surely in His anger.

Robert Burns (1759–1796).

DCLVII.

ON A CARICATURE REPRESENTING THREE HARROW BOYS IN A PAIR OF SCALES, OUTWEIGHING THREE ETONIANS.

> What mean ye by this print so rare,
>   Ye wits, of Eton jealous,
> But that we soar aloft in air,
>   While ye are heavy fellows?
>   *Right Hon. George Canning* (1770–1827).

[This appeared in the Eton school magazine called *The Microcosm*, and was replied to in the following epigram by Hook, then a boy at Harrow.]

---o---

DCLVIII.

REPLY TO THE ABOVE.

> Cease, ye Etonians! and no more
>   With rival wits contend:
> Feathers, we know, will float in air,
>   And bubbles will ascend.
>   *Theodore Edward Hook* (1788–1841).

---o---

DCLIX.

ON TWINING, THE TEA-MERCHANT.

> It seems as if Nature had curiously plann'd
>   That men's names with their trades should agree;
> There's Twining the Tea-man, who lives in the Strand,
>   Would be whining, if robb'd of his T.
>   *Theodore Edward Hook.*

DCLX.

ON A CERTAIN NOBLEMAN DESERTING HIS CAUSE AGAINST A MR. CUMMING.

Cease your humming;
The case is "on";
Defendant's *Cumming*,
Plaintiff's—gone!
Theodore Edward Hook (1788–1841).

---o---

DCLXI.

ON FLOWERS AND FRUITS.

That plants feel attachments grave Darwin believ'd,
And Seward opin'd that he was not deceiv'd;
But if Flowers can love in their natural state,
We beg to contend that the Fruits can bear hate;—
And our reason for this will be surely thought fair,
Since the very first Apple destroy'd the first Pair.

Anon.

[From *John Bull* (1825).]

---o---

DCLXII.

TO A YOUNG LADY,

Who asked him to Write Something Original for her Album.

An original something, dear maid, you would win me
To write—but how shall I begin?
For I fear I have nothing original in me—
Excepting Original Sin.

Thomas Campbell (1777–1844).

DCLXIII.

On Grapes and Gripes.

In Spain, that land of monks and apes,
The thing called wine doth come from grapes;
But, on the noble river Rhine,
The thing called gripes doth come from wine.

Samuel Taylor Coleridge (1772–1834).

[From J. C. Young's *Journal*. Coleridge, whilst boating on the Rhine, had partaken of a draught of Hockheimer, and this was the result.]

DCLXIV.

On an Exchange.

We pledged our hearts, my love and I,—
   I in my arms the maiden clasping;
I could not tell the reason why,
   But, oh! I trembled like an aspen.

Her father's love she bade me gain;
   I went, and shook like any reed!
I strove to act the man—in vain!
   We had exchanged our hearts indeed.

Samuel Taylor Coleridge.

DCLXV.

On Pius Æneas.

Virgil, whose magic verse enthrals,—
   And who in verse is greater?
By turns his wand'ring hero calls,
   Now *pius*, and now *pater*.

But when prepared the worst to brave,
  An action that must pain us,
Queen Dido meets him in the cave,
  And dubs him *dux Trojanus*.

And well he changes thus the word
  On that occasion, sure;
Pius Æneas were absurd,
  And *Pater* premature!

James Smith (1775–1839).

["It is worthy of remark," says Barham, "that the piece of sound criticism contained in these lines is to be attributed to Addison. On reading the sixth number of *The Tatler*, where the subject is discussed, he at once detected Steele to be the author, having himself pointed out to him the poet's nicety of taste in varying the epithet with the circumstances."]

DCLXVI.

ON BEING OBLIGED TO LEAVE A PLEASANT PARTY, FROM THE WANT OF A PAIR OF BREECHES TO DRESS FOR DINNER IN.

Between Adam and me the great difference is,
  Though a paradise each has been forced to resign,
That he never wore breeches till turn'd out of his,
  While, for want of my breeches, I'm banish'd from mine.

Thomas Moore (1779–1852).

DCLXVII.

Dialogue between a Dowager and her Maid.

"I want the *Court Guide*," said my Lady, "to look
 If the house, Seymour Place, be at 30 or 20."
"We've lost the *Court Guide*, ma'am, but here's the *Red Book*,
 Where you'll find, I dare say, Seymour *Places* in plenty!"

Thomas Moore (1779–1852).

[In allusion, of course, to the number of appointments held by gentlemen of the Seymour family.]

—o—

DCLXVIII.

A Joke Versified.

"Come, come," said Tom's father, "at your time of life,
 There's no longer excuse for thus playing the rake.
It is time, you should think, boy, of taking a wife."—
 "Why, so it is, father—whose wife shall I take?"

Thomas Moore.

[The story is told of R. B. Sheridan and his son.]

—o—

DCLXIX.

On the Superiority of Machinery.

A mechanic his labour will often discard,
 If the rate of his pay he dislikes;
But a clock—and its case is uncommonly hard—
 Will continue to work, tho' it strikes!

Thomas Hood (1798–1845).

DCLXX.

ON THE HALF-FARTHINGS.

" Too small for any marketable shift,
   What purpose can there be for coins like these ? "—
Hush, hush, good Sir !—Thus charitable Thrift
   May give a Mite to him who wants a cheese !

Thomas Hood (1798–1845).

DCLXXI.

ON ATHOL BROSE.

Charm'd with a drink which Highlanders compose,
   A German traveller exclaim'd with glee,—
" Potztausend ! sare, if dis is Athol Brose,
   How goot dere Athol Boetry must be ! "

Thomas Hood.

DCLXXII.

ON THE ABBEY CHURCH AT BATH.

These walls, so full of monument and bust,
Show how Bath-Waters serve to lay the dust.

Dr. Harrington.

DCLXXIII.

AT FINGERS' END.

The Latin word for " cold," one ask'd his friend ;
" It is," said he—" 't is at my fingers' end."

Anon.

[From *Elegant Extracts* (1805).]

DCLXXIV.

ON THE LONG SPEECHES OF THE FRENCH DEPUTIES ON THE LIBERTY OF THE PRESS.

The French enjoy freedom, they say;
  And where is the man who can doubt it?
For they have, it is clear, every day,
  The freedom of talking about it.

Anon.

DCLXXV.

WRITTEN IN THE WAITING-ROOM AT THE OFFICE OF THE SECRETARY OF STATE.

In sore afflictions sent by God's commands,
In patience Job the great example stands;
But in these days a trial more severe
Had been Job's lot, if God had sent him here.

Anon.

DCLXXVI.

ON A TALL DULL MAN,

Who invited the Writer to make Verses on Him.

Unlike my subject now shall be my song:
It shall be witty, and it shan't be long.

Philip Stanhope, Lord Chesterfield (1694–1773).

[Sir Thomas Robinson is the person here satirized.]

Miscellaneous.

DCLXXVII.

ON ONE GILES.

By one decisive argument
Giles gain'd his lovely Kate's consent
　　To fix the bridal day.
"Why in such haste, dear Giles, to wed?
I shall not change my mind," she said,—
"But then," says he, "I may."

Anon.

DCLXXVIII.

ON A LAME BEGGAR.

"I am unable," yonder beggar cries,
"To stand or move."　If he say true, he lies.

John Donne (1573–1631).

DCLXXIX.

ON THE LATIN GERUNDS.

When Dido found Æneas would not come,
She mourn'd in silence, and was Di-do-dum.

Richard Porson (1759–1808).

[Porson wrote the above in proof of the assertion that he could rhyme upon anything. See his *Life* by Watson (1861).]

DCLXXX.

On a certain Count Going to Italy and Leaving an Opera Score behind Him.

He has quitted the Countess—what can she wish more?
She loses one husband, and gets back a score.
                         Samuel Rogers (1765-1855).

---o---

DCLXXXI.

On some Bad Roads.

I'm now arriv'd—thanks to the Gods!—
 Through pathways rough and muddy,—
A certain sign that makin' roads
 Is no this people's study.

Altho' I'm no wi' Scripture cramm'd,
 I'm sure the Bible says
That heedless sinners shall be damn'd,
 Unless they mend their ways.
                         Robert Burns (1759-1796).

[The roads in question were between Kilmarnock and Stewarton, but the epigram is, unfortunately, only too general in its application.]

---o---

DCLXXXII.

On One run over by an Omnibus.

Killed by an omnibus—why not?
 So quick a death a boon is:
Let not his friends lament his lot—
 Mors omnibus communis.
                         Henry Luttrell (1770-1851).

DCLXXXIII.
ON AILING AND ALE-ING.

Come, come, for trifles never stick :
Most servants have a failing ;
Yours, it is true, are sometimes sick,
But mine are always ale-ing.

Henry Luttrell (1770–1851).

[A versification of one of his own jokes.]

---o---

DCLXXXIV.
ON PICKING POCKETS.

" These beer-shops," quoth Barnabas, speaking in alt,
" Are ruinous—down with the growers of malt ! "
" Too true," answers Ben, with a shake of the head,
" Wherever they congregate, honesty 's dead.
That beer breeds dishonesty causes no wonder ;
'T is nurtur'd in crime—'t is concocted in plunder ;
In Kent, while surrounded by flourishing crops,
I saw a rogue picking a pocket of hops ! "

James Smith (1775–1839).

---o---

DCLXXXV.
ON PANES AND PAINS.

Beneath the Piazza two wags chanced to pass,
Where a shop was adorned by an acre of glass.
Quoth Tom, *sotto voce*, " Hail, Burnett & Co. !
Success now-a-days is dependent on show."
" Not so," answered Richard, " here industry reigns ;
Success is dependent on using great *panes*."

James Smith.

DCLXXXVI.

On a certain Tanner.

A Bermondsey tanner would often engage
   In a long tête-à-tête with his dame,
While trotting to town in the Kensington stage,
   About giving their villa a name.

A neighbour, thus hearing the skin-dresser talk,
   Stole out, half an hour after dark,
Pick'd up on the roadway a fragment of chalk,
   And wrote on the palings—" *Hide* Park ! "

James Smith (1775–1839).

DCLXXXVII.

Impromptu under a Marquee at Fleming House.

When Parliament people petition their friends,
The state of the poll on the canvass depends;
But here we submit to a diff'rent control,—
The state of the canvas depends on the pole !

James Smith.

DCLXXXVIII.

To a Lady.

Howell and James, in taste correct,
   Unfold their silken pack,
From which a pattern I select
   Of lavender and black.

If you dislike it, you'll not press
  Your lip to Lethe's cup;
For, should you quarrel with the dress,
  You'll never make it up.
                    James Smith (1775–1839).

DCLXXXIX.

ON THE AMERICAN RIVERS.

In England rivers all are males—
  For instance, Father Thames—
Whoever in Columbia sails
  Finds them ma'amselles or dames.

Yes, there the softer sex presides,
  Aquatic, I assure ye,
And Mrs. Sippy rolls her tides
  Responsive to Miss Souri.
                    James Smith.

DCXC.

ON AN INVOLUNTARY CONJUROR.

As strong in the fist as a ditcher or hedger,
Tom lifts single-handed a counting-house ledger.
Says Dick, "This is mere sleight-of-hand, it is plain;
You only can do it by *ledger*-de-main."
                    James Smith.

DCXCI.

ON WESTMINSTER BRIDGE.

As late the Trades' Unions, by way of a show,
O'er Westminster Bridge strutted five in a row,
"I feel for the bridge," whisper'd Dick, with a shiver;
"Thus tried by the mob, it may sink in the river."
Quoth Tom, a crown lawyer, "Abandon your fears;
As a bridge, it can only be tried by its *piers*."

James Smith (1775–1839).

DCXCII.

ACTOR AND FISHMONGER.

An actor one day, at a fishmonger's shop
  In the city, stood kicking his heels,
And cried, "I espy an indifferent crop;
  You've nothing but turbots and eels.

"Your benefits bring you a bumper, my lad,
  But still it must give you the spleen.
I find in your house not a *plaice* to be had,
  And yet not a *sole* to be seen."

James Smith.

DCXCIII.

ON THE NEW COOK ON TRIAL AT FLEMING HOUSE.

My Lord, an objection I've plump'd on:
  Your sentence must yet be delay'd;
The hearing can't take place at Brompton,
  The venue's improperly laid.

Then nonsuit this case : be impartial,
And send it to Portsmouth instead ;
In trying a cook by Court-martial,
The Court must be held at *Spit*head.

James Smith (1775-1839).

DCXCIV.

IN SEASON.

At Brompton I, when winter reigns,
  Great-coated, quaff my wine ;
But when red Phœbus tans the plains,
  I under canvas dine.

My glass I to each season shape,
  Nor keep, in either, Lent :
My drink when winter frowns is Cape,
  My summer beverage Tent.

James Smith.

DCXCV.

ON MACLISE'S PORTRAIT OF MACREADY AS MACBETH.

Maclise's Macready's Macbeth
  As a picture defies all attacks ;
Yet, uniting these three in a breath,
  It is only a view of *Al-macks.*

Laman Blanchard (1803-1865).

DCXCVI.

ON A PICTURE CALLED "THE DOUBTFUL SNEEZE."

The Doubtful Sneeze! a failure quite—
A winker half, and half a gaper—
Alas! to paint on canvas here
What should have been on tissue paper!

Thomas Hood (1798–1845).

[From *The London Magazine* (1823).]

DCXCVII.

A REFLECTION.

When Eve upon the first of Men
The apple press'd with specious cant,
Oh! what a thousand pities then
That Adam was not Adamant!

Thomas Hood.

DCXCVIII.

ON THE PURSUIT OF LETTERS.

The Germans for learning enjoy great repute,
But the English make Letters still more a pursuit;
For a Cockney will go from the banks of the Thames
To Cologne for an O, and old Nassau for M's.

Thomas Hood.

Miscellaneous.

DCXCIX.

On a Late Cattle-Show at Smithfield.

Old Farmer Bull is taken sick,
Yet not with any sudden trick
　　Of fever, or his old dyspepsy;
But having seen the foreign stock,
It gave his system such a shock,
　　He's had a fit of cattle-epsy!

Thomas Hood (1798–1845).

DCC.

Good Advice.

This gardener's rule applies to youth and age :—
When young "sow wild oats," but when old "grow sage."

Henry James Byron.

DCCI.

Grammatical.

The least drop in the world I do not mind :
"Cognac" 's a noun I never yet declin'd.

Henry James Byron.

DCCII.

Military.

Smart soldiers like to be well tighten'd in :
Loose habits would destroy all discipline.

Henry James Byron.

DCCIII.

ON SEEING A GREAT COMMANDER EFFEMINATELY DRESSED AT A BALL.

'T is said that our soldiers so lazy have grown,
  With pleasure and plenty undone,
That they more for carriage, than courage, are known,
  And scarce know the use of a gun.

Let them say what they will, since it nobody galls,
  And exclaim out still louder and louder,
But there ne'er was more money expended in ball,
  Or a greater consumption of powder!

Anon.

[From *Elegant Extracts* (1805).]

DCCIV.

TO A PRETTY GIRL.

A lass, whose name was Mary Ware,
  And who could boast of beauty,
Of Love full oft had found the care.
A friend, to save her from his snare,
  Thus did a friendly duty.

" Fair maid, my lesson now regard,
  A lesson good and rare;
One word is all—and that not hard—
From husbands bad your surest guard;—
  Fair maid, it is—Be-*Ware!*

Anon.

[From *The Literary Chronicle* (1825).]

DCCV.

TO A RICH LADY.

I will not ask if thou canst touch
    The tuneful ivory key;—
Those silent notes of thine are such
    As quite suffice for me.

I'll make no question if thy skill
    The pencil comprehends;—
Enough for me, love, if thou still
    Canst draw—thy dividends.

Anon.

[From *Punch.*]

DCCVI.

ON RECEIVING A BRACE OF SNIPES.

My thanks I'll no longer delay
    For the birds which you shot with such skill;
But though there was nothing to pay,
    Yet each of them brought in his bill!

I mean not, my friend, to complain;
    The matter is certainly right;
And when bills such as these come again,
    I will always accept them at sight!

Anon.

DCCVII.
ON ONE PETER.

Poor Peter was in ocean drown'd,
    A harmless quiet creature;
And when at last his corpse was found
    It had become salt-petre.

Anon.

DCCVIII.
ON JEKYLL'S BEING NEARLY THROWN BY A VERY SMALL PIG.

As Jekyll walk'd out in his gown and his wig,
He happen'd to tread on a very small pig:
"Pig of Science," he said, "or else I am mistaken,
For surely thou art an abridgment of Bacon."

Anon.

DCCIX.
TO AN UNKIND MAID.

To win the maid the poet tries,
And sometimes writes on Julia's eyes;—
She likes a verse—but, cruel whim,
She still appears averse to him.

Anon.

DCCX.
ON THE RIVER HANS-SUR-LESSE, IN BELGIUM.

Old Euclid may go to the wall,
    For we've solved what he never could guess,—
How the fish in the river are small,
    But the river they live in is Lesse.

Anon.

DCCXI.

ON A GAMBLER.

"I'm very much surpris'd," quoth Harry,
"That Jane a gambler thus should marry."
"I'm not at all," her sister says;
"You know he has such winning ways!"

Anon.

DCCXII.

ON BALLS AND OPERAS.

If by their names we things should call,
　It surely would be properer,
To term a singing piece a *bawl*,
　A dancing piece a *hopperer!*

Anon.

DCCXIII.

ON TWO GUNMAKERS.

Two of a trade can ne'er agree—
　Each worries each if able;
In Manton and in Egg we see
　That proverb proved a fable.

Each deals in guns, whose loud report
　Proclaims the fact I'm broaching;
Manton's are made for lawful sport,
　And Egg's are best for poaching.

James Smith (1775–1839).

BOOK XI.

Compliments.

DCCXIV.

To the Memory of Spenser.

Here plac'd near Chaucer, Spenser claims a room,
As next to him in merit, next his tomb.
To place near Chaucer, Spenser lays a claim,
Nearer his tomb, but nearer far his fame.
With thee, our English verse was rais'd on high,
But now declin'd, it fears with thee to die.

Anon.

[From Pettigrew's *Chronicles*, where it is given as a translation of the Latin epitaph to Spenser which adorned his monument in Westminster Abbey before it was demolished by the Puritans.]

DCCXV.

On the Countess of Pembroke.

Underneath this sable hearse
Lies the subject of all verse,
Sidney's sister, Pembroke's mother;—

Death, ere thou hast slain another
Fair and learn'd and good as she,
Time shall throw his dart at thee.

Ben Jonson (1574–1637).

[From *Underwood's*. Mary Herbert, Countess of Pembroke, was the sister of Sir Philip Sidney, who dedicated to her his *Arcadia*, and on whom she wrote an *Elegy* and a *Pastoral Dialogue*. She also translated some of the Psalms into English, and a tragedy called *Anthony* from the French.]

DCCXVI.

HOW ROSES BECAME RED.

Roses at first were white,
 Till they could not agree
Whether my Sappho's breast
 Or they more white should be.

But being vanquisht quite,
 A blush their cheeks bespred;
Since which, believe the rest,
 The roses first came red.

Robert Herrick (1591–1674).

DCCXVII.

TO HIS MISTRESS.

Shall I tell you how the rose at first grew red,
And whence the lily whiteness borrowèd?
You blush'd, and straight the rose with red was dight,
The lily kiss'd your hand, and so was white.

Before such time, each rose had but a stain,
And lilies nought but paleness did contain;
You have the native colour, these the dye,
And only flourish in your livery.
Anon.

[From *Wit Restored* (1658).]

—o—

DCCXVIII.

ON A LADY WHO WRIT IN PRAISE OF MYRA.

While she pretends to make the graces known
Of matchless Myra, she reveals her own:
And when she would another's praise indite,
Is by her glass instructed how to write.
Edmund Waller (1605–1687).

—o—

DCCXIX.

TO CHAPMAN, ON HIS HOMER.

Thou ghost of Homer, 't were no fault to call
His the translation, thine the original;
Did we not know 't was done by thee so well,
Thou makest Homer Homer's self excel.
Anon.

[From *Wit Restored* (1658). Chapman's version of Homer—even now, perhaps, the most Homeric of all English translations—appeared in 1596.]

DCCXX.

To Pope, on his Homer.

So much, dear Pope, thy English Iliad charms,
As pity melts us, or as passion warms,
That after-ages shall with wonder seek
Who 't was translated Homer into Greek.
Anon.

[From *The Grove* (1721). Pope's translation of the *Iliad* was produced in 1720.]

———o———

DCCXXI.

Under Milton's Picture before his "Paradise Lost."

Three poets, in three distant ages born,
Greece, Italy, and England did adorn ;
The first in loftiness of thought surpass'd,
The next in majesty, in both the last.
The force of Nature could no further go ;
To make a third she join'd the former two.

John Dryden (1631–1701).

[For an excellent criticism on this once-praised epigram, see *Guesses at Truth*. The three poets meant are Homer, Virgil, and Milton, the first and last of whom are by no means happily characterized. "Loftiness of thought" cannot be ascribed to Homer, nor can it be attributed with great appropriateness to Milton, who was rather a scholar than a thinker.]

DCCXXII.

ON BUCKINGHAMSHIRE'S MONUMENT TO DRYDEN.

This Sheffield rais'd.   The sacred dust below
Was Dryden once.   The rest who does not know?

Alexander Pope (1688–1744).

[Apparently imitated from the Latin epitaph by Stroza, quoted on a previous page.]

---o---

DCCXXIII.

ON HEARNE, THE ANTIQUARY.

"Pox on 't," says Time to Thomas Hearne,
"Whatever I forget, you learn."

Anon.

[From *A Collection of Epigrams* (1727). This is a felicitous tribute to Hearne's great antiquarian lore. He was born in 1698 and died in 1735.]

---o---

DCCXXIV.

ON THE ABOVE.

"Hang it," quoth Hearne, in furious fret,
"Whate'er I learn, you soon forget."

Gilbert West (1705–1756).

DCCXXV.

ON MISS BIDDY FLOYD;

Or, The Receipt to Form a Beauty.

When Cupid did his grandsire Jove entreat
To form some Beauty by a new receipt,
Jove sent, and found far in a country scene
Truth, innocence, good-nature, look serene:
From which ingredients first the dexterous boy
Pick'd the demure, the awkward, and the coy.
The Graces from the court did next provide
Breeding, and wit, and air, and decent pride:
These Venus clears from every spurious grain
Of vice, coquet, affected, pert, and vain.
Jove mix'd up all, and his best clay employ'd;
Then call'd the happy composition *Floyd*.

Jonathan Swift (1667–1745).

[Miss Floyd is said to have been connected with the Berkeley family. In 1712 her face was sadly disfigured by small-pox.]

---o---

DCCXXVI.

TO MRS. HOUGHTON OF BORMOUNT, ON HER PRAISING HER HUSBAND TO DR. SWIFT.

You always are making a god of your spouse;
But this neither reason nor conscience allows:
Perhaps you will say, 't is in gratitude due,
And you adore him, because he adores you.
Your argument's weak, and so you will find;
For you, by this rule, must adore all mankind.

Jonathan Swift.

DCCXXVII.

Written on a White Fan borrowed from a Lady.

> Flavia the least and slightest toy,
> Can with resistless art employ.
> This fan in meaner hands would prove
> An engine of small force in love;
> Yet she, with graceful air and mien,
> Not to be told, or safely seen,
> Directs its wanton motions so,
> That it wounds more than Cupid's bow,
> Gives coolness to the matchless dame,
> To every other breast—a flame.
>
> *Francis Atterbury* (1662–1732).

[From Nichols' *Select Collection of Poems* (1782). The lady was Miss Osborne, afterwards the Bishop's wife.]

DCCXXVIII.

On the Countess of Manchester at Paris.

> When haughty Gallia's dames, that spread
> O'er their pale cheeks an artful red,
> Beheld this beauteous stranger there,
> In native charms divinely fair,
> Confusion in their looks they showed,
> And with unborrow'd blushes glowed.
>
> *Joseph Addison* (1672–1719).

[The above lines were engraved on Addison's toasting-glass at the Kit-Kat Club. The lady celebrated in them was the wife of the English ambassador at Paris, when that city was visited by Addison.]

DCCXXIX.
ON BISHOP HOUGH.

A Bishop, by his neighbours hated,
Has cause to wish himself translated;
But why should Hough desire translation,
Loved and esteemed by all the nation?

Yet if it be the old man's case,
I'll lay my life I know the place;
'T is where God sent some that adore him,
And whither Enoch went before him.
Alexander Pope (1688–1744).

[Bishop Hough died in 1743, after having held several sees in succession. He was Bishop of Worcester at the time this epigram was written.]

DCCXXX.
WRITTEN ON GLASS, WITH LORD CHESTERFIELD'S DIAMOND PENCIL.

Accept a miracle instead of wit :—
See two dull lines by Stanhope's pencil writ.
Alexander Pope.

DCCXXXI.
ON LADY MARY WORTLEY MONTAGU.

Here, stopt by hasty death, Alexis lies,
Who cross'd half Europe, led by Wortley's eyes.
Alexander Pope.

[Pope, says Carruthers, expressed in one of his letters to Lady Wortley Montagu, then in the East, his desire, real or fanciful, to meet her. "But," said the poet, "if my fate be such that this body of mine . . . . . be left behind on the journey, let the epitaph of Tibullus be set over it." The above lines are his version of the epitaph, for which see Tibull. Lib. i. Eleg. iv.]

DCCXXXII.

ON DRAWINGS OF THE STATUES OF APOLLO, VENUS, AND HERCULES, MADE FOR POPE BY SIR GODFREY KNELLER.

What God, what genius, did the pencil move,
  When Kneller painted these?
'T was friendship warm as Phœbus, kind as Love,
  And strong as Hercules.

Alexander Pope (1688–1744).

DCCXXXIII.

ON A CERTAIN LADY AT COURT.

I know a thing that's most uncommon;
  (Envy, be silent and attend!)
I know a reasonable woman,
  Handsome and witty, yet a friend.

Not warp'd by passion, aw'd by rumour,
  Not grave thro' pride, or gay through folly,—
An equal mixture of good humour,
  And sensible soft melancholy.

"Has she no faults then (Envy says), Sir?"
  Yes, she has one, I must aver;—
When all the world conspires to praise her,
  The woman's deaf, and does not hear.

Alexander Pope (1688–1744).

[The lady here addressed was Mrs. Howard, bedchamber woman to Queen Caroline, and afterwards Countess of Suffolk. She was mistress to George II., and, if a story told of her by Horace Walpole be correct, by no means worthy even to be called "good-humoured." Yet she was highly praised, not only by Pope, but by Lord Peterborough, in his well-known "Song by a Person of Quality," where her unconsciousness of the admiration she excited is again alluded to:—

"When so easy to guess who this angel should be,
  Would one think Mrs. Howard ne'er dreamt it was she?"]

DCCXXXIV.

Epitaph on Sir Godfrey Kneller, in Westminster Abbey (1723).

Kneller, by Heav'n, and not a master taught,
Whose art was nature, and whose pictures thought;
Now for two ages having snatch'd from Fate
Whate'er was beauteous, or whate'er was great,
Lies crown'd with princes' honours, poets' lays,
Due to his merit and brave thirst of praise.
Living, great Nature fear'd he might outvie
Her works, and, dying, fears herself may die.

Alexander Pope.

[The last two lines of this epitaph are copied directly from Cardinal Bembo's epitaph on Raphael :—

"Ille hic est Raphael. Timuit, quo sospite, vinci
Rerum Magna Parens, et moriente, mori."

Spence says that Pope thought these lines "the worst thing he ever wrote in his life."]

---o---

DCCXXXV.

EPITAPH INTENDED FOR SIR ISAAC NEWTON.

Nature and Nature's laws lay hid in night:
God said, Let Newton be! and all was light.
Alexander Pope (1688–1744).

[Referring to the last four words of this epigram, Warburton says :—" It had been better—'and there was light'—as more conformable to the reality of the fact, and to the allusion whereby it is celebrated." Intended for Sir Isaac Newton's monument in Westminster Abbey, it was passed over in favour of a pure Latin inscription. It was, however, engraved on a marble tablet in the room in which Sir Isaac was born, in the manor-house of Woolsthorpe. As originally written by Pope it ran :—

"Nature and all her works lay hid in night;
God said, Let Newton be, and all was light."

See Nichols' *Illustrations of Literary History*.]

---o---

DCCXXXVI.

ON SIR ISAAC NEWTON.

O'er Nature's laws God cast the veil of night:
Out blaz'd a Newton's soul, and all was light.
Allan Ramsay (1686–1758).

DCCXXXVII.

ON THE CELEBRATED DISPUTE BETWEEN THE ANCIENTS AND THE MODERNS.

Swift for the Ancients has argued so well,
'T is apparent from thence that the Moderns excel.

Mrs. Barker.

[From *Poems on Several Occasions* (1735). The reference is to Swift's *Battle of the Books*, a prose *jeu d'esprit*, published in 1704, in which the Dean took up the cause of "the Ancients" as against "the Moderns," in the controversy that then raged in literary circles. See No. CXXX., in Book II.]

DCCXXXVIII.

ON DR. BALGUY PREACHING A SERMON ON THE TEXT, "WISDOM IS SORROW."

If what you advance, my dear Doctor, be true,
That wisdom is sorrow—how wretched are you!

Joseph Warton (1722-1800).

DCCXXXIX.

ON A YOUNG LADY WISHING TO ASCEND IN A BALLOON.

Forbear, sweet girl, your scheme forego,
And thus our anxious troubles end;
Swiftly you 'll mount, full well we know,
And greatly fear you 'll not descend!

> When angels see a mortal rise,
> So beautiful, divine, and fair,
> They'll not release you from the skies,
> But keep their sister-angel there!
>
> *Anon.*

[From *An Asylum for Fugitive Pieces* (1785).]

DCCXL.

ON ANNE, COUNTESS OF SUNDERLAND.

> All Nature's charms in Sunderland appear,
> Bright as her eyes, and as her reason clear;
> Yet still their force, to men not safely known,
> Seems undiscover'd to herself alone.

Charles Montagu, Earl of Halifax (1661–1715).

[Compare with No. DCCXXXIII.]

DCCXLI.

ON THE DUCHESS OF ST. ALBANS (1703).

> The line of Vere, so long renown'd in arms,
> Concludes with lustre in St. Albans' charms.
> Her conquering eyes have made their race complete:
> They rose in valour, and in beauty set.

Charles Montagu, Earl of Halifax.

[The Duchess of St. Albans here distinguished was Diana de Vere, eldest daughter of Aubrey de Vere, last Earl of Oxford. The above lines were written for the toasting-glasses of the Kit-Cat Club.]

DCCXLII.

On the Lady Mary Churchill.

Fairest and latest of the beauteous race,
Blest with your parent's wit and her first blooming face,
Born with our liberties in William's reign,
Your eyes alone that liberty restrain.

Charles Montagu, Earl of Halifax.

[Also written for the Kit-Cat Club. The lady was the youngest daughter of the famous Duke of Marlborough.]

DCCXLIII.

To the Duchess of Beaufort.

Offspring of a tuneful sire,
Blest with more than mortal fire;
Likeness of a mother's face,
Blest with more than mortal grace;
You with double charms surprise,
With his wit, and with her eyes.

Anon.

[From *A Collection of Epigrams* (1727).]

DCCXLIV.

To the Hon. Mrs. Percival, with Hutcheson's Treatise on Beauty and Virtue.

Th' internal senses painted here we see;
They're born in others, but they live in thee.
O were our author with thy converse blest,
Could he behold the virtues of thy breast,
His needless labours with contempt he'd view,
And bid the world not read, but copy you.

Mrs. Grierson.

[From *A Collection of Epigrams* (1727). Francis Hutcheson, Professor at Glasgow, published his *Inquiry into the Original of our Ideas of Beauty and Virtue* in 1725.]

DCCXLV.

On a Lady's Wearing a Patch.

That little patch upon your face
   Would seem a foil to one less fair;
On you it hides a charming grace,
   And you, in pity, placed it there.

Anon.

[From *A Collection of Epigrams* (1727).]

DCCXLVI.

ON ONE SELINDA.

Selinda ne'er appears till night,
   And what won't female envy say?
But well she knows, she shines so bright,
   Her presence may supply the day.

Anon.

[From *A Collection of Epigrams* (1727).]

DCCXLVII.

ON ONE STELLA.

Venus whipt Cupid t' other day
   For having lost his bow and quiver;
For he had giv'n them both away
   To Stella, queen of Isis river.

" Mamma! you wrong me while you strike,"
   Cried weeping Cupid, "for I vow,
Stella and you are so alike,
   I thought that I had lent them you."

William Thompson.

[Little more, as Dodd points out, than a paraphrase of an epigram by Tebaldes, an Italian poet (1456–1538), a translation of which is given in *Delitiae Delitiarum.*]

DCCXLVIII.
ON ONE MOLLY SCOTT.

Minerva last week (pray let nobody doubt it)
Went an airing from Oxford, six miles or about it:
When she spied a young virgin so blooming and fair,
That " O Venus," she cried, " is your ladyship there?
Pray is not that Oxford? and lately you swore
Neither you, nor one like you, should trouble us more.
Do you keep thus your promise? and am I defied?"
The virgin came nearer and smiling replied:
" My goddess! what, have you your pupil forgot?"—
" Your pardon, my dear—is it you, Molly Scott?"

William Thompson.

DCCXLIX.
A YORKIST PRINCE TO A LANCASTRIAN LADY WITH THE PRESENT OF A WHITE ROSE.

If this pale rose offend your sight,
   It in your bosom wear;
'T will blush to find itself less white,
   And turn Lancastrian there.

But if thy ruby lip it spy,
   To kiss it shouldst thou deign,
With envy pale, 't will lose its dye,
   And Yorkist turn again.

William Somerville (1692–1742).
William Congreve (1670–1729).

[The first stanza is Somerville's, the second Congreve's. The lines are " supposed to have been written in the fifteenth century by the Duke of Clarence, of the House of York, and sent, with a white rose, to Lady Eliza Beauchamp, daughter of the Duke of Somerset, and of the House of Lancaster." See Halford's *Nugæ Metricæ*.]

---o---

DCCL.

ON A BEAUTIFUL YOUTH, STRUCK BLIND BY LIGHTNING.

>Sure 't was by Providence design'd
>   Rather in pity than in hate,
>That he should be, like Cupid, blind,
>   To save him from Narcissus' fate.

Oliver Goldsmith (1728-1774).

---o---

DCCLI.

ON JAMES QUIN, IN BATH CATHEDRAL.

That tongue which set the table in a roar,
And charm'd the public ear, is heard no more;
Clos'd are those eyes, the harbingers of wit,
Which spoke, before the tongue, what Shakspeare writ;
Cold are those hands which, living, were stretched forth
At friendship's call to succour modest worth.
Here lies James Quin. Deign, reader, to be taught
(Whate'er thy strength of body, force of thought,
In Nature's happier mould however cast)
To this complexion thou must come at last.

David Garrick (1716-1779).

[See Nos. CCCXX. and CCCXXI.]

DCCLII.

ON CLAUDIUS PHILLIPS, THE MUSICIAN, WHO DIED IN
POVERTY.

Phillips, whose touch harmonious could remove
The pangs of guilty pow'r and hapless love,
Rest here distress'd by poverty no more,
Here find that calm thou gav'st so oft before.
Sleep undisturb'd within this peaceful shrine,
Till angels wake thee with a note like thine.

David Garrick (1716–1779).

DCCLIII.

VERSES WRITTEN ON A BOOK CALLED "FABLES FOR THE
FEMALE SEX," BY EDWARD MOORE.

While here the poet paints the charms
  Which bless the perfect dame,
How unaffected beauty warms,
  And wit preserves the flame;

How prudence, virtue, sense agree
  To form the happy wife—
In Lucy and her book I see
  The Picture and the Life.

David Garrick.

[Edward Moore, the dramatist (1712–1757), author of that very ghastly play, *The Gamester*, published his *Fables* in 1744.]

DCCLIV.

On a Lady Embroidering.

Arachne once, as poets tell,
    A goddess at her art defied,
But soon the daring mortal fell
    The hapless victim of her pride.

O, then, beware Arachne's fate;
    Be prudent, Chloe, and submit;
For you'll more surely feel her hate
    Who rival both her art and wit.

David Garrick (1716–1779).

DCCLV.

On Barry and Garrick as King Lear.

The town has found out different ways
    To praise its different Lears;
To Barry it gives loud huzzas,
    To Garrick only tears.

A king? Aye, every inch a king—
    Such Barry doth appear:
But Garrick's quite another thing;
    He's every inch King Lear.

Richard Kendal.

[From *The Poetical Register* (1810-11). Spranger Barry, Garrick's rival in popularity, if not in powers, was born in 1719 and died in 1777.]

DCCLVI.

ON ONE MOLLY SLEIGH.

Minerva, wand'ring in a myrtle grove,
Accosted thus the smiling Queen of Love:
" Revenge yourself, you 've cause to be afraid,
Your boasted pow'r yields to a British maid:
She seems a goddess—all her graces shine;
Love lends her beauty which eclipses thine."
" Each youth, I know," says Venus, "thinks she 's me;
Immediately she speaks, they think she 's thee:
Good Pallas, thus you 're foil'd as well as I."
" Ha, ha!" cries Cupid; "that 's my Molly Sleigh."
Allan Ramsay (1685–1758).

[Compare with No. DCCXLVIII.]

DCCLVII.

ON RECEIVING AN ORANGE FROM A LADY.

Now Priam's son, thou may'st be mute,
   For I can blithely boast with thee;
Thou to the fairest gave the fruit,
   The fairest gave the fruit to me.
Allan Ramsay.

[The lady was Miss Grace Lockhart, afterwards Countess of Aboyne (d. 1738).]

DCCLVIII.

ON RICHARDSON'S "CLARISSA."

This work is Nature's; every tittle in 't
She wrote, and gave it Richardson to print.
David Graham (b. about 1726).

[From Nichols' *Literary Anecdotes*. *Clarissa* appeared in 1748, and at once took "the town" by storm. It has since been highly praised by every critic, from Macaulay downwards, and has been reduced by E. S. Dallas to the dimensions of a three-volume novel.]

---o---

DCCLIX.

ON LORD COBHAM'S GARDENS.

It puzzles much the sage's brains
 Where Eden stood of yore;
Some place it in Arabia's plains,
 Some say it is no more.

But Cobham can these tales confute,
 As all the curious know;
For he has prov'd beyond dispute
 That Paradise is Stow.

Nathaniel Cotton (1707–1788).

---o---

DCCLX.

ON SEEING A YOUNG JACOBITE LADY DRESSED WITH ORANGE RIBBONS.

Say, lovely traitor, where's the jest
Of wearing Orange on thy breast,
While that breast upheaving shows
The whiteness of the rebel rose?

Philip Stanhope, Lord Chesterfield (1694–1773).

[Said to have been written impromptu, at a ball in Dublin Castle. In the *Asylum for Fugitive Pieces* it is ascribed to a Mr. John St. Leger.]

DCCLXI.

ON THE DUCHESS OF DEVONSHIRE CANVASSING FOR VOTES
FOR FOX (1780).

 Array'd in matchless beauty, Devon's Fair
  In Fox's favour takes a zealous part;
 But oh! where'er the pilfrer comes—beware!
  She supplicates a vote, and steals a heart!

Anon.

[The Duchess of Devonshire distinguished herself at the Westminster Election of 1780 by giving a kiss for each vote she succeeded in obtaining for Charles James Fox, who owed his success entirely to her efforts.]

DCCLXII.

ON SOME SNOW THAT MELTED ON A LADY'S BREAST.

 Those envious flakes came down in haste,
  To prove her breast less fair:
 Grieving to find themselves surpass'd,
  Dissolv'd into a tear.

Anon.

[From Nichols' *Select Collection of Poems* (1782).]

DCCLXIII.

ON TWO LADIES WHO WERE DROWNED WHILST WALKING ON THE SEA-SHORE.

Thou swelling sea, what now can be thy boast,
  By whose fell floods such barbarous deeds were done,
In whose curst waves two Venuses are lost?
  Two you have taken, though you gave but one!

Anon.

[From Nichols' *Select Collection of Poems* (1782).]

---o---

DCCLXIV.

ON MRS. BARTON.

At Barton's feet the God of Love
  His arrows and his quiver lays,
Forgets he has a throne above,
  And with this lovely creature stays.

Not Venus' beauties are more bright,
  But each appear so like the other,
That Cupid has mistook the right,
  And takes the nymph to be his mother.

Anon.

[From Nichols' *Select Collection of Poems* (1782); written on the toasting-glasses of the Kit-Cat Club. Mrs. Barton was a niece of Sir Isaac Newton.]

DCCLXV.

ON THE BEAUTIFUL MISSES GUNNING.

Sly Cupid perceiving our modern beaux's hearts
Were proof to the sharpest and best of his darts,
His power to maintain, the young urchin, grown cunning,
Has laid down his bow and now conquers by Gunning.

Anon.

[The Misses Gunning were two Irish beauties, who blazed as the comets of more than one season, and ended by making very brilliant marriages.]

DCCLXVI.

ON BEING ASKED WHICH OF THREE SISTERS WAS MOST BEAUTIFUL.

When Paris gave his voice, in Ida's grove,
For the resistless Venus, queen of love,
'T was no great task to pass a judgment there,
When she alone was exquisitely fair.

But here, what could his ablest judgment teach,
When wisdom, power, and beauty reign in each?
The youth, nonpluss'd, behov'd to join with me,
And wish the apple had been cut in three.

Robert Fergusson (1750–1774).

[A similar idea runs through a Greek epigram by Ruffinus, translated by Graves in *The Festoon.*]

DCCLXVII.
To Lady Brown.

When I was young and débonnaire,
The brownest nymph to me was fair;
But now I'm old, and wiser grown,
The fairest nymph to me is Brown.
George, Lord Lyttelton (1709–1773).

[From *An Asylum for Fugitive Pieces* (1786), where it is described as an extempore effort and attributed to Lord Lyttelton.]

DCCLXVIII.
Inscription for a Bust of Lady Suffolk in a Wood at Stowe.

Her wit and beauty for a court were made:
But truth and goodness fit her for a shade.
George, Lord Lyttelton.

[Henrietta, Countess of Suffolk, died in 1767.]

DCCLXIX.
To Madame de Damas, on her Learning English.

Though British accents your attention fire,
You cannot learn so fast as we admire.
Scholars like you but slowly can improve,
For who would teach you but the verb I love?
Horace Walpole, Earl of Orford (1717–1797).

[This does not figure in the works of Walpole, but is generally understood to be his work.]

DCCLXX.

TO MADAME DU CHATELET, WHEN ON A VISIT TO STRAWBERRY HILL.

When beauteous Helen left her native air,
Greece for ten years in arms reclaim'd the fair:
Th' enamour'd boy withheld his lovely prize,
And stak'd his country's ruin 'gainst her eyes.
Your charms less baneful, not less strong appear:
We welcome any peace that keeps you here.

Horace Walpole, Earl of Orford (1717–1797).

---o---

DCCLXXI.

ON SEEING A CROYDON BELLE IN COURT AT KINGSTON, DURING THE ASSIZES.

Whilst petty offences and felonies smart,
Is there no jurisdiction for stealing a heart?
You, my fair one, will cry, "Laws and court, I defy you!"
Concluding no *Peers* can be summon'd to try you.
But think not, fair Shorey, this plea will secure ye,
Since the Muses and Graces will just make a jury.

Anon.

[From *Select Epigrams* (1797).]

---o---

DCCLXXII.

REPLY TO THE ABOVE.

Sir, the lady must smile, and your menace deride,
For the jury you mention are all on her side.

Anon.

DCCLXXIII.

IMPROMPTU :

After reading the Story of Ulysses and the Sirens.

> When Emily, sweet maid, appears,
> More dangerous charms surprise;
> What then avails to stop our ears,
> Unless we shut our eyes?
>
> Anon.

[From *Select Epigrams* (1797).]

DCCLXXIV.

ON THE DEATH OF DR. SECKER, ARCHBISHOP OF CANTERBURY.

> While Secker liv'd he show'd how seers should live,
> While Secker taught, heav'n open'd to our eye :
> When Secker gave we knew how angels give,
> When Secker died we knew e'en saints must die.
>
> Anon.

[From *Elegant Extracts* (1805). See the note to No. CCXIV.]

DCCLXXV.

ON THE EARL OF DORSET.

> By fav'ring wit Mæcenas purchas'd fame :
> Virgil's own works immortaliz'd his name ;
> A double share of fame is Dorset's due,
> At once a patron and a poet too.
>
> Anon.

[From *Elegant Extracts* (1805). The poet here intended is Charles Sackville, Earl of Dorset (1637–1706), author of some graceful lyrics.]

DCCLXXVI.

TO A LADY WHO SENT HIM COMPLIMENTS ON A TEN OF HEARTS.

Your compliments, dear lady, pray forbear;
Old English services are more sincere.
You send Ten Hearts—the tithe is only mine;—
Give me but One and burn the other Nine.

Anon.

[From Dodsley's *Collection of Poems*.]

DCCLXXVII.

TO A BEAUTIFUL GIRL, ON HER PRINCIPLES OF LIBERTY AND EQUALITY.

How Liberty! girl, can it be by thee nam'd?
Equality, too! hussy, art not asham'd?
Free and equal, indeed, while mankind thou enchain'st,
And over their hearts as a despot so reign'st.

Robert Burns (1759–1796).

[Dr. Johnson made a Latin epigram very similar in point upon a young Whig lady friend of his.]

DCCLXXVIII.

On Miss Jean Scott.

O had each Scot of ancient times
   Been Jeanie Scott as thou art,
The bravest hearts on English ground
   Had yielded like a coward.

Robert Burns (1759-1796).

———o———

DCCLXXIX.

On Seeing Mrs. Kemble as Yarico.

Kemble, thou cur'st my unbelief
   In Moses and his rod;
At Yarico's sweet note of grief
   The rock with tears had flow'd.

Robert Burns.

[The Mrs. Kemble here celebrated was the wife of the Stephen Kemble who played Falstaff without "stuffing." She appeared at Dumfries, in the opera of *Inkle and Yarico*, in 1794.]

———o———

DCCLXXX.

To Lord Nelson, on the Night-cap he had Lent the Author taking Fire.

Take your night-cap again, my good lord, I desire,
   For I wish not to keep it a minute:
What belongs to a Nelson, where'er there's a fire,
   Is sure to be instantly in it.

John Wolcot (1738-1819).

[This arose out of an accident which happened to Wolcot whilst on a visit to Lord Nelson at his seat at Merton.]

DCCLXXXI.

INSCRIBED ON A SUMMER-HOUSE IN THE GROUNDS OF HOLLAND HOUSE.

Here Rogers sat, and here for ever dwell,
To me, those pleasures that he sings so well.
Henry Vassal, Lord Holland (1773–1840).

[Rogers' *Pleasures of Memory* appeared in 1792.]

DCCLXXXII.

TO A LADY.

Die when you will, you need not wear
At Heaven's court a form more fair
   Than Beauty here on earth has given:
Keep but the lovely looks we see,
The voice we hear, and you will be
   An Angel ready made for heaven.
Thomas Moore (1779–1852).

[This is merely a versification of the remark said to have been made by Lord Herbert of Cherbury to a nun at Venice: "Moria pur quando vuol, non e bisogno mutar ni faccia ni voce per esser un Angelo!" Compare it with the following.]

DCCLXXXIII.

ON A BEAUTIFUL AND VIRTUOUS YOUNG LADY.

Sleep soft in dust, wait the Almighty's will,
Then rise unchang'd and be an angel still.
Anon.

[From *Elegant Extracts* (1805).]

DCCLXXXIV.
ON A LADY.

With women and apples both Paris and Adam
    Made mischief enough in their day :—
God be prais'd that the fate of mankind, my dear madam,
    Depends not on *us*, the same way.

For, weak as I am with temptation to grapple,
    The world would have doubly to rue thee;
Like Adam, I'd gladly take *from* thee the apple,
    Like Paris, at once give it *to* thee.

Thomas Moore (1779–1852).

DCCLXXXV.
TO CHLORIS.

Chloris, I swear, by all I ever swore,
That from this hour I shall not love thee more.
"What! love no more? oh, why this alter'd vow?"
Because I *cannot* love thee *more*—than *now*!

Thomas Moore.

DCCLXXXVI.
ON MOORE'S TRANSLATIONS FROM ANACREON.

Oh! mourn not for Anacreon dead,
Oh! weep not for Anacreon fled;
The lyre still breathes he touch'd before,
For we have one Anacreon Moore.

Thomas, Lord Erskine (1748–1823).

[See the note to No. CLXIX.]

DCCLXXXVII.

TO LADY PAYNE,

On his Complaining of Illness at her House.

'T is true I am ill, but I need not complain;
For he never knew pleasure that never knew *Payne*.

Thomas, Lord Erskine (1748–1823).

―o―

DCCLXXXVIII.

ON MISS TREE (MRS. BRADSHAW).

On this Tree when a nightingale settles and sings,
The Tree will return her as good as she brings.

Henry Luttrell (1770–1851).

[Quoted by Rogers in his *Table Talk* (1856), where he calls it "quite a little fairy tale." Miss Tree was a noted vocalist in her day.]

―o―

DCCLXXXIX.

ON GEORGE COLMAN THE YOUNGER.

Within this monumental bed
Apollo's favourite rests his head:
  Ye Muses, cease your grieving.
A son the father's loss supplies;—
Be comforted; though Colman dies,
  His "Heir-at-Law" is living.

James Smith (1775–1839).

[The comedy of *The Heir-at-Law* was produced in 1797. Its author, Colman the younger, died in 1836; father in 1794.]

DCCXC.

To Miss Edgeworth.

We everyday bards may "Anonymous" sign;
That refuge, Miss Edgeworth, can never be thine.
Thy writings, where satire and moral unite,
Must bring forth the name of their author to light.
Good and bad join in telling the source of their birth,
The bad own their edge, and the good own their worth.

James Smith (1775–1839).

[Maria Edgeworth was born in 1767, and died in 1849. "Her extraordinary merit," said Sir James Mackintosh, "both as a moralist and a woman of genius, consists in her having selected a class of virtues far more difficult to treat as the subject of fiction than others."]

DCCXCI.

On Mr. Strahan, the King's Printer.

Your lower limbs seem'd far from stout,
    When last I saw you walk;
The cause I presently found out,
    When you began to talk.

The power that props the body's length,
    In due proportion spread,
In you mounts upwards, and the strength
    All settles in the head.

James Smith.

[The subject of these lines was so delighted with them, that he immediately made a codicil to his will, bequeathing three hundred pounds to Smith.]

DCCXCII.

To a Lady, with a Present of a Walking-Stick.

A compliment upon a crutch
Does not appear to promise much;
A theme no lover ever chose
For writing billet-doux in prose,
Or for an amatory sonnet;
But this I may comment upon it.
Its heart is whole, its head is light;
'T is smooth and yielding, yet upright.
In this you see an emblem of the donor,
Clear and unblemish'd as his honour;
Form'd for your use, framed to your hand,
Obedient to your last command.
Its proper place is by your side,
Its main utility and pride
To be your prop, support, and guide.
John Hookham Frere (1769–1846).

[The lady here addressed was Jemima, Dowager Countess of Errol, to whom the writer was afterwards married.]

DCCXCIII.

On Miss Vassal, at a Masquerade.

Imperial nymph! ill-suited is thy name
To speak the wonders of that radiant frame;
Where'er thy sovereign form on earth is seen,
All eyes are Vassals—thou alone a Queen.
Anon.

[Miss Vassal became the wife of the third Lord Holland. The above was written in 1786.]

DCCXCIV.

ON PROFESSOR AIREY, THE ASTRONOMER, AND HIS BEAUTIFUL WIFE.

Airey alone has gain'd that double prize
   Which forc'd musicians to divide the crown :
His works have rais'd a mortal to the skies,
   His marriage vows have drawn an angel down.

Sydney Smith (1771–1845).

[The allusion to Dryden's *Alexander's Feast* is obvious :—

" Let old Timotheus yield the prize,
   Or both divide the crown ;
He rais'd a mortal to the skies,
   She drew an angel down."]

DCCXCV.

ON THE PORTRAIT OF A LADY,

Taken by the Daguerreotype.

Yes! there are her features! her brow, and her hair,
   And her eyes, with a look so seraphic,
Her nose, and her mouth, with the smile that is there,
   Truly caught by the Art Photographic!

Yet why should she borrow such aid of the skies,
   When, by many a bosom's confession,
Her own lovely face, and the light of her eyes,
   Are sufficient to make an impression?

Thomas Hood (1798–1845).

DCCXCVI.

ON ONE LAURA.

"Tell me," said Laura, "what may be
The difference 'twixt a clock and me."
"Laura," I cried, "Love prompts my powers
  To do the task you've set them:
A clock reminds us of the hours,
  You cause us to forget them."

Anon.

DCCXCVII.

ON A YOUNG LADY WITH GREY HAIRS.

Mark'd by extremes, Susannah's beauty bears
Life's opposite extremes—youth's blossoms and grey hairs.
Meet sign for one in whom combined are seen
Wisdom's ripe fruit and roses of fifteen.

Anon.

DCCXCVIII.

ON A MODERN ACTRESS.

"Miss Neilson's 'benefit,'" one says:
  I ask to what the phrase refers;
For, sure, when such an artist plays,
  The "benefit" is ours, not hers.

Anon.

BOOK XII.

Translations and Imitations.

DCCXCIX.

ON ONE WITH A LONG NOSE.

Beware, my friend! of crystal brook
Or fountain, lest that hideous hook,
   Thy nose, thou chance to see;
Narcissus' fate would then be thine,
And self-detested thou wouldst pine,
   As self-enamoured he.

William Cowper (1731–1800).

[From the Greek of Lucillius, who "flourished" in the second century.]

DCCC.

ON ONE WEARING FALSE HAIR.

They say that thou dost tinge (O monstrous lie!)
The hair that thou so raven-black dost buy.

Richard Garnett.

[From the Greek of Lucillius.]

DCCCI.

ON A MISER.

A miser in his chamber saw a mouse,
And cried, dismay'd, "What dost thou in my house?"
She with a laugh, "Good landlord, have no fear,
'T is not for board but lodging I came here."

Richard Garnett.

[From the Greek of Lucillius.]

---o---

DCCCII.

ON AN UGLY WOMAN.

Gellia, your mirror's false; you could not bear,
If it were true, to see your image there!

Anon.

[From the Greek of Lucillius.]

---o---

DCCCIII.

ON WIVES.

All wives are bad,—yet two blest hours they give,
When first they wed, and when they cease to live.

John Herman Merivale.

[From the Greek of Palladas (about A.D. 370).]

---o---

DCCCIV.

ON AN INANIMATE ACTRESS.

Thou hast a score of parts not good,
    But two divinely shown :
Thy Daphne a true piece of wood,
    Thy Niobe a stone.

Richard Garnett.

[From the Greek of Palladas.]

DCCCV.

ON DOCTOR MEAD.

When Mead reach'd the Styx, Pluto started and said,
"Confound him! he's come to recover the dead."

Anon.

[Imitated from Palladas. See No. CCLXIX.]

DCCCVI.

ON A GERMAN SCHOLAR.

The Germans in Greek
Are sadly to seek :
Not five in five score,
But ninety-five more,—
All, save only Hermann,
And Hermann's a German.

Richard Porson (1759–1808).

[Imitated from epigrams by Phocylides and Demodocus. See Nichols' *Illustrations of Literary History.*]

DCCCVII.

ON A SLOW RUNNER AND SWIFT EATER.

You feed so fast, and run so very slow,
Eat with your legs, and with your grinders go!

Robert Bland.

[From the Greek of Lucian (about A.D. 160).]

---o---

DCCCVIII.

ON A MERCENARY BEAUTY.

Golden the hive, and yet 't is true
Bees wrought it not from gold, but dew.
Dewy thy kiss, and yet 't is told,
Its birth is not from dew, but gold.

Richard Garnett.

[From the Greek of Macedonius.]

---o---

DCCCIX.

ON ONE DICK.

With nose so long and mouth so wide,
And those twelve grinders side by side,
Dick, with very little trial,
Would make an excellent sun-dial.

Anon.

[Attributed to the Emperor Trajan.]

DCCCX.

ON ONE WITH A LONG NOSE.

Dick cannot blow his nose whene'er he pleases,
   His nose so long is, and his arm so short;
Nor ever cries, God bless me! when he sneezes—
   He cannot hear so distant a report.

John Herman Merivale.

[From the Greek.]

DCCCXI.

ON ONE RUFUS.

By dealings hateful to an honest man,
Poor Rufus swells to rich Rufinian:
Which sounding style might well expanded be,
Nor yet proportioned to his roguery.

Richard Garnett.

[From the Greek.]

DCCCXII.

TO A LADY.

I send thee myrrh, not that thou mayest be
By it perfumed, but it perfumed by thee.

Richard Garnett.

[From the Greek.]

DCCCXIII.
On an Incapable Person.

Fortune advanced thee that all might aver
That nothing is impossible to her.

Richard Garnett.

[From the Greek.]

---o---

DCCCXIV.
On the Cappadocians.

A viper bit a Cappadocian's hide;
But 't was the viper, not the man, that died.

Anon.

[From the Greek. Goldsmith may have had this in his mind when he wrote, in his *Elegy on a Mad Dog*:

"The man recovered of the bite,
The dog it was that died."]

---o---

DCCCXV.
On a Certain Partnership.

Damon, who plied the Undertaker's trade,
With Doctor Crateas an agreement made.
What linens Damon from the dead could seize
He to the Doctor sent for bandages;
While the good Doctor, here no promise-breaker,
Sent all his patients to the Undertaker.

Anon.

[From the Greek.]

DCCCXVI.

ON DORIS.

Of Graces four, of Muses ten,
   Of Venus's now two are seen ;
Doris shines forth to dazzled men,
    A Grace, a Muse, and Beauty's queen ;—
But let me whisper something more :—
The Furies now are likewise Four.
                                Anon.

[The first four lines of this are from the Greek of an anonymous author ; the concluding couplet has been added by the anonymous translator, thus converting a compliment into a satire.]

DCCCXVII.

ON A PROFESSOR WITH A SMALL CLASS.

Hail, Aristides, Rhetoric's great professor !
Of wondrous words we own thee the possessor.
Hail ye, his pupils seven, that mutely hear him—
His room's four walls, and the three benches near him !
                                Anon.

[From the Greek.]

DCCCXVIII.

ON FORTUNE.

Fortune, men say, doth give too much to many :
And yet she never gave enough to any.
              Sir John Haryngton (1561–1612).

[From the Latin of Martial.]

DCCCXIX.
To an Ill Reader.

The verses, Sextus, thou dost read, are mine ;
But with bad reading thou wilt make them thine.

Sir John Haryngton (1561–1612).

[From the Latin of Martial (b. about A.D. 40).]

———o———

DCCCXX.
Of Galla's Goodly Periwig.

You see the goodly hair that Galla wears ;
  'T is certain her own hair : who would have thought it ?
She swears it is her own : and true she swears,
  For hard by Temple Bar last day she bought it.
So fair a hair upon so foul a forehead,
Augments disgrace, and shows the grace is borrowed.

Sir John Haryngton.

[Founded on Martial. A somewhat similar idea runs through the lines translated from Lucillius, above (No. DCCC.).]

———o———

DCCCXXI.
On a Curious Fellow.

In all thy humour, whether grave or mellow,
Thou 'rt such a touchy, testy, pleasant fellow ;
Hast so much wit, and mirth, and spleen about thee,
There is no living with thee, or without thee.

Joseph Addison (1672–1719).

[From the Latin of Martial.]

DCCCXXII.

To a Lady.

Whilst in the dark on thy soft hand I hung,
And heard the tempting siren in thy tongue,
What flames, what darts, what anguish I endur'd !—
But, when the candle enter'd, I was cur'd.

Sir Richard Steele (1671–1729).

[Founded on the Latin of Martial.]

—o—

DCCCXXIII.

The Obligation.

To John I ow'd great obligation ;
   But John unhappily thought fit
To publish it to all the nation :
   Sure John and I are more than quit.

Matthew Prior (1664–1721).

[Imitated from Martial.]

—o—

DCCCXXIV.

On New-Made Honour.

A friend I met, some half-hour since—
   " Good-morrow, Jack ! " quoth I ;
The new-made knight, like any prince,
   Frown'd, nodded, and pass'd by :

When up came Jem:—" Sir John, your slave !"
" Ah ! James ; we dine at eight—
Fail not——" (low bows the supple knave)—
" Don't make my lady wait."
The king can do no wrong ! As I'm a sinner,
He's spoilt an honest tradesman, and my dinner.
Richard Harris Barham (1778–1845).

[Imitated from Martial.]

DCCCXXV.
ON A CERTAIN JACK.

Jack writes severe lampoons on me, 't is said—
But he writes nothing who is never read.
Dr. Hodgson.

[From the Latin of Martial.]

DCCCXXVI.
OF KATE AND BELL.

Kate's teeth are black, while lately Bell's are grown;
Bell buys her teeth, and Kate still keeps her own.
Dr. Hodgson.

[From the Latin of Martial.]

DCCCXXVII.
ON A DOCTOR.

A Doctor lately was a Captain made ;
It is a change of title, not of trade.
William Hay.

[From the Latin of Martial. See No. DCCCLVI.]

DCCCXXVIII.

ON A CERTAIN FOP.

His lordship bought his last gay birthday dress,
And gay it was, for fourscore pound or less.
Is he so good at buying cheap? you say;—
Extremely good, for he does never pay.

William Hay.

[From the Latin of Martial.]

———o———

DCCCXXIX.

ON A VICIOUS PERSON.

He called thee vicious, did he? Lying elf!
Thou art not vicious; thou art Vice itself.

Fletcher.

[From the Latin of Martial.]

———o———

DCCCXXX.

ON A CERTAIN LADY SUSAN.

Of rank, descent, and title proud,
  Mere gentry Lady Susan could not bear;
She'd wed but with a Duke, she vow'd,—
  And so absconded with a player.

Nathaniel Halhed.

[From the Latin of Martial.]

DCCCXXXI.

To an Author.

In spite of hints, in spite of looks,
Titus, I send thee not my books.
The reason, Titus, canst divine?
I fear lest thou shouldst send me thine.

Richard Garnett.

[From the Latin of Martial.]

---o---

DCCCXXXII.

On an Atheist.

That there's no God, John gravely swears
And quotes in proof his own affairs;
For how should such an atheist thrive,
If there were any God alive?

Anon.

[From the Latin of Martial. See the *Westminster Review* for 1853.]

---o---

DCCCXXXIII.

On one Paul.

Paul so fond of the name of a poet is grown,
With gold he buys verses, and calls them his own.
Go on, Master Paul, nor mind what the world says;
They are surely his own for which a man pays.

Anon.

[From the Latin of Martial.]

DCCCXXXIV.

ON ANGER.

Anger's a kind of gain that rich men know:
It costs them less to hate than to bestow.

Anon.

[From the Latin of Martial.]

DCCCXXXV.

ON A PARASITE.

Angling for dinner, Charles, at every line
  I read him, puts me to the blush :
"Delicious!" "charming!" "exquisite!" "divine!"
  "Hush, Charles, you've earned your victuals, hush!"

Anon.

[From the Latin of Martial.]

DCCCXXXVI.

ON A DINER-OUT.

Jack boasts he never dines at home,
  With reason too, no doubt ;
In truth, Jack never dines at all
  Unless invited out.

Anon.

[From the Latin of Martial.]

DCCCXXXVII.

ON A NEWLY-MADE BARONET.

Though I do "Sir" thee, be not vain, I pray;
I "Sir" my monkey Jacko every day.

Anon.

[From the Latin of Martial.]

—o—

DCCCXXXVIII.

ON A GENERAL LOVER.

We know not why you for the fair
So many billet-doux prepare;
But this we know, a billet-doux
No fair one ever penned for you.

Anon.

[From the Latin of Martial.]

—o—

DCCCXXXIX.

ON SPONGE.

Lend Sponge a guinea! Ned, you'd best refuse,
And give him half. Sure, that's enough to lose.

Anon.

[From the Latin of Martial. See No. CDXXXIII.]

—o—

DCCCXL.

ON DR. JOHN FELL, BISHOP OF OXFORD.

I do not love thee, Doctor Fell;
The reason why, I cannot tell:
But this I know, and know full well—
I do not love thee, Doctor Fell.

Anon.

[From the Latin of Martial. Dr. Fell died in 1686.]

---o---

DCCCXLI.

ON A WINE MERCHANT.

The vilest of compounds while Balderdash vends,
And brews his dear poison for all his good friends;
No wonder they never can get him to dine,—
He's afraid they'd oblige him to drink his own wine.

Anon.

[From the Latin of Martial.]

---o---

DCCCXLII.

ON A BAD PREACHER WHO WROTE WELL.

So ill you preach, a Bishop you might be,
But that you write too well to hold a see.
'T is not enough to fear success in one:
To be a Bishop both must be ill done.

Richard Simpson.

[From the Latin of Sir Thomas More.]

DCCCXLIII.
On Papal Claims.

The Pope claims back to Apostolic sources,
But when I think of Papal crimes and courses,
It strikes me the resemblance is completer
To Simon Magus than to Simon Peter.

Anon.

[John Owen has a Latin epigram founded on very much the same idea.]

DCCCXLIV.
On Law and Physic.

Physic brings health, and Law promotion,
   To followers able, apt, and pliant;
But very seldom, I've a notion,
   Either to patient or to client.

Anon.

[From the Latin of John Owen.]

DCCCXLV.
On a certain Marcus.

Why durst thou offer, Marcus, to aver
Nature abhorr'd a vacuum?—confer
But with your empty skull, then you'll agree
Nature will suffer a vacuity.

Anon.

[From the Latin of John Owen.]

DCCCXLVI.

ON ONE BEAU CLINCHER.

Because I'm silent, for a fool
    Beau Clincher doth me take;
I know he's one by surer rule,
    For—I heard Clincher speak.

Dr. Walsh.

[Stated in *Select Epigrams* (1757) to be imitated from Owen. See No. CDXLV.]

---o---

DCCCXLVII.

ON A LAWYER AND HIS WIFE.

How fitly join'd the lawyer and his wife!
He moves at bar, and she at home, the strife.

Anon.

[From the Latin of Peter Giles; Englished in *The Poetical Farrago* (1794).]

---o---

DCCCXLVIII.

ON POPE JULIUS II.

Thy father Genoese, thy mother Greek,
Born on the seas: who truth in thee would seek?
False Greece, Liguria false, and false the sea:
False all: and all their falsehoods are in thee.

Anon.

[From the Latin of George Buchanan (1506-1582).]

DCCCXLIX.

To an Enemy.

Thou speak'st always ill of me,
I always speak well of thee.
But spite of all our noise and pother,
The world believes nor one nor t' other.

Anon.

[From the Latin of George Buchanan.]

---o---

DCCCL.

On a certain Doletus.

Doletus writes verses, and wonders—ahem!—
When there's nothing in him, that there's nothing in them.

Anon.

[From the Latin of George Buchanan.]

---o---

DCCCLI.

Of Pride.

If thou wilt needs be proud, mark this, friend mine,
Of good deeds be not proud—they are not thine:
But when thou playest the knave, in ill deeds grown,
Be proud of those ill deeds, they are thine own.

John Heywood (1506–1565).

[A Latin distich by Nicholas Baxius has some resemblance to the first part of this quatrain.]

DCCCLII.

ON FRANCIS CHARTRES.

Here Francis Chartres lies. Be civil;
The rest God knows—perhaps the devil!
Alexander Pope (1688-1744).

[From the Latin of Hercules Stroza, on Joannes Mirandola. See *Delitiae Delitiarum :—*

"Joannes jacet hic Mirandola; cætera norunt
Et Tagus et Ganges, forsan et Antipodes."

"You know," Pope is represented as saying, in Spence's *Anecdotes* (1820), "I love short inscriptions, and that may be the reason why I like the epitaph on the Count of Mirandola so well. Some time ago I made a parody of it for a man of very opposite character." This was the infamous Colonel Chartres, whose name, however, was by-and-by deleted, to make way for that of the Lord Coningsby, who impeached Harley, Earl of Oxford, in 1715.]

—o—

DCCCLIII.

ON A CERTAIN ARTHUR.

Arthur, they say, has wit; for what?
For writing? No; for writing not.
Jonathan Swift (1667-1745).

[Perhaps imitated from a distich by Jean de Cisinge (1434-1472), an Hungarian writer.]

—o—

DCCCLIV.

On Praise after Death.

If only when they're dead, you poets praise,
I own I'd rather have your blame always.

Anon.

[Translated in the *Quarterly Review* from the Latin of Euricius Cordus (d. 1538). See Martial, VIII. 69; also No. DCCCLXVIII.]

DCCCLV.

On a Bald Man.

If by your hairs your virtues numbered be,
Angels in heav'n were not more pure than thee.

Anon.

[From the Latin of N. Paterson (about 1678.)]

DCCCLVI.

On a Butcher becoming a Leech.

Sosil, the butcher, has become a leech. 'T is nothing new,
For what he did when butchering, as doctor he will do.

Anon.

[Translated in the *Quarterly Review* from the Latin of Georgius Anselmus (d. 1528). See No. DCCCXXVII.]

DCCCLVII.

ON A WEAK-WILLED FELLOW.

Tom, weak and wavering, ever in a fright
Lest he do something wrong, does nothing right.

Richard Simpson.

[From the Latin of Paschasius.]

DCCCLVIII.

ON LEO X.'S SALE OF INDULGENCES.

Leo lack'd the last sacrament. "Why," need we tell?
He had chosen the chalice and paten to sell.

Anon.

[Translated in the *Quarterly Review* from the Latin of Sannazaro (1458–1530).]

DCCCLIX.

ON ONE GABRIEL.

Black locks hath Gabriel, beard that's white,
   The reason, sir, is plain;
Gabriel works hard, from morn to night,
   More with his jaw than brain.

Anon.

[From *The Spirit of the Public Journals* (1806). It is a free translation of an epigram by Macentinus, printed in *Delitiae Delitiarum*.]

DCCCLX.

ON A CERTAIN DAMON.

To Damon's self his love's confined;
   No harm I therein see;
This happiness attends his choice;
   Unrivall'd he will be.

Anon.

[This is only a free rendering of an epigram by Paul Thomas, Sieur de Maisonnette, given in *Delitiae Delitiarum*.]

DCCCLXI.

ON THE SCOTCH AND THE SWISS.

No one longs half so much as a Scot or a Swiss
For his home when abroad; and the reason is this—
Of all those who live absent from home there is not
One from home half so long as a Swiss and a Scot.

Anon.

[From the Latin.]

DCCCLXII.

ON A CERTAIN SPINTEXT.

As Spintext one day, in the mansion of prayer,
Was declaiming a sermon he'd stolen from Blair,
A large mastiff dog began barking aloud;
"Turn him out," cried the doctor, enraged, to the crowd.
"And why?" answered one; "in my humble belief
He's an excellent dog, for he barks at a thief."

Anon.

[From the French of Guichard.]

DCCCLXIII.

ON AN AUTHOR-CRITIC.

Damis, an author cold and weak,
 Thinks as a critic he's divine;
Likely enough; we often make
 Good vinegar of sorry wine.

Anon.

[From the French of Guichard. Shenstone says somewhere:—" A poet that fails often becomes a morose critic; weak white wine makes excellent vinegar."]

―――o―――

DCCCLXIV.

ON A LADY RARELY SEEN EXCEPT AT MIDNIGHT OPERAS AND BALLS.

Young Cliton has set me a difficult task,—
For Phillis's age he's thought proper to ask,
 Of whose doings town talk is not thrifty.
She's twenty at most, if you reckon her days;
If her nights, then, as far as I know of her ways,
 She's not far from the wrong side of fifty.

Peter Onslow.

[From the French of Gombauld.]

DCCCLXV.

ON ONE THERSANDES.

That you cannot get rid of Thersandes, you say,
   Though you've tried to accomplish it fifty times o'er:
I'll put you at once, my good friend, in the way,—
   Do but lend him ten pounds, and you'll ne'er see him more.

Anon.

[From the French of Gombauld.]

DCCCLXVI.

A GENERAL RULE.

   Sir, I admit your general rule
   That every poet is a fool;
   But you yourself may serve to show it,
   That every fool is not a poet.

Alexander Pope (1688-1744).

[This has been attributed to Swift. It is really an admirable translation from the French of Scèvole de Sainte Marthe (1536-1650). So Prior:—

   Yes, every poet is a fool,
     By demonstration Ned can show it;
   Happy, could Ned's inverted rule
     Prove every fool to be a poet.]

DCCCLXVII.

ON A WORTHLESS FELLOW.

Here lies a man who into highest station,
  By dint of bribes and arts, contrived to slide;
And ne'er one service rendered to the nation,
  Except the lucky day on which he died.
Anon.

[From the French of Brebœuf.]

---o---

DCCCLXVIII.

PRAISE PREMATURE.

" Praise premature is idle breath ;
No fame is just till after death ! "
  So Clodio is for ever crying.
" Excuse me, Clodio, then," say I ;
" I rate not your applause so high,
  To think of earning it—by dying ! "
Samuel Bishop (1731–1795).

[From the writer's *Works* (1796) ; imitated from the French of Rabatin de Bussy, who founded his in turn on Martial—" To Vacerra" (bk. viii. 69). See No. DCCCLIV.]

---o---

DCCCLXIX.

ON A STATUE OF JUSTICE BEING MOVED INTO THE MARKET-PLACE.

" Tell me why Justice meets our eye,
Raised in the market-place on high ? "
" The reason, friend, may soon be told :
'T is meant to show she 's to be sold."
Anon.

[From the French of Furetière.]

DCCCLXX.

ON A DOCTOR.

You say, without reward or fee
   Your uncle cured me of a dangerous ill;
I say, he never did prescribe for me;
   The proof is plain—I'm living still.

Anon.

[From the French of Nicholas Boileau (1636-1711.)]

DCCCLXXI.

ON A PROUD PRELATE.

A prelate, in whose motley-colour'd mind
Humility and pride were found combin'd,
Prostrate in sickness, while his spirit sank,
Could not, in that last hour, forget his rank;
But breathed to Heaven this prayer of penitence,
" O Lord! have mercy on my Eminence!"

Lord Neaves (1800-1876).

[From the French of Boursault.]

DCCCLXXII.

ON A CERTAIN LORD.

A lord of senatorial fame
   Was by his portrait known outright,
For so the painter play'd his game,
   It made one even yawn at sight.

" 'T is he—the same—there's no defect
But want of speech," exclaimed a flat ;
To whom the limner—" Pray reflect ;
'T is surely not the worse for that."
Anon.

[From the French of Jean Baptiste Rousseau.]

———o———

DCCCLXXIII.

ON PIRON, BY HIMSELF.

Here lies Piron—a man of no position,
Who was not even an Academician.
Anon.

[Piron wrote this, in French, to revenge himself for his exclusion from the Academy, against whom he directed a perfect shower of epigrams. His *Works* were published in 1776. He was born in 1689, and died in 1773.]

———o———

DCCCLXXIV.

ON A FRENCH TRAGEDY, IN WHICH A HISSING SERPENT WAS INTRODUCED, AND WHICH WAS DAMNED.

What rivalry in magic power is this !
No fear of these their due laudation missing :
One artist makes a pasteboard serpent hiss ;
A greater still sets crowds of men a-hissing.
Lord Neaves (1800–1876).

[From the French of Piron.]

DCCCLXXV.

ON VOLTAIRE RE-WRITING TWO OF CREBILLON'S
TRAGEDIES.

No doubt of it : if Adam, our first father,
   Had felt this forward rhymster's foolish rage,
Leaving the apple, he'd have ventur'd rather
   In some more widespread mischief to engage.

Dissatisfied with this fair frame of Nature,
   Whose charms to other ears so clearly speak,
He'd have pulled down the work of his Creator,
   And built it up again within the week.

Lord Neaves (1800–1876).

[From the French of Piron. Crebillon, the dramatist, was born in 1674, and died in 1762.]

DCCCLXXVI.

ON A CERTAIN DAMIS.

Damis says, modestly, he must forego
   For wit or eloquence all claim to praise :
What Damis thinks I own I do not know,
   But I agree with him in all he says.

Lord Neaves.

[From the French of Piron.]

DCCCLXXVII.

ON THE SEVEN SACRAMENTS.

Whatever Rome may strive to fix,
The sacraments are only six.
This truth will palpably appear,
When o'er the catalogue you run:
For surely of the seven, 't is clear,
Marriage and Penance are but *one*.

Anon.

[From the French of Marshal Saxe (1696-1750).]

DCCCLXXVIII.

ON ONE WHO WAS ALWAYS IN THE FEAR OF DEATH.

Thrice happy Damon! Fate has stopp'd his breath!
He's now deliver'd from the fear of death.

Anon.

[From the French of Lebrun (1729-1807).]

DCCCLXXIX.

ON A BAD WRITER WHO COMPOSED THE EPITAPH OF A GOOD POET.

On Stephen's tomb thou writ'st the mournful line:
Why lived he not, alas! to write on thine?

Anon.

[From the French of Lebrun.]

DCCCLXXX.

On Job.

Sly Beelzebub took all occasions
To try Job's constancy and patience;
He took his honours, took his health;
He took his children, took his wealth,
His servants, horses, oxen, cows,—
But cunning Satan did *not* take his spouse.

But Heaven, that brings out good from evil,
And loves to disappoint the devil,
Had predetermined to restore
Twofold all Job had before,—
His servants, horses, oxen, cows;—
Short-sighted devil, *not* to take his spouse!

Samuel Taylor Coleridge (1772–1834).

[Several versions of these lines are in existence. The lines themselves have been traced to an epigram by Coquard, called "Misère de Job."]

———o———

DCCCLXXXI.

On Tiraqueau, the Lawyer.

Tiraqueau, while drinking water,
Has an annual son or daughter;
Wine or beer he ne'er partook,
Yet he writes an annual book.
Large already is the score,
And we look for many more.
But if he, on water merely,
Can achieve these wonders yearly,
What if wine, with gen'rous fire,
Should a larger aim inspire?

Such increase his works might gain
As the world could scarce contain,
And 't would be a task bewildering
Where to put his books and children.
                              Anon.

[From the French of De Cailly. Tiraqueau, the great French lawyer, had the reputation of producing a book yearly, whilst his wife presented him with a baby with equal regularity. The fact of his being a teetotaler also added point to the many sarcasms that were levelled at his *libri* and *liberi*.]

—o—

DCCCLXXXII.

ON DACIER AND HIS WIFE.

When Dacier, jointly with his learned wife,
Has children of the flesh that spring to life,
I'm quite disposed, as much as any other,
To hold that Madame Dacier is the mother.

But when good Dacier and his wife combin'd
Produce their books, those children of the mind,
I own I feel an inclination rather
To hold that Madame Dacier is the father.
                              Anon.

[From the French of De Cailly.]

—o—

DCCCLXXXIII.

ON A COQUETTE.

" How blest," my dear brother, said Sylvia one day,
" Should I be would you quit this bad habit of play;
    Do you mean to extinguish it never?"

"When you cease to coquet, I'll quit play," he replied:
"Ah! plainly I see, my dear brother," she cried,
   "You're determined to gamble for ever!"
Anon.

[From the French of De Cailly.]

---o---

DCCCLXXXIV.

ON A DR. JULEP.

His long speeches, his writings, in prose and in rhyme,
Dr. Julep declares are but meant to kill time.
What a man is the doctor! for, do what he will,
He something or somebody wishes to kill.
Anon.

[From the French of Fabian Pillet.]

---o---

DCCCLXXXV.

ON FOLLY.

  The world of fools has such a store,
    That he who would not see an ass
  Must bide at home and bolt his door,
    And break his looking-glass.
Anon.

[From the French of La Monnoye.]

---o---

DCCCLXXXVI.

ON THE DUKE OF ANJOU.

Nay, marvel not, ye Flemings brave,
If your choice duke two noses have:
'T is meet and right such double grace
Should decorate a double face.

Anon.

[From the French. This Duke of Anjou was one of the many suitors of Queen Elizabeth, and was elected Prince of the Low Countries by the Flemings.]

—o—

DCCCLXXXVII.

ON MISS PRUE.

" I never give a kiss," says Prue,
  " To naughty man, for I abhor it."
She will not give a kiss, 't is true;
  She 'll take one though, and thank you for it.

Thomas Moore (1779–1852).

[From the French.]

—o—

DCCCLXXXVIII.

TO A CRUEL FAIR ONE.

'T is done; I yield; adieu, thou cruel fair!
  Adieu, th' averted face, th' ungracious check!
I go to die, to finish all my care,
  To hang.—To hang?—yes—round another's neck.

James Henry Leigh Hunt (1784–1859).

[From the French.]

DCCCLXXXIX.

ON A CERTAIN ÆGLE.

Ægle, beauty and poet, has two little crimes;
She makes her own face, and does not make her rhymes.

Lord Byron (1788–1824).

[From the French.]

DCCCXC.

ON A SPONGE AND SLANDERER.

You never dine at home at all, but sponge upon your friends,
And, when you speak, the poison'd stream of slander never ends.
So we may say that day by day, on this or that pretence,
Your mouth you never open but at other men's expense.

Lord Neaves (1800–1876).

[From the French.]

DCCCXCI.

ON A NOMINATION TO THE LEGION OF HONOUR.

In ancient times—'t was no great loss—
They hung the thief upon the cross:
But now, alas!—I say 't with grief—
They hang the cross upon the thief.

Anon.

[From the French.]

DCCCXCII.

ON TALLEYRAND.

Seven cities boasted Homer's birth, 'tis true,
But twenty boast of not producing you.

Anon.

[From the French. See No. CXI.]

DCCCXCIII.

ON ONE WHO OWED HIM MONEY.

My debtor Paul looks pale and harass'd;
  Thinks he on means to pay his bill?
Oh, no! he only is embarrass'd
  For means to be my debtor still.

Anon.

[From the French. See No. CDXXXV.]

DCCCXCIV.

ON ADAM AND EVE.

Whilst Adam slept, Eve from his side arose:
Strange! his first sleep should be his last repose!

Anon.

[From the French.]

DCCCXCV.

ON A LADY WHO PAINTED.

Say, which enjoys the greatest blisses,
John, who Dorinda's picture kisses,
Or Tom, his friend, the favoured elf,
Who kisses fair Dorinda's self?

Faith, 'tis not easy to divine,
  While both are thus with raptures fainting,
To which the balance should incline,
  Since Tom and John both kiss a painting.
Anon.

[From the German of Lessing (1729–1781).]

---o---

DCCCXCVI.
ON THE ABOVE.

Nay, surely John's the happiest of the twain,
Because—the picture cannot kiss again.
Anon.

[From the same.]

---o---

DCCCXCVII.
ON ONE LUCINDA.

A long way off Lucinda strikes the men:
  As she draws near,
  And one sees clear,
A long way off one wishes her again.
Anon.

[From the German of Lessing.]

---o---

DCCCXCVIII.
ON ONE GRUDGE AND HIS MONEY.

Grudge leaves the poor his whole possessions—nearly :—
He means his next of kin shall weep sincerely.
Anon.

[From the German of Lessing.]

DCCCXCIX.
ON A DEAF AND DUMB WIFE.

"How strange, a deaf wife to prefer!"—
"True, but she's also dumb, good sir."

Anon.

[From the German of Lessing.]

CM.
ON ONE NIGER.

"He's gone at last—old Niger's dead!"
   Last night 't was said throughout the city.
Each quidnunc gravely shook his head,
   And half the town cried, "What a pity!"

The news prov'd false—'t was all a cheat;
   The morning came the fact denying;
And all the town to-day repeat
   What half the town last night was crying.

Anon.

[From the German of Lessing.]

CMI.
ON A VOLUME OF EPIGRAMS.

Point in his foremost epigram is found:
Bee-like, he lost his sting at the first wound.

Anon.

[From the German of Lessing.]

CMII.

ON MEDICAL ADVICE.

"Better to roam the fields for health unbought,
Than fee the doctor for a nauseous draught."
This maxim long I happily pursued,
And fell disease my health then ne'er pursued;
But to be more than well at length I tried—
The doctor came at last—and then I died!

Anon.

[From the German.]

---o---

CMIII.

ON A YOUTH WHO WAS NOT TO BE ALLOWED TO MARRY UNTIL HE HAD REACHED YEARS OF DISCRETION.

Poor Stephen is young, and lacks wisdom, 't is said,
   And therefore still longer must tarry;
If he waits though, methinks, till he 's sense in his head,
   I will be sworn that he never will marry.

Anon.

[From the Italian.]

---o---

CMIV.

ON A LIAR.

One single truth, before he died,
   Poor Dick could only boast:
"Alas, I die!" he faintly cried,
   And then gave up the ghost.

Anon.

[From the Italian.]

NOTICES

OF

THE EPIGRAMMATISTS.

ADDISON, JOSEPH (1672–1719), was appointed Under-Secretary of State in 1706, and Secretary of State in 1717. He published *The Campaign* in 1704, and volumes of *Poems* in 1712 and 1716. His prose works include contributions to *The Spectator*, *The Tatler*, and *The Guardian;* *The Freeholder*, and a treatise on *The Evidences of the Christian Religion*. His opera of *Rosamund* was produced in 1706, his tragedy of *Cato* in 1713, and his comedy of *The Drummer* in 1715. His *Works* were collected in 1765, and his *Life* has been written by Johnson and Miss Aikin.

ALDRICH, HENRY, D.D. (1647–1710), was Dean of Christ Church, Oxford, and wrote, in addition to several works on architecture, an *Artis Logicae Compendium*.

ASHBY-STERRY, J. A living writer, author of a book of essays entitled *Tiny Travels* and a volume of social verse entitled *Boudoir Ballads*.

ATTERBURY, FRANCIS, D.D. (1662–1732), was made Bishop of Rochester in 1713. He was tried and outlawed in 1722 on the charge of being concerned in a Jacobite conspiracy. He wrote four volumes of *Sermons* (1740), and a Latin translation of *Absalom and Achitophel* (1682). His *Works* appeared in 1789-98; his *Memoirs* in 1723. Volumes of his *Correspondence* were issued in 1768 and 1783.

BANCROFT, THOMAS (d. about 1600), published *Two Bookes of Epigrammes and Epitaphs* in 1639. He wrote, among other works, *The Glutton's Feaver* and *The Heroical Lover*. He is described as "of Catherine Hall, Cambridge," and was much esteemed as an epigrammatist in his day.

BARBER, MARY, published in 1735 *Poems on Several Occasions*.

BISHOP, SAMUEL (1731-1795), was appointed Head Master of Merchant Taylors' School, London, in 1783. He was also Rector of St. Martin Outwich. His *Poetical Works* appeared in 1796.

BLANCHARD, LAMAN (1803-1865), published a variety of tales, essays, and sketches, a selection from which was issued, with a *Memoir* by Lord Lytton, in 1849. His *Poems* appeared in 1876.

BLESSINGTON, MARGUERITE, COUNTESS OF (1790-1849), was twice married,—first to a Captain Farmer, in 1817; afterwards to Charles Gardiner, Earl of Blessington, who died in 1829. A leader of fashion, her gaieties ran her into debt, and she took to literature as a profession. Among the best of her works are her *Conversations with Lord Byron*, her books of travel, *The Repealers* and a few other novels. Her *Life* was written by Madden.

BRERETON, JANE (1685-1740), wrote a number of poetic pieces, which were published in her *Life and Letters* in 1744. See Brydges' *Censura Literaria*.

BROOKS, CHARLES SHIRLEY (1815–1874), succeeded Mark Lemon as Editor of *Punch* in 1870, and retained the office until his own death, four years later. He published several novels, including *Aspen Court, The Silver Cord, The Gordian Knot,* and *Sooner or Later.* Among his contributions to the drama were *The Creole* and *Our Governess.* A selection from his contributions to *Punch* was edited by his son in 1875.

BROOME, WILLIAM (see the note to No. CXXXIX).

BROUGHAM AND VAUX, HENRY BROUGHAM, LORD (1779–1868), was educated at Edinburgh University, and joined the Scottish bar, which he left in 1807. In 1810 he entered the House of Commons; twenty years afterwards he became Lord Chancellor. Among his works were *Discourses of Natural Theology* (1835), *Dissertations on Scientific Subjects* (1839), *Historic Sketches of the Statesmen of George III.'s Time* (1839–43), *Political Philosophy* (1840), *Lives of Men of Letters and Science* (1845), and *Contributions to the Edinburgh Review* (1857). His autobiography appeared in 1871.

BROWN, THOMAS (d. 1704), was educated at Oxford, and was for some time a schoolmaster in the country. He afterwards went to London, and embarked in literature. His *Works* were edited in 1760 by Dr. Drake; they were first collected in 1707.

BROWN, SIR WILLIAM. A physician of Lynn, in Norfolk.

BUCKINGHAMSHIRE, JOHN SHEFFIELD, DUKE OF (1649–1721), wrote *The Vision,* and certain minor poems and lyrics, published with a *Memoir* in 1723.

BUDGELL, EUSTACE (1685–1736), was at one time a member of the Irish Parliament and an Under-Secretary of State; during his latter years, however, his fortunes declined; he got into debt and into discredit, and eventually committed suicide. He was suspected of forging a will in his own favour—a circumstance alluded to by Pope in a well-known couplet. Budgell is best known in literature as a contributor to Addison's *Spectator*.

BURNS, ROBERT (1759-1796), published his first volume of poems in 1786, coming again before the world in 1787 and 1793 with a second and a third edition of it. The first complete edition of his *Works* was that of Currie, in 1800; the most recent is that of Scott Dalgleish, 1877-8. The events of Burns's life are too well known to need recital. See the biographies and criticisms by Chambers, Alexander Smith, Lockhart, Cunningham, Carlyle, and Professor Wilson.

BURTON, DR. (see note to No. CCLXVII).

BUTLER, SAMUEL (1600-1680), was the son of a gentleman farmer, and spent the early years of his life as tutor in families of good position. He was by-and-by appointed Secretary to the Earl of Carbery, and, afterwards, Steward of Ludlow Castle. The first part of his great poem, *Hudibras*, was published in 1663, the second part in 1664, and the third in 1778. The poet's latter years were spent in London, and were marked by poverty and neglect. His *Posthumous Works* appeared in 1715, the *Remains* in 1759. See the *Life* by Dr. Johnson, and the criticism by Hazlitt.

BYROM, JOHN (1691-1763), was the son of a Manchester linen-draper, was educated at Cambridge, and studied, if he did not practise, medicine. He obtained his livelihood chiefly by shorthand writing, on the subject of which he wrote a work, called *Universal English Shorthand* (1767). His *Poems* appeared in 1773. See the *Biographia Britannica*.

BYRON, GEORGE GORDON, LORD (1788-1824), first appeared as a poet in 1807, when he published his *Hours of Idleness*,

Notices of the Epigrammatists. 353

a savage review of which stung him into the composition of his famous satire, *English Bards and Scotch Reviewers*. That, as well as his *Hints from Horace*, contains much that is brilliantly epigrammatic. *Beppo* and *Don Juan* are written in a different vein, but are also full of the most exquisitely worded epigram in the language. As a poem of pure persiflage, *Don Juan* is of course unrivalled. Byron's biography was written by Moore, Galt, and others. For criticism, the essays by Macaulay, Brimley, Kingsley, and Swinburne may be recommended.

BYRON, HENRY JAMES (b. 1835), has produced over a hundred dramatic pieces, ranging from *Cyril's Success*, *Our Boys*, *Married in Haste*, *An English Gentleman*, *An American Lady*, *Old Soldiers*, *Old Sailors*, *Weak Woman*, and other comedies, to extravaganzas like *The Maid and the Magpie*, *Little Don Cæsar de Bazan*, and *Little Dr. Faust*. He has published two stories, *Paid in Full* and *A Bad Debt*, and was for some time Editor of *Fun*.

CAMPBELL, THOMAS (1777-1844), published the *Pleasures of Hope* in 1799, *Gertrude of Wyoming* in 1809, *Theodric* in 1824, and two volumes of short poems in 1803 and 1842. He is most highly esteemed, of course, for his martial lyrics, which have fire and vigour. His epigrammatic powers were but slight. He produced several prose works. See his *Life* by Beattie (1849).

CANNING, RIGHT HON. GEORGE (1770-1827), was educated at Eton and Oxford, and entered life as a barrister. Returned to Parliament in 1793 as member for Newport, Isle of Wight, he was, three years afterwards, appointed Under-Secretary of State under Pitt. When the latter resigned office, in 1801, Canning joined the opposition to the Addington Administration, and when Pitt again took office, in 1804, accepted the Treasurership of the Navy. In the Portland Ministry of 1807 Canning was Minister for Foreign Affairs; in 1814 he went as ambassador to Lisbon; and in 1816 he was made

A A

President of the Board of Control, under the Liverpool *régime*. In 1822 he was again entrusted with the Foreign Secretaryship. He was called on to form a Ministry in 1827, but died in August of the same year. His contributions to literature are to be found chiefly in the pages of *The Anti-Jacobin.* See the *Cornhill Magazine* for 1867.

CAREY, MRS.

CAYLEY, GEORGE JOHN. Author of *The Bridle Roads of Spain* and *Sir Reginald Mohun;* the former a charming book of travel, the latter a poem of some power.

CHESTERFIELD, PHILIP DORMER STANHOPE, EARL OF (1694-1773), studied at Cambridge, and afterwards entered Parliament as member for St. Germains. He was made Privy Councillor in 1727, was sent in 1728 as ambassador to Portugal, and in 1730 was appointed Steward of the Household. In 1745 he went as ambassador to the Hague; his next appointment being to the Lord-Lieutenancy of Ireland. In 1746 he became one of the principal Secretaries of State, but resigned in 1748. He was seized with deafness in 1752, and the remainder of his days was passed in comparative seclusion. He was a contributor to *The Craftsman* and *The World*, and wrote a series of *Letters to his Son*, to which, curiously enough, he owes his present fame. His *Works* were collected in 1777, when his *Memoir* was published by Dr. Maty. His *Letters* were edited by Lord Stanhope in 1845.

CHEYNE, DR.

CLARKE, WILLIAM (1696-1771), was Chancellor of Chichester Cathedral, and noted for his "exquisite taste and diversified erudition."

COLERIDGE, SAMUEL TAYLOR (1772-1834), published *Christabel* in 1816, *The Ancient Mariner* in 1798, and a volume of *Poems* in 1794. His dramas of *The Fall of Robespierre*,

Remorse, and *Zapolya* appeared in 1794, 1813, and 1818 respectively. His prose publications included *The Friend* (1812), *Biographia Literaria* (1817), and *Aids to Reflection* (1825). His *Works* appeared in 1847, and his *Life* was written by Gillman (1838). For criticisms, see the essays by Mr. Swinburne and Principal Shairp.

CONGREVE, WILLIAM (1670-1729), was lucky enough to obtain early in life positions under Government which ensured for him a handsome income and the *entrée* to society. His first comedy, *The Old Bachelor*, was produced when he was twenty-three; *The Double Dealer* followed in 1694, *Love for Love* in 1695, and *The Way of the World* in 1700. His only tragedy, *The Mourning Bride*, was performed in 1697. His *Poems* appeared in 1710; his *Memoirs* in 1730. See the criticisms by Thackeray, Macaulay, and Hazlitt.

COTTON, NATHANIEL (1707-1788), was a physician as well as a poet, and had Cowper under his skilful and tender care. His *Various Pieces in Prose and Verse* appeared in 1791.

CROLY, REV. GEORGE (1780-1860), Rector of St. George's, Walbrook, London, wrote a comedy called *Pride shall have a Fall*, and a tragedy called *Catiline*. His poetical productions were numerous, including *Paris in* 1815, *The Angel of the World*, and *The Modern Orlando*. He was also voluminous as a romancist, biographer, and historian. His *Poems* were collected in 1830.

CUNNINGHAM, JOHN (1729-1773), actor and poet, wrote *May-Eve*, *Content*, and other poems and lyrics. See Campbell's *Specimens*.

CURRAN, JOHN PHILPOT (1750-1817), was called to the Irish bar in 1775, and entered the Irish Parliament in 1782, retiring from it before the Union, to which he was strongly opposed. He held the Mastership of the Rolls in Ireland from 1806 till 1813. He was an effective speaker, being distinguished for his brilliancy of retort.

DAVIES, SIR JOHN (1570-1626), was made Solicitor-General for Ireland in 1603 and King's Serjeant in 1616. He wrote *Orchestra* (1590), *Hymns of Astraea* (1599), *Nosce Teipsum* (1599), and various other poems. His *Poetical Works* were published in 1773 by T. Davies, and in 1876 by A. B. Grosart. See the *Life* by Chalmers (1786).

DENHAM, SIR JOHN (1615-1668), produced a tragedy called *The Sophy*, and a poem called *Cooper's Hill*. His *Poems and Translations* were issued in 1709. See Johnson's *Lives of the Poets*.

DIBDIN, THOMAS (1771-1841), was the son of Charles Dibdin, the famous song writer, was also a composer of very lively ditties, as well as the author of numerous dramatic pieces. He published his *Reminiscences* in 1828. They are chiefly theatrical.

DOBSON, AUSTIN, is well known as the author of *Vignettes in Rhyme* and *Proverbs in Porcelain*, two volumes of miscellaneous and social verse.

DODDRIDGE, PHILIP, D.D. (1702-1751), ministered during most of his life to a dissenting congregation at Northampton, where he presided also over a theological seminary. His principal prose work is *The Rise and Progress of Religion in the Soul* (1750). His *Sermons* appeared in 1826, his *Memoirs* in 1766, and *Life* in 1831.

DODSLEY, ROBERT (1703-1764), was originally a footman, but having a strong literary bias, became a bookseller and publisher, in which latter capacity he produced his well-known collections of *Poems* and *Plays*. His own works include *The Muse in Livery* (1732), and some minor poems; besides various plays, some of which were very successful, but none of which have survived their author. His works were collected under the title of *Trifles* (1748) and *Miscellanies* (1772).

DONNE, JOHN, D.D. (1573-1631), was educated at Oxford and Cambridge, and for many years of his life resided with various persons of title and position. Late in his career he took orders, and rose to be Dean of St. Paul's. His principal productions are *The Pseudo-Martyr* (1610), *Essays in Divinity* (1651), and *Sermons* (1640-9). His poems include elegies, satires, and miscellaneous lyrics of the metaphysical order. His *Works* were issued in 1635. See the *Life* by Dean Alford (1839).

DRUMMOND, WILLIAM (1585-1649), spent most of his life on his estate at Hawthornden, near Edinburgh, occasionally travelling on the Continent. He wrote voluminously in verse, and many of his sonnets are remembered. One of the best of his productions is a humorous poem called *Polemo-Middinia* (1691). His most familiar work is his *Notes of the Conversations of Ben Jonson* (1619). See the *Life* by Cunningham (1833).

DRYDEN, JOHN (1631–1701), after receiving his early education at Westminster School, was elected to a scholarship at Cambridge in 1650, and in 1654 succeeded to a small estate worth £60 per annum. He was appointed poet laureate in 1670, but deprived of the office at the Revolution. His works comprise satires, such as *Absalom and Achitophel* and *Macflecknoe;* argumentative poems, such as *Religio Laici* and *The Hind and the Panther;* and plays, such as *All for Love* and *The Conquest of Granada*. His translation of Virgil appeared in 1697. His *Works* have frequently been reprinted. See the *Life* by Scott, and the criticisms by Clough and Lowell

ELIOT, JOHN, is supposed to be the author of a volume of *Poems and Epigrams* published in 1658.

ELLIOTT, EBENEZER (1781-1849), is famous as the poet of the Anti-Corn-Law agitation. His *Works* were collected in 1834, 1840, and 1876.

ERSKINE, THOMAS, LORD (1750–1823), entered at Lincoln's Inn in 1775, and was immediately and conspicuously successful as a barrister. He was returned for Portsmouth in 1783, and was made Attorney-General in 1786. He was eventually Lord Chancellor. He was famous in his time as the defender of Tom Paine and Queen Caroline in their well-known trials. He was equally celebrated as a wit, his epigrammatic efforts being numerous and excellent.

EVANS, ABEL, D.D. (circa 1700), was "of St. John's College, Oxford," and was an intimate friend of Pope and other celebrities of the time. He was celebrated in his day as a writer of epigrams, few of which are now in existence.

FERGUSSON, ROBERT (1750–1774), was the author of a volume of *Poems* published in 1773. His biography was written by Peterkin and Irving.

FITZPATRICK, GENERAL RICHARD (1748–1815), is remembered as one of the contributors to *The Rolliad*. He was Secretary of War in 1783 and 1806.

FREEMAN, THOMAS (b. about 1590), published two books of epigrams—*Rubbe and a Great Cast*, and *Runne and a Great Cast, the Second Bowle*—both in 1614.

FRERE, JOHN HOOKHAM (1769–1846), esteemed as a diplomatist, is remembered as the translator of the plays of Aristophanes, and as the author of a humorous poem entitled *The Monks and Giants* (1817–18). He was also a contributor to *The Anti-Jacobin*. His *Works* were recently collected.

FULLER, FRANCIS (circa 1691), was "of St. John's College, Cambridge."

GARNETT, RICHARD, has published *Idylls and Epigrams* (1869), and other works.

GARRICK, DAVID (1716-1779), made his *début* on the stage in 1741, at Ipswich, appearing in London later in the same year. He was received with great applause as Richard III., and ever afterwards maintained his position as the leading actor in England. His plays include *The Lying Valet, Miss in her Teens,* and others. His *Poetical Works* were issued complete in 1785. See the *Lives* by Davies (1780) and Fitzgerald (1872).

GAY, JOHN (1688-1732), is celebrated as the author of *The Beggar's Opera*, which had an enormous success when first performed. The sequel, called *Polly*, was never produced. Gay also wrote several other pieces for the stage. Among his poetical works, first issued collectively in 1720, are *Trivia, Fables,* and *Rural Sports*. See the *Life* by Coxe, and Thackeray's *Humourists*.

GOLDSMITH, OLIVER (1728-1774), began life as a medical student, but quickly settled down to the career of a literary man. He produced his comedies of *The Good-natured Man* and *She Stoops to Conquer* in 1768 and 1773. His poems, *The Traveller* and *The Deserted Village*, appeared in 1764 and 1770, and his immortal novel, *The Vicar of Wakefield*, in 1766. His miscellaneous prose works are too numerous to be mentioned. See the *Lives* by Prior, Irving, and Forster.

GRAHAM, DAVID (b. about 1726), was a member of St. John's College, Cambridge, and a barrister-at-law.

GRAVES, REV. RICHARD (1715-1804), Scholar of Pembroke and Fellow of All Souls' Colleges, Oxford, was Rector of Claverton from 1750 till his death. His epigrams appear in *Euphrosyne; or, Amusements on the Road of Life* (1776). He also edited *The Festoon* (1767), a collection of ancient and modern epigrams.

GRAY, THOMAS (1716-1771), passed most of his mature years at Cambridge, his life at which was varied only by a visit now and then to London, or to other parts of the United Kingdom. He was for some years Professor of Modern History at his University. His *Poems* have been edited by Mitford, Moultrie, and others. The standard biography is by Mason. For criticism, see W. C. Roscoe's *Essays*.

GRIERSON, MRS.

HALIFAX, CHARLES MONTAGU, EARL OF (1661-1715), was at once a poet and a patron of poets—"fed," as Pope said, "with soft dedications all day long." He was co-author with Prior of *The City and Country Mouse*. His *Miscellanies* appeared in 1716. See Johnson's *Lives of the Poets*.

HANNAY, JAMES (1827-1873), was for some years Editor of the *Edinburgh Courant*, and was afterwards British Consul at Barcelona. His epigrams are printed in his *Sketches and Criticisms* (1865). He wrote *Satire and Satirists*, *Essays in the Quarterly*, *A Course of English Literature*, and *Studies on Thackeray;* besides two novels—*Singleton Fontenoy* and *Eustace Conyers*.

HARRINGTON, DR.

HARYNGTON, SIR JOHN (1561-1612), was educated at Eton and Cambridge, and was a distinguished courtier. His epigrams, "most elegant and wittie," many of which are from Martial, appeared in 1633. He also wrote *The Metamorphosis of Ajax* (1596), and a translation of Ariosto's *Orlando Furioso*.

HEATH, JOHN (b. about 1585), was admitted perpetual Fellow of New College, Oxford, in 1607. His *Two Centuries of Epigrams* appeared in 1610.

HEATH, ROBERT, published in 1650 *Clarastella, together with Poems, Occasional Elegies, Epigrams, and Satyrs*. Nothing is known of his life.

HEBER, REGINALD (1783-1826), was appointed Bishop of Calcutta in 1823. His poems include *Palestine* (1803) and *Lines on the War* (1809). They were collected in 1812. His *Life* was written by his widow, his *Memoirs* by Potter and Taylor.

HENLEY, REV. JOHN (1692-1756), better known as Orator Henley, was celebrated in his day as a preacher and political lecturer. He was the author of a *Universal Grammar*, and a poem on *Queen Esther*.

HERRICK, ROBERT (1591-1674), was presented to the vicarage of Dean Prior, Devonshire, in 1629. His *Noble Numbers* came out in 1647, his *Hesperides* in 1648. His *Poems* have been edited by Carew, Hazlitt, and A. B. Grosart. See also the selection by F. T. Palgrave.

HERVEY, LORD JOHN (1696-1743), immortalized by Pope as Sporus, lives in his *Memoirs of the Reign of George II*. His *Life* was written by John Wilson Croker. He was successively Chamberlain and Lord Privy Seal, and was satirized by Pope in a familiar passage.

HEYWOOD, JOHN (d. 1565), was, we are told, a favourite of Henry VIII.'s, and of his daughter Mary, owing to his faculty for telling amusing stories. Nothing more is known of him, except that he left England on the accession of Elizabeth, and died abroad. His epigrams were frequently reprinted.

HICKS. A barrister, of whom some anecdotes may be read in J. C. Young's *Diary*.

HOADLEY, JOHN.

HOGARTH, WILLIAM (1697–1764), the famous painter, is believed to have written no other epigram than that which is given in this volume. His "Harlot's Progress" appeared in 1733, his "Enraged Musician" in 1741, his "Marriage à la Mode" in 1745, and his "March to Finchley" in 1748. A handsome edition of his works was published in 1820–22. See the *Life* by Nichols, and the essay by G. A. Sala.

HOLLAND, HENRY RICHARD VASSALL FOX, LORD (1773–1840), held the post of Lord Privy Seal in the Grenville Ministry, and became Chancellor of the Duchy of Lancaster in 1830. He also held office under Lords Grey and Melbourne. His publications include *Memoirs of the Whig Party* and a *Life of Lope de Vega*.

HOME, JOHN (1724–1808), was a Scotch presbyterian minister, but considerable scandal being caused by the production of his play of *Douglas* (1756), he resigned his living, and retired into private life. In 1778 he obtained a captaincy in the militia. He wrote three other plays, called *The Fatal Discovery*, *Alonzo*, and *Alfred*, as well as a *History of the Rebellion of* 1745. See the *Life* by Mackenzie.

HOOD, THOMAS (1798–1845), began life in a counting-house, which he, by-and-by, deserted for an engraver's office. He took to literature, definitely, in 1821, when he became connected with *The London Magazine*. From that time to his death he was a constant contributor to *Belles Lettres* and the press. He died in 1845. His chief works are *The Plea of the Midsummer Fairies*, a poem too little appreciated, and *Tylney Hall*, a novel; his comic publications were legion. He was for some time editor of *The New Monthly Magazine*.

HOOK, THEODORE EDWARD (1788–1841), was appointed in 1813 Accountant-General and Treasurer of the Mauritius, from which island he returned in 1818. He started the *John Bull* newspaper in 1820. His works consist chiefly of novels, of which *Sayings and Doings* (1824), *Gilbert Gurney* (1835), and *Jack Brag* (1837) are the principal. His *Life and Remains* appeared in 1848.

HOPKINS, JOHN (b. about 1525), assisted Thomas Sternhold in translating the Psalms into English metre. He is believed to have been a clergyman, and to have resided in Suffolk, but otherwise nothing is recorded of him.

HUGMAN, R.

HUNT, JAMES HENRY LEIGH (1784-1859), began his literary career as a contributor to *The Examiner*, started by his brother in 1808. After suffering imprisonment for certain strictures on the Regent, he started *The Indicator* and *The Companion*, and, later still, in 1834, *The London Journal*. His poems include *The Story of Rimini*, *Captain Sword and Captain Pen*, *The Legend of Florence*, and *The Palfrey*. His prose works include *Men, Women, and Books* (1847), *A Jar of Honey* (1848), his *Autobiography* (1850), *The Religion of the Heart* (1853), and *The Royal Court Suburb* (1855). His *Letters* were published in 1862.

JEKYLL, JOSEPH, was a "man of society" of his time and a celebrated wit. Next to nothing is known of his career. We are not even sure about his Christian name.

JENNER, EDWARD, M.D. (1749-1823), will always be famous in the annals of medicine, and indeed of society, as the discoverer of vaccination, which may be said to have been conclusively established in 1796. It was in 1798 that Jenner published his *Inquiry into the Cause and Effect of the Variolae Vaccinae*. In 1802 he was voted a grant of £10,000, and in 1807 a second grant of £20,000, in recognition of his services to the country.

JOHNSON, DR. SAMUEL (1709-1784), published his first work— his satire of *London*—in 1738, and *The Vanity of Human*

Wishes in 1749. His tragedy, *Irene*, was produced in 1749 also ; whilst his world-renowned *Dictionary of the English Language* followed in 1765, his *Rasselas* in 1759, and his *Lives of the Poets* in 1779–81. His edition of the plays of Shakespeare appeared in 1768. His contributions to *The Rambler* and *The Idler* have placed his name in the front rank of essayists. Besides Boswell's *Life*, his biography has been written by Hawkins and Russell. See also Macaulay's *Biographies* and Carlyle's *Essays*.

JONSON, BEN (1574-1637), served as a soldier in the Low Countries, and afterwards as an actor in London. He then took to writing for the stage, and produced *Every Man in his Humour, Volpone, The Silent Woman, The Alchemist, Sejanus, Catiline*, and other plays. He was Poet Laureate under James I. and Charles I., for whom he wrote some masques, and from whom he received a pension. He died, however, in great poverty. The best edition of his *Works* is that superintended by Gifford (1816). See the biographies by Gifford, Procter, and Cunningham and Bell.

JORDAN, THOMAS, was poet to the city of London from 1671 to 1684. He was also a dramatist and an actor. See Lowndes' *Bibliographer's Manual* and the *Biographia Dramatica*.

KENDAL, REV. RICHARD, was of Peterhouse, Cambridge.

LAMB, CHARLES (1775–1834), was educated at Christ's Hospital, London, and afterwards (in 1792) obtained a clerkship in the East India House, which he retained until within a few years of his death (1825). His first publication was in the shape of a few *Poems* (1797) ; then followed *Rosamond Grey*, a romance (1798) ; *John Woodvil*, a tragedy (1801); after which came the *Essays of Elia*, collected into a volume (1823), the *Last Essays of Elia* being published in 1833. Lamb was part-author with his sister Mary of *Tales from Shakespeare* and *Poetry for Children*. His *Life* was written by Serjeant Talfourd and by B. W. Procter.

LANDOR, WALTER SAVAGE (1775–1864), was educated at Rugby and Oxford, married in 1811, and thereafter resided on the Continent, chiefly at Florence, where he died. He published a volume of *Poems* in 1796, *Gebir* in 1797, *Count Julian* in 1812, *Imaginary Conversations* in 1824, another volume of *Poems* in 1831, *Pericles and Aspasia* in 1836, *The Pentameron* in 1837, *Hellenics* in 1847, *Last Fruits off an Old Tree* in 1853, and *Dry Sticks Fagoted* in 1858. His *Life* has been written by John Forster.

LANSDOWNE, GEORGE GRANVILLE, LORD (1667–1735), wrote *The She-Gallants*, *The Jew of Venice*, *Heroic Love*, *The British Enchanters*, and various miscellaneous poems. For his biography, see Johnson's *Lives of the Poets*.

LETTSOM, JOHN COAKLEY, M.D. (1744–1815), wrote many works on medical subjects. His *Life* was written by Pettigrew (1817).

LOCKER, FREDERICK, is the author of a volume of *London Lyrics* (1857), which has run into several editions, and the editor of *Lyra Elegantiarum*, a collection of *vers de société*.

LOVER, SAMUEL (1797–1868), was notable as dramatist, novelist, and song-writer. His best known work is *Rory O'More*. Next in popularity comes *Handy Andy*. See the *Life* by Bayle Bernard.

LUTTRELL, HENRY (1770–1851), is remembered as the author of *Advice to Julia*, *Crockford House*, and various fugitive pieces of verse, the best of which may be seen in Mr. Locker's *Lyra Elegantiarum*. See also the *Diaries* of Moore and Greville.

LYTTELTON, GEORGE, LORD (1709–1773), entered Parliament in 1730, occupied several high offices of state, and was raised to the peerage in 1759. His most celebrated work is his *Letters from a Persian in England to his Friend in Ispahan* (1735). His poems include *Blenheim* and *The Progress of Love*. His *Life* has been written by Phillimore.

MALLET, DAVID (1700–1765), was at one time tutor in the family of the Duke of Montrose, at another under-secretary to the new Prince of Wales. He afterwards received a pension from the second Duke of Marlborough, and was rewarded for some flattering verses on Lord Bute by the Keepership of the Book of Entries for the Port of London. He wrote *William and Margaret* (1727), *A Life of Bacon* (1740), and many other works.

MANSEL, HENRY LONGUEVILLE, D.D. (1820–1871), was appointed in 1855 Reader in Moral Philosophy in Magdalen College, Oxford, and, in 1858, Bampton Lecturer, his subject being "The Limits of Religious Thought." In 1859 he became Waynflete Professor of Philosophy, and in 1866 Regius Professor of Ecclesiastical History and Canon of Christ Church. In 1868 he accepted the Deanery of St. Paul's. His *Lectures on History* appeared in 1861-2, his *Philosophy of the Conditioned* in 1866. His humorous satire, *Phrontisterion*, appeared with his *Letters, Lectures, and Reviews* in 1873.

MARVEL, ANDREW (1620–1628), became assistant-secretary to Milton in 1657, and was chosen in 1660 to represent Hull in Parliament. He was a strong supporter of the Republican party and principles. He wrote a very amusing satire on Holland, with some miscellaneous lyrics of first-rate quality. His *Works* were published with a *Life* in 1772, also in 1776.

MASON, WILLIAM (1725–1797), will be best remembered as the friend and biographer of Gray. He was educated at

Oxford, and, taking orders, became Precentor of York Cathedral. His chief poem is *The English Garden* (1772). He also produced two tragedies, called *Caractacus* and *Elfrida*. His *Memoirs of Gray* were published in 1775.

MATHEWS, CHARLES (1776–1835), the well-known actor and entertainer ; whose *Life* has been written by Mr. Edmund Yates. See also the memoirs edited by the actor's wife. Mathews was the father of the late (and no less celebrated) Charles James Mathews.

MONTAGU, LADY MARY WORTLEY (1690-1762), accompanied her husband to Constantinople in 1716, and wrote thence her famous *Letters*, first printed in 1763. In 1737 she separated from Mr. Montagu, and resided for many years in Italy. Her *Town Eclogues* (1716) were the occasion of a notorious literary quarrel, in which Pope and Swift took part. Her *Poetical Works* were collected in 1768 ; her *Works* were issued by Dallaway in 1803, and by Lord Wharncliffe in 1836.

MOORE, THOMAS (1779-1852), was educated at Dublin University, and in 1798 entered himself at the Middle Temple, London. In 1803 he was appointed to a Government post at Bermuda, but soon left that place to return to England, where he resided and laboured as a man of letters during the remainder of his life, save during a stay of a few years in Paris. His *Life* has been written by R. H. Montgomery ; see also his *Diary*, edited by Lord Russell. His *Odes of Anacreon* appeared in 1800, his first volume of original poetry in 1801, his *Lalla Rookh* in 1817. See Roscoe's *Essays*.

MORE, SIR THOMAS (1478-1535), was made Privy Councillor in 1516, Speaker of the House of Commons in 1523, and Lord Chancellor in 1529. The first English version of his *Utopia* (by Robinson) was printed in 1551. His *Epigrammata* were issued at Basle in 1520, and may be found translated in part in Pecke's *Parnassi Puerperium* (1659). See the *Lives* by Cayley, Emily Taylor, and Sir James Mackintosh; also, Campbell's *Lives of the Chancellors.*

NEAVES, CHARLES (Lord) (1800-1876), was a Scotch Judge of Session. His *Songs and Verses* (originally contributed to *Blackwood's Magazine*) appeared in 1869. His work on *The Greek Anthology* was published in 1874.

NUGENT, ROBERT CRAGGS, EARL (d. 1788).

O'CONNELL, DANIEL (1775-1847), the celebrated Irish agitator, was called to the bar in 1798, and was elected member of Parliament for Clare in 1828, for Kerry County in 1830, for Dublin in 1836, for Kilkenny in the same year (having been unseated on petition), for Dublin again in 1837, and for Cork County in 1841. In that year he was indicted for seditious conspiracy, and sentenced to imprisonment and a fine—a judgment which was, however, reversed. He published *A Memoir of Ireland* and a few pamphlets. His *Life* was written by his son and by Fagan.

OLDYS, WILLIAM (1687-1761), spent most of his life as a bookseller's drudge. He was dissolute in his habits, yet contrived to publish several valuable works, *e.g.*, *The British Librarian* (1737), a *Life of Raleigh* (1738), a translation of Camden's *Britannia*, and *The Harleian Miscellany*.

OUTRAM, GEORGE (1805-1856), a Scotch lawyer, published a volume of *Lyrics, Legal and Miscellaneous*.

PARNELL, THOMAS (1679-1718), was Archdeacon of Clogher in the Irish Church. His *Life* was written by Goldsmith; his *Poems* were collected in 1773. See Johnson's *Lives of the Poets*.

PARROT, HENRY, was the author of a volume entitled *Laquei Ridiculosi; or, Springes for Woodcocks*, published in 1613. See Warton's *History of English Poetry*. The facts of Parrot's life are wholly unknown.

POPE, ALEXANDER (1688–1744), first came before the public in 1709 with a volume of *Pastorals;* then came *An Essay on Criticism* (1711), *The Rape of the Lock* (1712), his translation of *The Iliad* (1820), his edition of the works of Shakespeare (1725), his translation of *The Odyssey* (1725), *The Dunciad* (1728), the *Essay on Man* (1732), *Moral Essays* (1735), and many other works. See the editions by Elwin and Ward. For criticism, consult Lowell's *Study Windows* and Leslie Stephen's *Hours in a Library*.

PORSON, RICHARD (1759–1808), the famous scholar, was educated at Cambridge, and became Fellow of Trinity College there in 1782. He resigned his fellowship in 1792, and was afterwards appointed Regius Professor of Greek in the University. In 1806 he was preferred to the Librarianship of the London Institution. His *Opera Philologica et Critica* were issued in six volumes under the editorship of Dr. Kidd. His *Biography* was written by Watson (1861); see also the shorter memoirs by Weston, Clarke, and Turton.

PRIOR, MATTHEW (1664–1721), was educated at Cambridge, and introduced to Court in 1688 by the Earl of Dorset. Appointed Secretary to the Embassy to the Hague in 1690, he obtained in succession several similar posts. In 1701 he entered Parliament. In 1711 he was charged with treason in connection with the negotiations for peace with France, imprisoned, and released after a confinement of two years. A collected edition of his *Works* appeared in 1718, his *Memoirs* in 1722. See Thackeray's *Humourists*, and the *Lives* by Johnson and Mitford.

PYNE.

RAMSAY, ALLAN (1686-1758), followed the trade of wig-maker up to his thirtieth year, when he commenced business as a bookseller. He also opened the first circulating library in Scotland. His first publication was some additional stanzas to the old poem of *Christis Kirk of the Grene*. His *Gentle Shepherd* was published in 1725 ; his collected *Poems* were issued in 1731 and 1800. See the *Life* by Chalmers.

RELPH, JOSIAH (1712-1743), was educated at Glasgow University, became a schoolmaster in Cumberland, and was afterwards admitted into the Church of England. His *Poems* were published at Carlisle in 1798.

ROCHESTER, JOHN WILMOT, EARL OF (1647-1680), was educated at Oxford, and, going to Court, was made one of the gentlemen of the bedchamber by Charles II. In 1665 he served under the Earl of Sandwich in the naval fight off Bergen. The remainder of his career was that of a courtier, with a love and a taste for letters. He wrote a tragedy called *Valentinian* and various poetical miscellanies. The story of his *Life and Death* was written by Bishop Burnet. See Johnson's *Lives*.

ROGERS, SAMUEL (1763-1855), was banker as well as poet, and is remarkable as one of the longest-lived of our singers. His first work appeared in 1786, and his last in 1822. *Columbus* was published in 1812, and *Jacqueline* in 1814. See Hayward's *Essays*, Roscoe's *Essays*, and Martineau's *Biographical Sketches*.

ROSE, SIR GEORGE, was master in chancery, bencher of the Inner Temple, and a Judge of the Court of Review. Some of the best of his *jeux d'esprit* were given in the course of an article on the subject in a recent volume of *Macmillan's Magazine*.

RUSSELL, T.

SCOTT, ROBERT, Master of Balliol College, Oxford.

SEDLEY, SIR CHARLES (1639-1701), the son of a Kentish baronet, opened his career somewhat riotously, but settled down by-and-by, and, becoming a member of Parliament, distinguished himself by his opposition to the oppressive measures of James II. He was the author of two plays called *The Mulberry Garden* (1668) and *Antony and Cleopatra* (1677), and various fugitive pieces. His works were printed in 1702, 1707, and 1722. See Jesse's *Reign of the Stuarts*.

SEWARD, THOMAS (d. 1790), father of Anna Seward the poetess, was prebendary of Salisbury and canon residentiary of Lichfield. He was a contributor to Dodsley's *Collection of Poems*, and edited the works of Beaumont and Fletcher.

SHAKESPEARE, WILLIAM (1564-1616). Shakespeare's plays were first collected in 1623. The leading editions are by Rowe (1709), Pope (1725), Theobald (1733), Johnson (1765), Malone (1790), Singer (1826), Collier (1841), Halliwell-Philipps (1851), Dyce (1857), Grant White (1857), Staunton (1858), Clarke (1860), Clark and Wright (1863), and Furnival (1877). See the criticisms by Coleridge, De Quincey, Dowden, Hallam, Hazlitt, Hunt, Lamb, Lowell, and Maginn.

SHERIDAN, RICHARD BRINSLEY (1751-1816), was returned to Parliament for Stafford in 1780, and did good service to the Whig party by his debating power. His comedies and other plays were brought out in the following order:—*The Rivals* (1775), *St. Patrick's Day* (1775), *The Duenna* (1775), *The School for Scandal* (1777), *A Trip to Scarborough* (1777), *The Critic* (1779), and *Pizarro* (1799). His *Works* appeared in a collected form in 1846. His *Life* was written by Moore.

SMITH, JAMES (1775–1839), was Solicitor to the Board of Ordnance and a member of the fashionable society of his time. He was co-author with his brother of the well-known *Rejected Addresses* and a collection of lyrics called *Horace in London* (1813). His *Memoirs and Remains* appeared in 1840.

SMITH, HORACE (1779–1849), was a stockbroker by profession, and was a much more voluminous writer than his brother James (*q. v.*), being the author of several novels, of which *Brambletye House* is perhaps the best. His *Tin Trumpet* (1836) is full of excellent satire. His *Poems* were collected in 1846.

SMITH, REV. SYDNEY (1771–1845), was educated at Oxford, and, entering the Church, officiated at Amesbury and Edinburgh before removing to London in 1803. Here he became known as a brilliant preacher and lecturer. He was afterwards preferred successively to the rectory of Foston-le-Clay, in Yorkshire, the living of Londesborough, a prebend's stall at Bristol, and the rectory of Combe Florey, in Somersetshire, and a canon's stall in St. Paul's Cathedral (1831). He was one of the earliest contributors to the *Edinburgh Review*, and published numerous sermons, and pamphlets, and speeches. His most familiar works are the *Letters of Peter Plymley* (1808), and *Sketches of Moral Philosophy* (1849). A selection from his writings appeared in 1855, and from his *Wit and Wisdom* in 1861. His *Works* appeared in 1839.

SNEYD.

SOMERVILLE, WILLIAM (1692–1742), was originally a well-to-do squire, but died in distressed circumstances. His chief works are *The Chase*, *Field Sports*, and a burlesque poem called *Hobbinol*. See Johnson's *Lives of the Poets*.

SUCKLING, SIR JOHN (1609–1641), was educated at Cambridge, and distinguished himself when young by fighting on the

Continent under the banner of the King of Sweden. Returning to England, he espoused the Royal cause, but, being detected in a plot to free Stafford from the Tower, was compelled to fly to France. His muse was as gay as his disposition, and as easy as his manners. His *Works* were collected in 1770, and his *Life* was written by a descendant, the Rev. Alfred Suckling (1836).

SWIFT, JONATHAN (1667–1745), was educated at Trinity College, Dublin, and took orders in 1694. He was by-and-by appointed to the vicarage of Laracor, in Ireland, and afterwards to the Deanery of St. Patrick's. His political writings include his pamphlets on *The Conduct of the Allies* (1712) and *The Panier Treaty* (1712). His *Drapier Letters* appeared in 1724. His *Gulliver's Travels* (1726) at once sprang into popularity. Among his other works may be named *The Tale of a Tub* (1704) and *An Argument against the Abolition of Christianity* (1708). His *Works* (including his *Poems*) were edited, with a *Memoir*, by Sir Walter Scott, in 1814. For criticism, see Thackeray's *Humourists* and Taine's *English Literature*.

TAYLOR, JOHN (1580–1654), commonly called "The Water-Poet," owing to his occupation, which was that of a waterman, had an uneventful career, save in his journey on foot from London to Edinburgh, the story of which is told in his *Pennyless Pilgrimage*. His *Works*, in prose and verse, were collected in 1630.

THOMPSON, WILLIAM (b. early in the eighteenth century), was Fellow of Queen's College, Oxford.

TOWNSHEND, REV. HENRY.

TRAPP, DR. JOSEPH (1679–1747), was the first Professor of Poetry at Oxford. His *Praelectiones Poeticae* appeared in 1718.

WADD, W.

WADDINGTON, SAMUEL. A living writer, who contributes frequently to the magazines.

WALLER, EDMUND (1605–1687), was a man of property and position, and, after leaving college, married a rich heiress. He then entered Parliament, of which he remained a member with scarcely an interruption during the reigns of Charles I., Charles II., and James II. His complete *Works* appeared in 1729; his *Poems* were edited by Robert Bell in 1866. See Johnson's *Lives of the Poets*.

WALPOLE, HORACE (1717–1797), was fourth Earl of Orford, and from various sinecures and other offices had an income of £4,000 a year. His literary work includes a *Catalogue of the Royal and Noble Authors of England* (1758), *Anecdotes of Painting* (1762), a romance called *The Castle of Otranto* (1705), *Historic Doubts on the Reign of Richard III.* (1768), and *Memoirs* and *Journals* of the Reigns of George II. and George III. His fame rests chiefly on his *Letters*. See the edition of 1857.

WALSH, WILLIAM (1663–1708), represented Worcestershire in Parliament, and was noted in his day both as poet and critic. Pope refers to him as "knowing Walsh" in a manner which testifies to the respect in which he was held. His works were unimportant: only one or two of his lyrics are now read.

WARBURTON, EGERTON.

WARTON, JOSEPH (1722–1800), was appointed Head Master of Winchester School in 1766; he was afterwards made a prebendary of St. Paul's. He published *Odes on several Subjects* (1746), an *Essay on the Genius of Pope* (1756), and editions of the *Works* of Pope and Dryden. His *Life* was written by Wood in 1806.

WARTON, THOMAS (1728–1790), was appointed Professor of Poetry at Oxford in 1757, Poet Laureate in 1785, and Camden Professor of History in the same year. His celebrated *History of English Poetry* issued from the press in 1774–8. His chief poem is *The Pleasures of Melancholy* (1745); he also wrote *The Triumph of Isis* (1749), *A Panegyric on Oxford Ale*, and other works, published complete in 1802. See Dennis's *Studies in English Literature*.

WELSTED, LEONARD (1689–1747), wrote *Epistles and Odes* (1724), *The Triumvirate, The Genius*, and other works published in 1787. He figures in *The Dunciad*.

WESLEY, SAMUEL (1662–1735), brother of the famous Methodists, was master of Tiverton School, and a clergyman in the Church of England. He published *Maggots; or, Poems on Several Subjects* (1685), a versified *History of the Old and New Testament*, a rhythmical *Life of Christ*, and other works.

WEST, GILBERT, LL.D. (1705–1756), translated the *Odes of Pindar* into English, and published a poem on *The Institution of the Garter*. He was also a contributor to Dodsley's *Collection of Poems*.

WHATELY, RICHARD (1787–1863), Archbishop of Dublin, published *Historic Doubts relative to Napoleon* (1819), *Some Difficulties in the Writings of St. Paul* (1828), *Elements of Logic* (1828), *Elements of Rhetoric* (1828), *Lectures on Political Economy* (1831), and other works. See the *Life* by his daughter.

WILLIAMS, SIR CHARLES HANBURY (1709–1759), courtier and diplomatist, wrote *Poems* (1763) and *Odes* (1775), republished with the remainder of his works in 1822. He was notable in his day as a producer of society verse of a satirical character.

WOLCOT, JOHN (1738–1819), began life as a medical assistant, but afterwards entered the Church, and obtained preferment in Jamaica. He soon returned to England, however, and resumed his former profession. From that time to his death he distinguished himself by pouring out a crowd of prose pamphlets and rhythmical lampoons. His most important work is *The Lousiad* (1786). Only a few of his miscellaneous pieces are now remembered, though his pseudonym of "Peter Pindar" is still famous. His *Works* were published in 1794-1801.

WYNTER, DR.

YATES, EDMUND HODGSON (b. 1831). A living writer, well-known as a novelist and journalist. He was editor of *Temple Bar* for several years. Among his best fictions are *Broken to Harness*, *Kissing the Rod*, and *Black Sheep*.

YOUNG, EDWARD (1684–1765), was, in early years, tutor to the Duke of Wharton. In 1730 he obtained a living in Hertfordshire, and married a daughter of the Earl of Lichfield. In 1761 he was made Clerk of the Closet to the Dowager Princess of Wales. His prominent publications were *The Revenge*, a tragedy (1721), *The Universal Passion* (1725), and *Night Thoughts* (1742). His *Works* were first published in 1737; his *Life* has been written by Mitford (1834), Doran (1851), and Thomas (1852).

INDEX OF WRITERS.

[The figures refer to the pages on which epigrams by the writers will be found.]

Addison, Joseph, 280.
Aldrich, Henry, 252.
Ashby-Sterry, J., 213, 233.
Atterbury, Francis, 280.

Bancroft, Thomas, 242.
Barber, Mary, 285.
Bishop, Samuel, 43, 123, 166, 206, 219.
Blanchard, Laman, 267.
Blessington, Countess of, 77.
Brereton, Jane, 139.
Brooks, Charles Shirley, 42, 102, 226, 236.
Broome, William, 171.
Brown, Thomas, 49, 88, 198.
Brown, Sir William, 107.
Brougham and Vaux, Lord, 34.
Buckinghamshire, Duke of, 4, 152.
Budgell, Eustace, 155.
Burns, Robert, 67, 144, 145, 146, 147, 177, **220**, 253, 262, 302, 303.
Burton, Dr., 115.
Butler, Samuel, 172.
Byrom, John, 6, 7, 61, 144.
Byron, Lord, 15, 25, 26, 28, 31, 69, 70, 74, 149, 150, 171, 224, 225, 233.
Byron, Henry James, 42, 249, 269.

Index of Writers.

Campbell, Thomas, 255.
Canning, George, 34, 254.
Carey, Mrs., 243.
Cayley, George John, 207.
Chesterfield, Lord, 260, 295.
Cheyne, Dr., 119.
Clarke, William, 244.
Coleridge, Samuel Taylor, 84, 154, 240, 256.
Congreve, William, 201, 290.
Cotton, Nathaniel, 295.
Croly, George, 197.
Cunningham, John, 153.
Curran, John Philpot, 20.

Davies, Sir John, 192.
Denham, Sir John, 49.
Dibdin, Thomas, 165, 233.
Dobson, Austin, 85.
Doddridge, Philip, 194.
Dodsley, Robert, 99.
Donne, John, 209, 261.
Dryden, John, 3, 216, 217.
Drummond, William, 1.

Eliot, John, 164.
Elliott, Ebenezer, 194.
Erskine, Lord, 25, 72, 237, 305, 306.
Evans, Abel, 105, 133.

Fergusson, Robert, 128, 210, 298.
Fitzpatrick, Richard, 15.
Freeman, Thomas, 82, 242.
Frere, John Hookham, 15, 18, 308.
Fuller, Francis, 151.

Garnett, Richard, 69, 85, 170, 178, 182, 203, 226.
Garrick, David, 62, 63, 64, 137, 188, 291, 292, 293.
Gay, John, 247.

Index of Writers.

Goldsmith, Oliver, 101, 291.
Graham, David, 294.
Graves, Richard, 87, 121, 163, 185, 187, 188.
Gray, Thomas, 93.
Grierson, Mrs., 288.

Halifax, Earl of, 286, 287.
Hannay, James, 142, 162, 170, 236.
Harrington, Dr., 259.
Haryngton, Sir John, 81, 172, 190, 203, 241.
Heath, John, 151, 155, 158.
Heath, Robert, 172, 242.
Heber, Reginald, 108.
Henley, John, 60.
Herrick, Robert, 98, 157, 178, 185, 188, 193, 209, 275.
Hervey, Lord, 131.
Heywood, John, 47, 157, 164, 172, 179, 190, 215, 241, 242.
Hicks, 223.
Hill, Aaron, 201, 234.
Hoadley, John, 186.
Hogarth, William, 136.
Holland, Lord, 71, 72, 192, 304.
Home, John, 12.
Hood, Thomas, 36, 37, 78, 79, 192, 221, 222, 250, 258, 259, 268, 269, 309.
Hook, Theodore Edward, 21, 71, 74, 150, 222, 254, 255.
Hopkins, John, 92.
Hugman, R., 217.

Jekyll, Joseph, 35, 127, 128, 235.
Jenner, Edward, 117.
Johnson, Samuel, 58.
Jonson, Ben, 48, 120, 159, 160, 164, 275.
Jordan, Thomas, 166.

Kendal, Richard, 293.

Lamb, Charles, 19, 22.

Index of Writers.

Landor, Walter Savage, 32, 220, 221.
Lansdowne, Lord, 253.
Lettsom, Dr., 117.
Locker, Frederick, 250.
Lover, Samuel, 225.
Luttrell, Henry, 27, 30, 43, 78, 262, 263, 306.

Mallet, David, 171, 196.
Mansel, Henry Longueville, 110, 111.
Marvel, Andrew, 2.
Mason, William, 66.
Mathews, Charles, 25.
Montagu, Lady Mary Wortley, 61.
Moore, Thomas 23, 29, 30, 51, 76, 84, 140, 141, 157, 208, 258, 304, 305.
More, Sir Thomas, 102.

Neaves, Lord, 150, 239, 250.
Nugent, Lord, 174.

O'Connell, Daniel, 140.
Oldys, William, 50.
Outram, George, 102.

Parnell, Thomas, 252.
Parrot, Henry, 98, 177, 191, 204, 238.
Pope, Alexander, 4, 5, 52, 53, 54, 57, 58, 59, 92, 132, 165, 187, 195, 213, 247, 278, 281, 282, 283, 284.
Porson, Richard, 13, 14, 107, 108, 240, 261.
Prior, Matthew, 51, 82, 90, 91, 115, 179, 186, 191, 211, 212, 217, 218, 239, 246.
Pyne, 82.

Ramsay, Allan, 43, 200, 284, 294.
Relph, Josiah, 122, 156, 181.
Rochester, Earl of, 2, 154, 184, 198.

Rogers, Samuel, 27, 262.
Rose, Sir George, 80, 127, 209.
Russell, T., 102.

Scott, Dr. Robert, 96.
Sedley, Sir Charles, 3.
Seward, Thomas, 47.
Shakespeare, William, 143.
Sheridan, Richard Brinsley, 20, 224.
Smith, James, 29, 37, 71, 101, 127, 152, 167, 222, 257, 263, 264, 265, 266, 306, 307.
Smith, Horace, 167.
Smith, Sydney, 76, 248, 309.
Sneyd, 75.
Somerville, William, 290.
Suckling, Sir John, 249.
Swift, Jonathan, 54, 55, 59, 93, 100, 135, 195, 218, 237, 279.

Taylor, John, 238.
Thompson, William, 289, 290.
Townsend, Rev. Henry, 77, 104.
Trapp, Dr. Joseph, 107.

Wadd, 122.
Waddington, Samuel, 103, 167.
Waller, Edmund, 276.
Walpole, Horace, 7, 94, 230, 299.
Walsh, William, 73.
Warburton, Egerton, 185.
Warton, Joseph, 285.
Warton, Thomas, 144, 285.
Webbe, Egerton, 84.
Welsted, Leonard, 152.
Wesley, Samuel, 5, 50.
West, Gilbert, 278.
Whately, Archbishop, 79.

Williams, Sir Charles Hanbury, 6, 135.
Wolcot, John, 123, 158, 303.
Wynter, Dr., 18, 119.

Yates, Edmund Hodgson, 244.
Young, Edward, 134.

INDEX OF SUBJECTS.

[The figures refer to the pages on which the epigrams will be found.]

Actor and Fishmonger, 266.
Actress, A Modern, 310.
Actress, An Inanimate, 313.
Adam and Eve, 345.
Adams, John, Carrier, 149.
Addington Cabinet, The, 19.
Advice, Good, 269.
Ægle, A certain, 344.
Æneas, Pius, 256.
Ailing and Ale-ing, 263.
Ainsworth, Harrison, 81.
Airey, Professor, and his Wife, 309.
Album, Written in an, 208.
Alchemists, 159.
Alderman, An, 153.
"Ἄλλος ἄλλο λέγει, 103.
All Saints', 244.
Alone and Weary, 229.
American Rivers, The, 265.
Ancients and Moderns, 56.

Andrews, Miles Peter, 66.
Anger, 323.
Anjou, Duke of, 343.
Anti-Corn Law Bill, The, 38.
April Fool, An, 168.
Arthur, A certain, 329.
Artist, An, 148.
Art-Unions, 250.
Atalanta, 197.
Athanasian Creed, The, 102.
Atheist, An, 322.
Athole Brose, 259.
Atkinson, Two Rogues called, 144.
Atlantic Cable, Laying of the, 40.
Atterbury, Bishop, 90, 91.
Attorney, A Foolish, 167.
Author, A Bad, 82.
Author-Critic, An, 33.
Author, To an, 322.

Bad Preacher who Wrote Well, A, 325.
Bad Writer who Composed the Epitaph of a Good Poet, 339.
Bald Man, A, 330.
Balguy, Dr., 285.
Balls and Operas, 273.
Bank-notes being made a Legal Tender, 17.
Bankrupt turned Preacher, 193.
Banks and Paper Credit of Scotland, 235.
Bard, An Anonymous, 150.
Barringtons, The Two, 94.
Barry and Garrick, 293.
Barton, Mrs., 297.
Bath Abbey Church, 259.
Beau, A Venerable, 171.
Beaufort, Duchess of, 287.
Beautiful and Virtuous Young Lady, 304.
Beautiful Lady with Loud Voice, 204.
Beauty, A Made-up, 211.
Beauty, A Mercenary, 314.
Beggar, A Lame, 261.
Benevolent Neutrality, 230.
Bentinck, Lord George, 35.
Bentley, Dr., 52.
Bentley, Jun., 138.
Bibulus, A certain, 172.
Blackmore, Sir Richard, 51.

Blue Stockings, 202.
Bobadil, One, 161.
Borrower, A, 175.
Bragged of Knowledge, One who, 158.
Breeches, A Want of, 257.
Bright, Mr. Jacob, 42.
Broadhurst the Poet, 55.
Broome, William, 60.
Brougham, Lord, 34.
Brougham, Russell, Althorp, and Grey, 33.
Brown, Lady, 299.
Buckingham Reform Bill, The, 35.
Bufo, A certain, 68.
Bull, John, 233.
Bully, A, 180.
Burke, Edmund, 16.
Burlington, Lord, 131.
Burnet, Bishop, 60, 89.
Burton, Dr., 116.
Bury, Lady Charlotte, 78, 79.
Butcher becoming a Leech, A, 330.
Butler, Samuel, 50.
Byron, Lord, 71.
Byron's Marriage, 224, 225.

Cambridge, University of, 107.
Campbell of Netherplace, Mr., 148.
Canning, George, 15.
Cappadocians, The, 316.

Index of Subjects. 385

Carlisle, Earl of, 70, 71.
Caroline, Queen, 26, 133.
Carthy, the Translator, 54, 55.
Case of Conscience, A, 182.
Castlereagh, Lord, 28, 29.
Cattle-Show, A, 269.
Celia, A certain, 213.
Censorious Person, A, 181.
Chapel, Missing, by a Student, 112.
Chapman's Homer, 276.
Charles II., 2.
Charlotte, Queen, 25.
Chartres, Francis, 329.
Chatelet, Madame du, 300.
Chatterton, Thomas, 66.
Chesterfield, Lord, 281.
Cheyne, Dr., 118.
Chloe, 208.
Chloe and her Picture, 210.
Chloris, 305.
Church converted into a Law School, 97.
Churchill, Lady Mary, 287.
Cibber, Colley, 58.
Clarinda, 253.
Clement's Inn, and Statue in, 129.
Clergy, The, 100.
Clincher, One Beau, 327.
Cloris and Fanny, 207.
Cobbett, William, 69.
Cobbler and the Curate, The, 98.

Cobham's Garden, Lord, 295.
Codrus, One, 219.
Cognac, 269.
"Cold," Latin for, 259.
Collar, Inscription for a, 195, 247.
Colman the Younger, 306.
Cologne and the Rhine, 240.
Combe, John, 143.
Common, Enclosing a, 190.
Conceited Person, A, 157.
Congress at Vienna, The, 24.
Conjuror, An Involuntary, 265.
Cook, A, 266.
Cooke, the Actor, 235.
Coquette, A, 341.
Coroner who Hanged Himself, 162.
Count, A certain, 262.
Court Audience, A, 87.
Courtier, A, 112.
Coward, A, 156, 158.
Cowley, Mrs. Hannah, 67.
Coxcomb, A Conceited, 158.
Coxcomb, A Noted, 177, 178.
Craven Street, Strand, 127.
Croker, J. W., 141.
Cross Woman, A, 218.
Croydon Belle, A, 300.
Cruel Fair One, A, 343.
Cumberland, Duke of, 141.
Cumming's Case, 255.
Curious Fellow, A, 318.

c c

Index of Subjects.

Dacier and his Wife, 341.
Daguerreotype, The, 309.
Damas, Madame de, 299.
Damis, A certain, 338.
Damon, A certain, 332.
Dancing, Bad, to Good Music, 155.
Deaf and Dumb, 347.
Dean, A, 92.
Death, One who Feared, 339.
Delacourt the Poet, 55.
Delia, A certain, 206.
Dent, Dr., 95.
Derby (Lord) and Mr. Disraeli, 42.
Devonshire, Duchess of, 296.
Devotee, An Ignorant, 159.
Dick, One Named, 167.
Didactics in Poetry, 85.
Diner-out, A, 323.
Dispraise, Of, 179.
Doctor, A, 336.
Doctor, A, become Captain, 320.
Doctor, A certain, 124.
Doctor, A Valiant, 124.
Doctor who Used his own Recipe, A, 120.
Doctors and Undertakers, 124, 318.
Doctors' Consultation, 121.
Doctor's Motto, A, 121.
Doletus, A certain, 328.
Doris, One, 317.

Dorset, Earl of, 301.
Dorset, The Duke of, 134.
Doubtful Sneeze, The, 268.
Dove, John, Innkeeper, 145.
Dramatist, A, 86.
Dress, 226.
Dress v. Dinner, 245.
Drinker, An Unfair, 172.
Drinking, Five Reasons for, 252.
Drunken Courage, 242.
Drunken Landlord, A, 173.
Drunken Smith, A, 172.
Dryden's Monument, 278.
Dryden's Wife, 216.
Dublin, Castle of, 252.
Duck, Stephen, 59.
Dudley, Lord, 27.
Duke, A certain, 159.
Dumb Bells, 202.
Dunce, A, 178.
Dutch, The, 239.
Duties on Claret, The, 12.

Eater, A Small, 203.
Edgeworth, Miss, 307.
Edinburgh, 236.
Eldon, Lord, 125, 126.
Ellenborough, Lord, 142.
Elphinston's Martial, 67.
Emily, One, 301.
Empiric, Doctor, 120.
Enemy, An, 174, 328.
English Travellers, 149.

Index of Subjects. 387

Epigram, One who would fain Write an, 85.
Epigrams, A Volume of, 347.
Epitaph, An, 207.
Epitaph, Substitute for an, 171.
Eton Boys, 254.
Etough, Rev. Henry, 94.
Europe, The Balance of, 4.
Evans, Dr., 106.
Evening Dress, 203.
Evil, The Least, 232.
Exchange of Hearts, 256.
Exchequer and its Custodians, 5.

Fan, A, 280.
Farren, William, 138.
Fashion and Night, 245.
Fat Man, A Very, 106.
Fell, Dr., 325.
Fellow of All Souls, A, 113.
Fellow of Trinity College, A, 108.
Fiddler, A Bad, 155.
Flatman, Thomas, 50.
Flatterer, A, 181.
Flattery, 241.
Flowers and Fruits, 255.
Floyd, Biddy, 279.
Folly, 342.
Fool, A Laughing, 169.
Foolish Person, A, 165, 166.
Fool or Knave, To, 164.
Foote, Samuel, 135.

Foote's Marriage, 220.
Fop, A, 178.
Fop, A certain, 321.
Foppington, Dr., on Tailors, 177.
Foreknowledge, 248.
Fortune, 317.
French and English, 238.
French and Swiss, 239.
French Army, The, 8.
French Speeches, 260.
French Taste, 237.
French Tragedy, A, 337.
Friend, A False, 183.
Friend, Dr., 57.
Friendship, 241.
Friend who recommended Ass's Milk, 123.
Froude (Mr.) and Canon Kingsley, 80.

Gabriel, One, 331.
Galla's Goodly Periwig, 318.
Galloway, the Earl of, 144, 145.
Gambler, A, 273.
Garrow, a Barrister, 127.
Gasmakers, The, 24.
Gay's Epitaph, 247.
Gentleman of Seventy Marrying a Lady of Sixteen, On a, 171.
George I., 5.
George IV., 21, 22, 30, 31.

Index of Subjects.

George IV.'s Physicians, 117.
Georges, The Four, 32.
German Drinking, 240.
Gerunds, The Latin, 261.
Gibbs, One, 84.
Giles, One, 261.
Gin Act, 6.
Girl, A Pretty, 270, 302.
Gladstone, Mr., 42.
Goldsmith, Oliver, 63, 64.
Government, Under, 232.
Graceless Peer, A, 182.
Graham of Morsknowe, William, 146.
Grapes and Gripes, 256.
Grieve, James, a Laird, 147.
Grudge, One, and his Money, 346.
Grumus, On one, 182.
Gully, the Prize-Fighter, M.P., 37.
Gun-makers, Two, 273.
Gunning, The Misses, 298.

Hair, One wearing False, 311.
Hairs and Years, 212.
Hale, Archdeacon, 97.
Half-Farthings, The, 259.
Hampden Case, The, 97.
Hans-sur-Lesse, The River, 272.
Happy Home, The Only, 232.
Harrow Boys, The, 254.
Harte, Bishop, 93.

Head and Purse Vacant, 166.
Head, Sir Francis, 39.
Hearne, the Antiquary, 278.
Helen's Eyebrows, 211.
Henpecked Squire, A, 220.
Hill, Sir John, 62, 63, 120.
Hobhouse, Lord Broughton, 25.
Hog, One named, 150.
Holland, Philemon, 48.
Homer's Birthplace, 47.
Honey's Marriage, A Miss, 222.
Hood, Souter, 147.
Horse-racer, A, 176.
Host, A Mean, 185.
Hostess, A Mean, 186.
Hough, Bishop, 281.
Houghton, Mrs., 279.
House of Commons, The, 1, 44.
Howard, Mrs., 283.
Human Face, A New Use for the, 314.
Husband's Marriage, A Mr., 231.
Hypocrite, A, 163.

Idealism, Idle, 167.
Idle Fellow, A Very, 154.
Ignorance, Blessed, 242.
Ill, Deliverance from, 215.
Ill-favoured Woman, An, 205.
Incapable Person, An, 316.

Index of Subjects. 389

Inclosures, 251.
Intemperate Husband, An, 173.
Inverary, Inn at, 253.
Ireland, William Henry, 66.
Irish Sense, 237.

Jack, A certain, 190.
Jack, A certain, 320.
Jack and his Wife, 228.
Jacobite Lady dressed with Orange Ribbons, 295.
James I., 131.
Jeffrey, Lord, 75, 76.
Jekyll and the Pig, 272.
Jenner, England's Ingratitude to, 118.
Jewellery and Gambling, 248.
Job, 340.
John and his Wife, 217.
Joke Verified, A, 258.
Jowett, Dr., of Cambridge, 137.
Julep, A Dr., 342.
Julia's Choice, 206.
Julius II., Pope, 327.
Justice, A Statue of, 335.

Kate and Bell, 320.
Kemble, Mrs., as Yarico, 303.
Kenmare, Lord, 140.
Kennet, Bishop, 89.
Kingsley, Charles, 80.
Kit-Cat Club, The, 53.
Knave, A, 146.

Kneller, Sir Godfrey, 114, 282, 283.
Knighted, A Trifling Fellow being, 181.

Labour, Division of, 103.
Ladies' Accomplishments, 286.
Ladies Drowned whilst Walking on Sea-shore, 297.
Ladies, The, 198.
Lady, A, 304, 305, 315, 319.
Lady Embroidering, A, 293.
Lady often Seen at Balls, A, 333.
Lady who Beat her Husband, 229.
Lady who Sent him a Compliment, 302.
Lady whose Playing lacked Expression, A, 155.
Lady who Writ in Praise of Myra, A, 276.
Lady wishing to Ascend in a Balloon, 285.
Lady with Grey Hairs, A, 310.
Lake Poets, The, 77.
Landlord, Miserly, 186.
Lauder, Macpherson, Chatterton, and Ireland, 66.
Laughed at his Own Jokes, One who, 156.
Laura, One, 310.
Law and Physic, 326.
Law, The, 129.

Index of Subjects.

Lawyer, A certain, 128, 129.
Lawyer and his Wife, A, 327.
Lawyers and Gibbets, 128.
Lawyers and their Clients, 130.
Lawyers generally, 133.
Leach, Sir John, 45.
Legion of Honour, The, 344.
Lent or Borrowed, 105.
Leo X., 331.
Lesbia, A certain, 281.
Letters, the Pursuit of, 268.
Lettsom, Dr., 117.
Liar, A, 174, 348.
Library, A Fine, 83.
Life, The End of, 229.
Light-Witted Person, A, 164.
Lilburn, John, 48.
Living, Presentation to a, 99.
Lord, A certain, 147.
Lord, A certain, 336.
Lord, A certain, delivering his Speeches from his Seat, 44.
Lord Mouse, 188.
Lord's Arguments, A certain, 45.
Lords, House of, 244.
Lord's Passion for a Singer, A, 196.
Looking-Glass and Women, 207.
Love, 249.
Love and Marriage, 226.
Love, An Old, 213.

Love, Metamorphosis of, 249.
Lover, A General, 324.
Loving Couple, A, 189.
Lubin and his Wife, 217.
Lucinda, One, 346.
Lucy, One, 292.
Lyttelton, Lord, 61.

Macadam, John Loudon, 29, 30.
Machinery, 258.
Mackintosh, Sir James, 19.
Macklin, Charles, 163.
Macpherson, James, 66.
Macready as Macbeth, Maclise's Picture of, 167.
Mad for his Mistress, On One who feared he should run, 164.
Magic Line, A, 187.
Magistrate, A certain, 192.
Making it up, 264.
Malvern Waters, The, 116.
Man and a Clock, A, 241.
Manchester, The Duchess of, 280.
Marcus, A Certain, 326.
Marlborough, The Duke of, 132, 133.
Marquee, Impromptu under a, 264.
Marriage and Heraldry, 221.
Marriage-making, 225.

Index of Subjects. 391

Marriage of a Very Thin Couple, 225.
Marriage of Job Wall and Mary Best, 223.
Marriage of Mr. Lot and Miss Salter, 223.
Marriage v. Hanging, 219.
Marriages in Heaven, 98.
Married for Money, On One who, 200.
Married Men, 226.
Marston, John, 48.
Mausoleum, One who Built a, 179.
Mead, Dr., 116, 313.
Medical Advice, 348.
Merry Thoughts, 250.
Metaphysician, A Very Thin, 162.
Millers, Two, Bone and Skin, 144.
Milton, 277.
Milton, a Livery-Stable Keeper, 150.
Milton's Wife, 215.
Ministers and Habeas Corpus Act, 16.
Ministry of 1707, The, 4.
Mirror, A, 251.
Misers, 176, 183, 184, 185, 312.
Miss-Representation, 202.
Mistress, To his, 275.
Money, 245.

Montagu, Lady Mary Wortley, 281.
Moore, Modest, 85.
Moore-Smythe, James, 53.
Moore, Thomas, 73, 74, 75.
Moore's Anacreon, 305.
M.P.'s Speeches, A certain, 45.
M.P. who Gained his Seat by Losing his Character, 46.

Napoleon I., 20, 22, 25.
Nash, Beau, 138, 139.
Nash, John, 139.
Naturalization Bill, The, 7.
Ned and his Wife, 228.
Nell, A certain, 211.
Nelson, Lord, 303.
Newgate Windows, 242.
Newly-made Baronet, A, 324.
New-made Honour, 319.
Newton, Sir Isaac, 284.
Nicholas, The Czar, 39.
Niger, One, 347.
Nile, Victory of the, 17.
Nonsense, A Thoroughfare for, 169.
Northern Lights, 235.
Nose, One with a Long, 311, 315.

Obligation, The, 319.
O'Connell, Daniel, 140.
O'Keefe, John, 65.

Orange from a Lady, On receiving an, 294.
Originality, 255.
Owed Money, One who, 345.
Oxford Fees for Degrees, 110, 111.
Oxford, University of, 107.

Paine, Thomas, 68, 69.
Painted, A Lady who, 209, 345.
Painting Herself, A Lady, 210.
Palmerston and Derby, Lords, 41.
Palmerston and Urquhart, 41.
Panes and Pains, 263.
Papal Claims, 326.
Parasite, A, 322.
Parasites, 191.
Parish Clerk, A, with a Bad Voice, 154.
Paris Loan on England, 18.
Parr, Dr. Samuel, 65.
Parson, A certain, 100, 105.
Parson and his Portmanteau, 104.
Parson Beans, 98.
Parsons versus Doctors, 103.
Patch, A Lady wearing a, 388.
Patrons' Promises, 192.
Paul, One, 322.
Payne, Lady, 306.
Pedant, A, 179.
Peel, Sir Robert, 37, 38.

Peers and the Ploughboy, The, 101.
Pembroke, The Countess of, 274.
Perceval, Hon. Mrs., 288.
Percival, Colonel, 140.
Peter and his Wife, 221.
Peter (another) and his Wife, 228.
Peter, One, 272.
Peter, Randolph, 143.
Pfeiffer, Ida, 142.
Phillips, Claudius, 292.
Phillis's Age, 212.
Philo, One, 82.
Phryne, A certain, 209.
Physician, A Petit-maître, 124.
Picking Pockets, 263.
Piron's Epitaph, 337.
Pitt and Fox, 14.
Pitt, Earl of Chatham, 9.
Pitt, William, 11, 12, 13, 14, 15.
Plagiarist, A, 86.
Poem, A Bad, 84.
Poet, A certain, 83.
Poet, An Impecunious, 86.
Poetess, A Squinting, 84.
Poets and Fools, 334.
Poland, Insurrection in, 40.
Pollio, A certain, 163.
Pope's Homer, 60, 277.
Potter, Archbishop, 191.
Poverty, 243.
Praise after Death, 330.

Index of Subjects. 393

Praise Premature, 335.
Preacher, A certain, 100.
Preacher, A Dull, 101.
Predestination, 152.
Prelate, A Proud, 336.
Pretender, The, 76.
Pride, 328.
Princesse Dress, The, 213.
Prior, Matthew, 60, 61.
Prior's Epitaph, 246.
Priscus, A certain, 192.
Prodigal, A, 177.
Professor of Greek, A, 112.
Professor with a Small Class, A, 317.
Prue, Miss, 343.
Public-house, 247.
Puffed up, One, 193.
Purse-proud Blockhead, A, 160.

Quack, A, 122.
Quacks, 117, 118, 122.
Quack turned Curate, A, 99.
Queen's Life, Attempts on the, 36.
Quick, John, 136.
Quin, James, 136, 137, 291.

Radcliffe, Dr., 114, 115.
Radical, A, 162.
Radical Reformer, A, 170.
Reader, An Ill, 318.
Ready Penny, The, 227.

Reflection, A, 268.
Repartee, A, 168.
Rev. Doctor's Eyes, A, 102.
Richardson's "Clarissa," 294.
Rich Lady, A, 271.
Rich Man's Heir, A, 152.
Rich, the Manager, 136.
Roads, Bad, 262.
Robbery, A, 160.
Rockingham, Marquis of, 10.
Rogers, Samuel, 77, 78, 304.
Rook, A certain, 193.
Royal Marriage Act, The, 10.
Rufus, One, 315.
Run Over by an Omnibus, On One, 262.

Sabbath-breaker, A, 155, 156.
Sacraments, The Seven, 339.
Sappho, One, 275.
Scandal, 243.
Scholar about to Marry, A, 220.
Scholar, A German, 313.
Scholar who Married unfortunately, A, 214.
Scire Tuum Nihil Est, 250.
Scotch and the Swiss, The, 332.
Scotch Frugality, 236.
Scotchmen and Good Works, 236.
Scotchmen and their Country, 234.

Index of Subjects.

Scotch Weather, 234.
Scott, Miss Jean, 303.
Scott, One Molly, 290.
Scott, Sir Walter, 72.
Scribbler, A certain, 169.
Scribbletonius, One, 83.
Secker, Archbishop, 94, 301.
Secretary of State, Waiting on a, 260.
Selinda, One, 289.
Serjeants-at-Law, 128.
Sermon, A Bad, 102.
Sermon, A Long, 104.
Sermons, Robbery of, 104.
Service, The Only, 335.
Seymour Places, 258.
Sheepshanks, A Mr., 109.
Shelford, an Examiner, 110.
Shelley, Percy Bysshe, 71.
Sheridan, Dr. Thomas, 135.
Sherlock, both Doctors, 88.
Sherlock, the Elder, 88.
Shrew, A Fair, 203.
Sibthorp, Colonel, 140.
Singer, A Bad, 154.
Sisters, Three Beautiful, 298.
Slave to his Physician, One who was, 191.
Sleigh, One Molly, 294.
Slow Mover and Swift Eater, A, 314.
Snipes, On receiving a Brace of, 271.

Snow Falling on a Lady's Breast, 296.
Sold her Bed, One who, 231.
Soldiers, 269, 270.
Sot, An Ignorant, 174.
Sots, A Club of, 172.
Southey, Robert, 72.
South-Sea Bubble, The, 5.
Soyer, the Cook, 141.
Spendthrift, A, 176.
Spenser, Edmund, 274.
Spintext, A certain, 332.
Spoke Little, One who, 178.
Sponge, A certain, 324, 344.
Squinted, A Lady who, 205.
Squinted, On one who, 162.
St. Albans, The Duchess of, 286.
Stamp Duty on Receipts, 20.
Statesmen, Modern, 44.
Stealing a Pound of Candles, On, 160.
Stella, One, 289.
Stingy Fellow, A, 188.
Stingy Fop, A, 189.
Stingy Lord, A, 187.
Stout Elderly Lady, A, 204.
St. Paul's Cathedral, 249.
Strahan, King's Printer, 307.
Stupid Family, A, 165.
Suffolk, Lady, 299.
Sunderland, Countess of, 286.
Surplice Question, The, 222.
Susan, A Lady, 321.

Index of Subjects. 395

Swift, Dean, 285.
Sycophant, A, 166.
Sylla, A certain, 153.
Sylvia, A certain, 205.

Tadlow, Dr., 105, 106.
Talkativeness, Feminine, 200.
Talkative Old Maid, A, 201.
Talker, A Feminine, 201.
Talker, A Great, 164.
Talking Husband and Wife, 215.
Tall Dull Man, A, 260.
Talleyrand, 345.
Tanner, A certain, 264.
Tax on Burials, The Proposed, 11.
Theobald, Lewis, 52.
Thersandes, 334.
Thief and his Friends, 190.
Thompson, Dr., 115.
Thraso, A certain, 173.
Thuscus, One, 82.
Tiraqueau, the Lawyer, 340.
Toe, Dr., 108, 109.
Tofts, Mrs., 195.
Tom and his Wife, 218.
Tom's Morals, 170.
Tongue, A Sharp, 215.
Tongue versus Wit, 164.
Translation, A Bad, 68.
Trapp's Virgil, 68.
Traveller and the Gorilla, The, 170.

Travellers' Invention, 251.
Treason, 241.
Tree, Miss, 306.
Trifles, Verses called, 86.
Truth, 246.
Turncoat, A, 161.
Twining, the Tea Merchant, 254.

Ugly Woman, An, 312.
Undertaker, An, 180.
Union between Great Britain and Ireland, The, 18.
Unionists, 194.
Universities, The, 113.
Unkind Maid, An, 272.
Useless Man, A, 153.

Vain Man, A, 157.
Vanbrugh, Sir John, 133.
Vane's Speeches, 45.
Vassal, Miss, 308.
Verner, Colonel, 140.
Vernon, Admiral, 7.
Verulam (Lord) Knocking Down the Countess of Salisbury, 35.
Vicious Person, A, 321.
Vinegar Merchant, A, 161.
Virtue, 242.
Volatio, One, 194.
Voltaire, 134, 338.

Walcheren Expedition, The Leaders in the, 21.

Index of Subjects.

Walking-Stick, With a Present of a, 308.
Warren, Samuel, 80.
Watch Lost in a Tavern, 248.
Watson, Bishop, 95.
Wavering Man, A, 331.
Wellington, The Duke of, 23.
Welsh Poverty, 238.
Welsh Rabbit, 238.
Westminster Bridge, 266.
Wetherell, Sir Charles, 126.
Whigs and the Queen, The, 36.
Whigs and Tories, 43.
Whigs' Tenantry in Office, 44.
Widow, A Gay, 199.
Wife Deceased, A, 227.
Wife's Picture, His, 230.
Wilberforce, Bishop, 40.
William III., 2, 3.
William IV., 33.
Will of his Own, No, 230.
Wiseman, Cardinal, 96.
Wine in Season, 267.
Wine Merchant, A, 325.
Wives and their Wills, 217.
Wives in general, 224, 312.
Wolfe, General, 8.
Woman (Old) Marrying a Young Lad, 231.
Woman's Mind, A, 197.

Woman's Right, A, 227.
Women and Hymen, 199.
Women and "Intelligence," 200.
Women and their Whims, 197.
Women as Unionists, 177.
Women's Conquests, 199.
Women's Coquetry, 198.
Women's Faults, 136.
Women's Will, 204.
Wonder, A, 226.
Wood, Thomas, of Chiswick, 92.
Wordsworth, Dr. Christopher, 79.
World, The, 233.
Worm Doctor, A, 122.
Writer, A Bad, 152.
Writer, A Good, 151.
Writers who Carp at other Men's Books, 81.
Writing Master, A Left-handed, 151.
Wynter, Dr., 119.

Yorkist Prince to a Lancastrian Lady, 290.
Youth not allowed to Marry, 348.
Youth struck by Lightning, 291.

INDEX OF FIRST LINES.

	PAGE
A bishop, by his neighbours hated	281
A cobbler and a curate once disputed	98
A compliment upon a crutch	308
A doctor lately was a captain made	320
A doctor who, for want of skill	121
A duke once declared, and most solemnly too	86
A fellow that's single, a fine fellow's he	226
A fool and knave, with different views	206
A friend I met, some half-hour since	319
A haughty courtier, meeting in the streets	112
A lass, whose name was Mary Ware	270
A little garden little Jowett made	107
A long way off Lucinda strikes the men	346
A lord of senatorial fame	336
A lord that purposed for his more avail	190
A lovely young lady I mourn in my rhymes	207
A mechanic his labour will often discard	258
A minister's answer is always so kind!	192
A mirror has been well defined	251
A miser in his chamber saw a mouse	312
A parson of too free a life	103
A place under Government	232
A prelate, in whose motley-colour'd mind	336
A scholar was about to marry	220
A student, at his book so plast	214
A very pretty public stir	222
A viper bit a Cappadocian's hide	316

Index of First Lines.

	PAGE
A watch lost in a tavern! that's a crime	248
A Welshman and an Englishman disputed	238
A woman lately fiercely did assail	227
A year ago, you swore, fond she!	224
Accept a miracle instead of wit	281
Ægle, beauty and poet, has two little crimes	344
After such years of dissension and strife	221
Airey alone has gained that double prize	309
Alack, and well-a-day!	91
All-conquering, cruel Death, more hard than rocks	8
All men must be blind and deaf, ere thou praise win	179
All Nature's charms in Sunderland appear	286
All Newgate windows bay windows they be	242
All things you know: what all? If it be so	158
All wives are bad, yet to blest hours they give	312
Among the men, what dire divisions rise	199
An actor one day, at a fishmonger's shop	266
An arch wag has declar'd, that he truly can say	21
An original something, dear maid, you would win me	255
And, Doctor, do you really think	123
And thou extruded! Sadder this, and sadder!	42
And which is right? who knows? Do you?	103
And will Volatio quit this world so soon?	194
Andrews, 't is said, a comedy has writ	66
Anger's a kind of gain that rich men know	323
Angling for dinner, Charles, at every line	323
Arachne once, as poets tell	293
Are these the choice dishes the Doctor has sent us?	64
Array'd in matchless beauty, Devon's Fair	296
Arthur, they say, has wit; for what?	329
As both physic and verse to Phœbus belong	116
As Cyril and Nathan were walking by Queen's	95
As Father Adam first was fool'd	220
As Jekyll walk'd out in his gown and his wig	272
As late the Trades' Unions, by way of a show	266
As once the Pope with fury full	97
As Sherlock the elder with his jure divine	88

Index of First Lines.

	PAGE
As Spintext one day in the mansion of prayer	332
As strong in the fist as a ditcher or hedger	265
As Thomas was cudgell'd one day by his wife	218
As Tom was one day in deep chat with his friend	170
Ask not why Laura should persist	199
At Barton's feet the God of Love	297
At Brompton I, when winter reigns	267
At Christ Church " Marriage," play'd before the King	131
At Highgate, by salubrious air	123
Augustus at Rome was for building renown'd	139
Augustus still survives in Maro's strain	58
Be plain in dress, and sober in your diet	61
Because I'm silent, for a fool	327
Because on her way she chose to halt	223
Behold! a proof of Irish sense	237
Behold, ambitious of the British bays	59
Beneath the Piazza two wags chanced to pass	263
Beneath this marble stone there lies	135
Beneath this silent stone is laid	201
" Better to roam the fields for health unbought	348
Between Adam and me the great difference is	257
Beware, my friend! of crystal brook	311
Black locks hath Gabriel, beard that's white	331
Blogg rails against high birth. Yes, Blogg—you see	162
Bold and erect the Caledonian stood	12
Bright ran thy lines, O Galloway	145
Brougham writes his epitaph—to wit	34
Browne says that Pitt, so wise and good	12
Brutus unmoved heard how his Portia fell	228
By dealing hateful to an honest man	315
By fav'ring wit Mæcenas purchas'd fame	301
By one decisive argument	261
" By proxy I pray, and by proxy I vote "	182
By purchase a man's property is known	100
Cade, who had slain ten thousand men	120

Index of First Lines.

	PAGE
Carlisle subscribes a thousand pounds	70
Carthy, you say, writes well—his genius true	55
Cease, ye Etonians! and no more	254
Cease your humming	255
Celia, we know, is sixty-five	213
Charm'd with a drink which Highlanders compose	259
Charles keeps a secret well, or I'm deceived	174
Chloris, I swear, by all I ever swore	305
Cloris! if I were Persia's king	207
Come, come, for trifles never stick	263
"Come, come," said Tom's father, "at your time of life	258
Come, fill the South-Sea goblet full	5
Come hither, Sir John, my picture is here	229
Come, let us rejoice, merry hearts, at his fall	105
Condemn not in such haste	237
Conservatives of Hatfield House	35
Creed of St. Athanasius? No, indeed	102
Cries Ned to his neighbours, as onwards they prest	228
Cries she to Will, 'midst matrimonial strife	232
Cries Sylvia to a reverend Dean	98
Curio's rich sideboard seldom sees the light	189
Czar Nicholas cried, as he look'd in the glass	39
Czar Nicholas is so devout, they say	39
Dacus doth daily to his doctor go	191
Damis, an author cold and weak	333
Damis says, modestly, he must forego	338
Damon, who plied the undertaker's trade	316
"Dear Bell, to gain money, sure, silence is best	202
Dear ———, I'll gie ye some advice	148
Dear lady, think it no reproach	109
Deep, deep in Sandys' blundering head	6
Dick cannot blow his nose whene'er he pleases	315
Did he, who thus inscrib'd the wall	244
Did Milton's prose, O Charles, thy death defend?	52
Die when you will, you need not wear	304
Died from fatigue, three laundresses together all	126

Index of First Lines.

	PAGE
Died, Sir Charles Wetherell's laundress, honest Sue	126
"Do this," cries one side of St. Stephen's great hall	43
Doletus writes verses, and wonders—ahem!	328
Dunces, rejoice; forgive all censures past	115
Eldon was ask'd by one of note	125
England's ingratitude still blots	118
Entomb'd within this vault a lawyer lies	129
Fair Albion, smiling, sees her son depart	149
Fair, rich, and young? how rare is her perfection	203
Fairest and latest of the beauteous race	287
Famed for contemptuous breach of sacred ties	31
Fired with the thirst of Fame, thus honest Sam	85
Five letters his life and his death will express	174
Flavia the least and slightest toy	280
Folly and sense, in Dorset's race	134
Fool, to put up four crosses at your door	218
Foote, from his earthly stage, alas! is hurl'd	135
For Buckingham to hope to pit	35
For excuses, Anacreon old custom may thank	74
For physic and farces his equal there scarce is	62
For this her snuff-box to resign!	71
Forbear, sweet girl, your scheme forego	285
Fortune advanced thee that all might aver	316
Fortune, men say, doth give too much to many	317
Found dead, a rat—no case could sure be harder	126
Four forgers, born in one prolific age	66
Frank carves very ill, yet will palm all the meats	191
Frenchmen, no more with Britons vie	17
Friend! for your epitaphs I'm griev'd	57
Friend Hogg once promised me a pair of breeches	150
From ancient custom 't is (they say)	92
From no man yet you've run away!	124
From sunset to daybreak, when folks are asleep	5
"From wood to marble," Hawkins cried	12
Froude informs the Scottish youth	80

D D

Index of First Lines.

	PAGE
Full oft doth Mat with Topaz dine	51
Garrow, forbear! That tough old jade	127
Gellia, your mirror's false; you could not bear	312
George the First was always reckon'd	32
God bless the King—I mean the Faith's Defender	6
God has to me sufficiently been kind	227
God works a wonder now and then	129
Gold in Gripe's pocket is, and on Strut's coat	176
Gold is so ductile, learned chemists say	245
Golden the hive, and yet 't is true	314
"Good morning, dear Major," quoth Lieutenant B——	232
Good plays are scarce	74
Grudge leaves the poor his whole possessions nearly	346
Grumus ne'er saw, he says, a bearded ass	182
Had Cowley ne'er spoke, Killigrew ne'er writ	49
Hail, Aristides, Rhetoric's great professor!	317
Half your book is to an Index grown	82
"Hang it," quoth Hearne, in furious fret	278
Hard is the fate of every childless wife	231
Having finished his "Iliad"	42
He boasts about the truth, I've heard	175
He called thee vicious, did he? Lying elf!	321
He cannot be complete in aught	250
"He flatter'd in youth, he lampoon'd in his prime"	71
He has quitted the Countess—what can she wish more?	262
He is most happy sure that knoweth nought	242
He lived and died	162
He standeth well in his own conceit, each man tells	157
He thinks it might advance the nation's trade	177
He who a gold-finch strives to make his wife	226
He who in his pocket has no money	243
Her eyebrow box one morning lost	211
Her wit and beauty for a court were made	299
Here crumbling lies, beneath this mould	183
Here Francis Chartres lies. Be civil	329

Index of First Lines.

	PAGE
Here lies a Doctor of Divinity	108
Here lies a man who unto highest station . . .	335
Here lies Boghead among the dead	147
Here lies Johnnie Pigeon	145
Here lies my wife ! here let her lie !	216
Here lies Nolly Goldsmith, for shortness called Noll	63
Here lies one who was born and cried . . .	153
Here lies our sovereign lord the King . . .	2
Here lies Piron—a man of no position . . .	337
Here lies what had nor birth, nor shape, nor fame .	53
Here lieth one that was born once and cried . .	154
Here lives a man who, by relation	152
Here lyeth Robin Masters. Faith, 'twas hard .	180
Here mourning is all make-believe	199
Here plac'd near Chaucer, Spenser claims a room .	274
Here, reader, turn your weeping eyes . . .	34
Here Rogers sat, and here forever dwell . . .	304
Here Souter Hood in death does sleep . . .	147
Here, stopt by hasty death, Alexis lies . . .	281
Here, who but once in's life did thirst, doth lie .	172
Here's a happy new year ! but with reason . .	224
"He's gone at last—old Niger's dead !" . . .	347
His chimney smokes—it is some omen dire . .	184
His degradation is complete	46
His last great debt is paid. Poor Tom's no more .	176
His long speeches, his writings, in prose and in rhyme	342
His lordship bought his last gay birthday dress .	321
His son he cheats ; he leaves his bail i' th' lurch .	163
His work now done, he'll publish it, no doubt . .	68
How apt are men to lie ! how dare they say . .	201
"How blest, my dear brother," said Sylvia one day .	341
How capricious were Nature and Art to poor Nell !.	211
How comes it that Quibus should pass for a wit ? .	128
How D.D. swaggers—M.B. rolls !	103
How fitly join'd the lawyer and his wife ! . . .	327
How ill the motion to the music suits ! . . .	155
How kind has Nature unto Bluster been . . .	180

D D 2

	PAGE
How Liberty! girl, can it be by thee nam'd?	302
How like is this picture, you 'd think that it breathes	230
How monarchs die is easily explain'd	31
How old may Phillis be, you ask	212
"How strange, a deaf wife to prefer!"	347
How wisely Nature, ordering all below	200
Howell and James, in taste correct	264
I am his Highness' dog at Kew	247
"I am unable," yonder beggar cries	261
"I cannot comprehend," says Dick	167
I cannot praise the Doctor's eyes	102
I change, and so do women too	207
I could resign that eye of blue	208
I do not love thee, Doctor Fell	325
"I drink to thee, Tom." "Nay, thou drinkest *from* me, John	172
"I hardly ever ope my lips," one cries	178
I have kept your "Intelligence," madam, so long	200
"I have no hope," the Duke he says, and dies	90
I heard that Smug the smith, for ale and spice	172
I know a thing that 's most uncommon	282
"I laugh," a would-be sapient cried	169
I must confess that I was somewhat warm	54
"I never give a kiss," says Prue	343
"I owe," says Metius, "much to Colon's care	152
I send thee myrrh, not that thou mayest be	315
I sent for Radcliffe: was so ill	115
"I want the *Court Guide*," said my Lady, "to look	258
I was destroy'd by Wellington and Grey	15
I went to Frankfort and got drunk	240
I will not ask if thou canst touch	271
"I wish thou hadst a little narrow mouth, wife	215
I wonder'd not when I was told	234
"I wonder if Brougham thinks as much as he talks?"	34
"I would," says Fox, "a tax devise	20
If a man might know	248

Index of First Lines.

	PAGE
If all be true that I do think	252
If all you boast of your great heart be true . . .	159
If ancient poets Argus prize	205
If blocks can from danger deliver	19
If by their names we things should call	273
If by your hairs your virtues numbered be . . .	330
If Farren, cleverest of men	138
If heaven is pleased when sinners cease to sin . .	89
If it be true, on Watts's plan	168
If Kelly finds fault with the shape of your nose . .	63
If on penitence bent, you want to keep Lent . . .	96
If only when they're dead, you poets praise . . .	330
If this pale rose offend your sight	290
If thou wilt needs be proud, mark this, friend mine . .	328
If 't is true, as you say, that I've injur'd a letter . .	63
If what you advance, my dear Doctor, be true . .	285
If women reflected, oh scribbler, declare	207
" I'm glad to see you well."—" O faithless breath ! . .	99
I'm now arriv'd—thanks to the Gods !	262
I'm told, dear Moore, your lays are sung	78
" I'm very glad," to Ellenborough said	142
" I'm very much surpris'd," quoth Harry	273
Imperial nymph ! ill suited is thy name	308
In a church which is furnish'd with mullion and gable .	244
In all things that round him move	167
In all thy humour, whether grave or mellow . . .	318
In ancient times—'t was no great loss	344
In asserting that Z. is with villany ripe	44
In Craven Street, Strand, ten attorneys find place . .	127
In cutting, and dealing, and playing their cards . .	24
In digging up your bones, Tom Paine	69
In England rivers all are males	265
In Köln, a town of monks and bones	240
In merry old England it once was the rule . . .	58
In sore afflictions sent by God's commands . . .	260
In Spain, that land of monks and apes	256
In spite of hints, in spite of looks	322

Index of First Lines.

	PAGE
In systems as much out of sense as of season	68
In vain Clarinda night and day	253
In vain my affections the ladies are seeking	27
In vain, poor sable son of woe	129
In vino veritas, they say	13
Indians assert that wheresoe'er they roam	234
Indulgent Nature on each kind bestows	106
Is John departed, and is Lilburn gone?	48
It puzzles much the sage's brains	295
It seems as if Nature had curiously plann'd	254
It seems that the Scots	239
It sounds like paradox—and yet 't is true	209
I've dispatch'd, my dear madam, this scrap of a letter	117
"I've lost my portmanteau"	104
I've seen a man pluck geese on Shelford fen	110
Jack boasts he never dines at home	323
Jack, eating rotten cheese, did say	165
Jack his own merit sees: this gives him pride	157
Jack writes severe lampoons on me, 't is said	320
Jerry dying intestate, his relatives claim'd	230
Job, wanting a partner, thought he'd be blest	223
Joe hates a hypocrite: which shows	163
John Adams lies here, of the parish of Southwell	149
John Bull and Brother Jonathan	40
John ran so long, and ran so fast	176
John Scott was desired by two witty peers	101
Kate's teeth are black, while lately Bell's are grown	320
Kemble, thou cur'st my unbelief	303
Killed by an omnibus!—why not?	262
Kind Katherine to her husband kiss'd these words	204
Kind reader! take your choice to cry or laugh	171
Kneller, by Heaven, and not a master taught	283
Know we not all, the Scripture saith	228

Index of First Lines. 407

	PAGE
Lady, accept the gift a hero wore	70
Lalla Rookh	75
Landlord, with thee now even is the wine.	173
Last night thou didst invite me home to eat	185
Lend Sponge a guinea! Ned, you 'd best refuse	324
Leo lack'd the last sacrament. "Why," need we tell?	331
Let Hannibal boast of his conquering sway	161
Let Lyndhurst stride till hoarse and tired	35
Let none, because of its abundant locks	142
Lewis the living genius fed	133
Lie on! while my revenge shall be	174
Life is a jest, and all things show it	247
Light-finger'd Catch, to keep his hands in use	160
Light lay the earth on Billy's breast	177
Lo! here's the bride, and there's the tree	219
Lollius, with head bent back and close shut eyes	156
Long in the Senate had brave Vernon rail'd	7
Lord Erskine, at women presuming to rail	224
Lord Pam in the church (could you think it?) kneeled down	93
Love levels all—it elevates the clown	249
Lucetta's charms our hearts surprise	204
Lucia thinks happiness consists in state	200
Lysander talks extremely well	179
Maclise's Macready's Macbeth	267
Mark how the beaux, in fond amaze	212
Mark'd by extremes, Susannah's beauty bears	310
Mead's not dead, then, you say; only sleeping a little	116
Meek Francis lies here, friend: without stop or stay	91
Men dying make their wills, why cannot wives?	217
Men say you 're fair; and fair ye are, 't is true	209
Men take man of earthly things most excellent	241
Merit they hate, and wit they slight	4
Midas, they say, possess'd the art, of old	44
Mind but thy preaching, Trapp; translate no further	68
Minerva last week (pray let nobody doubt it)	290

	PAGE
Minerva, wand'ring in a myrtle grove	294
"Miss Neilson's 'benefit,'" one says	310
Money thou ow'st me : prithee fix a day	175
Moore always smiles whenever he recites	85
" My children ! to cope with the world and its tricks "	165
" My dear, what makes you always yawn ? "	229
My debtor Paul looks pale and harass'd	345
My dog, who picks up everything one teaches	42
" My dress, you 'll aver, is Economy's own	213
" My essay on Roads," quoth Macadam, "lies here	29
My friend and I did faithfully agree	182
My head and my purse had a quarrel of late	166
" My head, Tom's, confused with your nonsense and bother	169
My heart still hovering round about you	226
My Lord, an objection I've plumped on	266
My Lord complains that Pope, stark mad with gardens	187
My Lord feeds Gnatho ; he extols my Lord	191
My system, Doctor, is my own	119
" My wife's so very bad," cried Will	231
Nature and Nature's laws lay hid in night	284
Nay, marvel not, ye Flemings brave	343
Nay, surely John's the happiest of the twain	346
Neddy laugh'd loud at every word he spoke	156
Ned will not keep the Jewish Sabbath, he	155
Nerina's angel-voice delights	196
New friends are no friends ; how can that be true?	241
Nobles and Heralds, by your leave	246
No doubt of it : if Adam, our first father	338
No letter more full or expressive can be	9
No more by creditors perplext	193
No one longs half so much as a Scot or a Swiss	332
No Stewart art thou, Galloway	145
No : Varus hates a thing that's base	181
No wonder he is vain of coat or ring	178
No wonder that Oxford and Cambridge profound	113

Index of First Lines.

	PAGE
No wonder Tory landlords flout.	38
"Nothing is lighter than a feather, Kit"	164
Now Europe's balanc'd, neither side prevails	4
Now, Priam's son, thou may'st be mute	294
O had each Scot of ancient times	303
O thou whom Poetry abhors	67
O thou who read'st what's written here	208
O'er Nature's laws God cast the veil of night	284
Of all connections with great men	166
Of all hard-named gen'rals that caused much distraction	22
Of all speculations the market holds forth	157
Of a tall stature, and a sable hue	2
Of Augustus and Rome the poets still warble	11
Of Graces four, of Muses ten	317
Of miracles this is sans doute the most rare	178
Of rank, descent, and title proud	321
Of Rogers's "Italy," Luttrell relates	77
Offspring of a tuneful sire	287
Oft have we wondered that on Irish ground	16
Oh, Castlereagh! thou art a patriot now	28
Oh! mourn not for Anacreon dead	305
Oh! surely this horse had more wit than his master	243
Old Euclid may go to the wall	272
Old Farmer Bull is taken sick	269
Old Jacob, in his wondrous mood	3
Old Orpheus play'd so well, he mov'd old Nick	155
Old Parson Beans hunts six days of the week	98
Old South a witty Churchman, reckon'd	87
O'Leary was as poor as Job	189
On folly every fool his talent tries	14
On his death-bed poor Lubin lies	217
On Reason, Faith, and mystery high	138
On Stephen's tomb thou writ'st the mournful line	339
On this establishment how can we speak?	247
On this Tree when a nightingale settles and sings	306
On Waterloo's ensanguined plain	72

Index of First Lines.

	PAGE
" One Prior," and is this, this all the fame?	60
One Queen Artemisa, as old stories tell	148
One single truth, before he died	348
Only mark how grim Codrus's visage extends	219
Our Laureate Bob defrauds the King	72
Our morals as well as appearance must show	24
Our ships at the Nile have created such terror	17
Outrageous hourly with his wife is Peter	221
Oxford, beware of over-cheap degrees	110
" Oxford, no doubt you wish me well	111
Pamphlet, last week, in his fantastic fits	169
Parnassus' peaks still catch the sun	85
Paul, I have read your book, and, though you write ill	86
Paul so fond of the name of a poet is grown	322
Paulus, the famous quack, renowned afar	99
Perrault, the Frenchman, needs must prove	56
Philemon with translations so doth fill us	48
Phillips, whose touch harmonious could remove	292
Physic brings health, and Law promotion	326
Pius with Wiseman tries	96
Playwright, convict of public wrongs to men	48
Point in his foremost epigram is found	347
Pollio, who values nothing that's within	163
Pompous the boast, and yet a truth it speaks	236
Poor Peter was in ocean drown'd	272
Poor Stephen is young, and lacks wisdom, 't is said	348
Pope came off clean with Homer; but, they say	60
Pope Quin, who damns all churches but his own	137
Possessed of one great hall for state	131
" Pox on 't," says Time to Thomas Hearne	278
" Praise premature is idle breath	335
" Pray steal me not : I 'm Mrs. Dingley's	195
Quoth Dick to Tom, " This Act appears	10
Quoth Doctor Squill of Ponder's End	124

Index of First Lines. 411

	PAGE
Ralph is love-sick, and thinks he shall run mad	164
Rant is, they say, indicted for a wit	166
Reader, beware immoderate love of pelf	183
Ridway robb'd Duncote of three hundred pound	160
Rook, he sells feathers, yet he still doth cry	193
Roses at first were white	275
Said a thief to a wit, "There's no knowing one's friends	190
Said His Highness to Ned, with that grim face of his	141
Said vain Andrew Scalp, "My initials, I guess	157
Samuel Warren, though able, yet vainest of men	80
Say, lovely traitor, where's the jest	295
Say which enjoys the greatest blisses	345
Says Ainsworth to Colburn	81
Says Boney to Johnny, "I'm coming to Dover"	20
Says epicure Quin—"Should the devil in hell	137
Says great William Pitt, with his usual emotion	9
Scarce from Privation's dreary lap	162
Scotland! thy weather's like a modish wife	234
Scribbletonius, thy volumes, whene'er we peruse	83
See Clodio, happy in his own dear sense	158
"See," cry our ministerial blocks	16
"See, sir, here's the grand approach	132
See! yonder goes old Mendax, telling lies	174
Selinda ne'er appears till night	289
Seven cities boasted Homer's birth, 't is true	345
Seven cities warr'd for Homer, being dead	47
Seven wealthy towns contend for Homer dead	47
Shall I tell you how the rose at first grew red	275
Shelley styles his new poem "Prometheus Unbound"	71
Should Flatman for his client strain the laws	50
Should women sit in Parliament	202
"Silvia makes sad complaints; she's lost her lover"	205
Silvio, so strangely love his mind controls	113
Simplicity is best, 't is true	203
Sir, can you tell where young Pandorus lives	177

Index of First Lines.

	PAGE
Sir Godfrey and Radcliffe had one common way	114
Sir, I admit your general rule	334
Sir, the lady must smile, and your menace deride	300
Sleep soft in dust, wait the Almighty's will	304
Sly Beelzebub took all occasions	340
Sly Cupid perceiving our modern beaux's hearts	298
Smart soldiers like to be well tightened in	269
So bright is thy beauty, so charming thy song	195
So Castlereagh has cut his throat!—the worst	28
So gently in peace Alcibiades smil'd	23
So *He* has cut his throat at last!—He! who?	28
So ill you preach, a Bishop you might be	325
So many thousands for a house	188
So much, dear Pope, thy English Iliad charms	277
Sosil, the butcher, has become a leech. 'T is nothing new	330
So well deserv'd is Rogers' fame	77
Some envious Scot, you say, the apple threw	235
Some for the Ancients zealously declare	56
Soyer is gone! Then be it said	141
Spare me thy vengeance, Galloway	145
Sternhold and Hopkins had great qualms	154
Still hovering round the fair at sixty-four	171
"Stop thief," Dame Nature cried to Death	146
St. Paul has declar'd that when persons, tho' twain	225
Strange that the Duke, whose life was charm'd	23
Sturdy Tom Paine, biographers relate	69
Subdued by Death, here Death's great herald lies	180
Sure 't was by Providence designed	291
Swans sing before they die: 't were no bad thing	154
Swift for the Ancients has argued so well	285
Sylla declares the world shall know	153
Take your night-cap again, my good lord, I desire	303
Talk no more of the lucky escape of the head	33
Tax'd to the bone, thy loving subjects see	11
Tell, if you can, which did the worse	58

Index of First Lines. 413

	PAGE
Tell me from whom, fat-headed Scot	118
"Tell me," said Laura, "what may be	310
"Tell me why Justice meets our eye	335
Ten guineas Tom would borrow : I give five	175
Ten in the hundred the devil allows	143
Ten thousand tailors, with their length of line	105
Thanks for this miracle ! it is no less	184
That flesh is grass is now as clear as day	78
That he's ne'er known to change his mind	159
That he was born it cannot be denied	153
That ignorance makes devout, if right the notion	159
That little patch upon your face	288
That Picture-Raffles will conduce to nourish	250
That plants feel attachments grave Darwin believ'd	255
That there is falsehood in his looks	146
That there's no God, John gravely swears	322
That throat so vex'd by cackle and by cup	75
That tongue which set the table in a roar	291
That you cannot get rid of Thersandes, you say	334
The author, sure, must take great pains	2
The bench hath oft 'posed us, and set us a-scoffing	94
The braziers, it seems, are preparing to pass	26
The Chancellor, so says Lord Coke	125
The charity of Close-fist, give to fame	184
The church and clergy here, no doubt	100
The city feast inverted here we find	11
The death of the Queen has caused great perturbation	25
The Doubtful Sneeze ! a failure quite	268
The Earl of Chatham, with his sword drawn	21
The French enjoy freedom, they say	260
The French excel us very much in millinery	238
The French have taste in all they do	237
The Germans for learning enjoy great repute	268
The Germans in Greek	313
The gift by Nature boon supplied	170
The great debt of Nature he paid, as all must	136
The house a lawyer once enjoy'd	130

Index of First Lines.

	PAGE
The initials of Brougham, Russell, Althorp, and Grey	33
The intramural churchyard's reeking pale	97
The jolly members of a toping club	172
The King employ'd three doctors daily	117
The King, observing, with judicious eyes	107
The King of Great Britain was reckon'd before	5
The King to Oxford sent a troop of horse	107
The Latin word for "cold," one ask'd his friend	259
The Law and the Gospels you always have by you	181
The law decides questions of *Meum* and *Tuum*	129
The lawyers may revere that tree	128
The Leach you've just bought should first have been tried	45
The least drop in the world I do not mind	269
The line of Vere, so long renown'd in arms	286
The little boy, to show his might and pow'r	249
The lofty arch his high ambition shows	133
The modest bard, like many a bard unknown	150
The newspapers lately have taught us to know	202
The Paris cits, a patriotic band	18
The Parliament Grant to MacAdam, we find	30
The paviours bless his steps where'er they come	106
The preacher Maurus cries, "All evil is vain"	100
The Premier in, the Premier out	41
The privilege hard money to demand	17
The poor dear dead have been laid out in vain	79
The Pope claims back to Apostolic sources	326
"The Queen's with us," the Whigs insulting say	36
The readers and the hearers like my books	81
The reason why Dr. Dash squints, I suppose	162
The Regent, sir, is taken ill	30
The same allegiance to two kings he pays	88
The satyrs of old were satyrs of note	109
The Serjeants are a grateful race	128
The thresher Duck could o'er the queen prevail	59
The toast of each Briton in war's dread alarms	8
The Tories vow the Whigs are black as night	38
The town has found out different ways	293

Index of First Lines. 415

	PAGE
The truth to declare, if one may without shocking 'em	10
The turning of coats so common has grown	15
The verses, Sextus, thou dost read, are mine	318
The vilest of compounds while Balderdash vends	325
The way to make a Welshman thirst for bliss	238
The Whigs resemble nails. How so, my master?	44
The wish should be in form revers'd	62
The world is a bundle of hay	233
The world is like a rink, you know	233
The world of fools has such a store	342
Their care and pains the fair ones do bestow	198
There's none were fitter than thou to endite	151
There's this to say about the Scotch	236
There was a little Bart.	39
"These beer-shops," quoth Barnabas, speaking in alt	263
These heroes of Erin, abhorrent of slaughter	140
These Napoleon left behind	25
These walls, so full of monument and bust	259
They came and stole my garments	104
They came from the lakes, an appropriate quarter	77
They say his wit's refined. This is explain'd	141
They say, O'Keefe	65
They say that thou dost tinge (O monstrous lie!)	311
Th' internal senses painted here we see	288
This case is the strangest we've known in our life	231
This day, of all our days, has done	225
This house and inhabitants both well agree	252
This house is formed with art, and wrought with pains	179
This I may boast, which few e'er could	54
This is God's house; but 't is to be deplor'd	249
This pair in matrimony	222
This picture, placed these busts between	139
This quack to Charon would his penny pay	122
This Sheffield rais'd. The sacred dust below	278
This work is Nature's; every tittle in 't	294
Tho' George, with respect to the wrong and the right	161
Thomas is sure a most courageous man	156

Index of First Lines.

	PAGE
Those envious flakes came down in haste	296
"Those Evening Bells—those Evening Bells"	37
Those waters, so famed by the great Dr. Wall	116
Thou essence of dock, and valerian, and sage	62
Thou ghost of Homer, 't were no fault to call	276
Thou great descendant of the critic line	112
Thou hast a score of parts not good	313
Thou hast a swift-running tongue	164
Thou speak'st always ill of me	328
Thou swelling sea, what now can be thy boast	297
Though a railroad, learnèd Rector	101
Though British accents your attention fire	299
Though I do "Sir" thee, be not vain, I pray	324
Though matches are all made in heaven, they say	225
Though Nature thee of thy right hand bereft	152
Though Sir Edward has made many speeches of late	45
Though thou 'rt like Judas, an apostate black	19
Thoughtless that "all that 's brightest fades"	248
Thraso picks quarrels when he 's drunk at night	173
Three colonels, in three distant counties born	140
Three doctors, met in consulation	121
Three poets, in three distant ages born	277
Three traitors, Oxford, Francis, Bean	36
Thrice happy Damon! Fate has stopp'd his breath!	339
Through and through the inspirèd leaves	147
Through regions by wild men and cannibals haunted	142
Thuscus writes fair, without blur or blot	82
Thus Tophet look'd; so grinned the brawling fiend	93
Thus to the master of an house	187
Thus with kind words Sir Edward cheer'd his friend	183
Thy cellars, friend, may justly vaults be styled	185
Thy father Genoese, thy mother Greek	327
Thy flattering of me this followeth thereupon	241
Thy flattering picture, Phryne, 's like to thee	209
Thy nags (the leanest things alive)	186
Thy praise or dispraise is to me alike	164
Thy verses are eternal, O my friend	83

Index of First Lines.

	PAGE
Tiraqueau, while drinking water	340
'T is bad enough, in man or woman	251
'T is done; I yield; adieu, thou cruel fair!	343
'T is generous, Tibbald! in thee and thy brothers	52
'T is highly rational, one can't dispute	226
'T is said that Peel	38
'T is said that our soldiers so lazy have grown	270
'T is stated by a captious tribe	251
'T is true I am ill, but I need not complain	306
To a Swiss, a gay Frenchman in company said	239
To Damon's self his love's confined	332
"To fast and pray we are by Scripture taught	112
To half of Busby's skill in mood and tense	65
To have a thing is little, if you're not allowed to show it	250
To John I ow'd great obligation	319
To no one Muse does she her glance confine	84
To roar and bore of Northern wights	235
To rob the public two contractors came	144
To say the picture does to him belong	89
To tell us why banks thus in Scotland obtain	235
To the Church I once went	105
To the same sounds our parties two	43
To win the maid the poet tries	272
To wonder now at Balaam's ass were weak	44
Tomkins will clear the land, they say	170
Tom praised his friend, who changed his state	229
Tom, weak and wavering, ever in a fright	331
Tom Wood of Chiswick, deep divine	92
Too small for any marketable shift	259
Traitor to God, and Rebel to thy pen	49
Treason doth never prosper; what's the reason?	241
Truth, they say, lies in a well	246
'T was in his carriage the sublime	51
'T was the Russian's conscription, the papers declare	40
'Twixt Footman Tom and Dr. Toe	108
Two lawyers, when a knotty case is o'er	130
Two millers thin	144

E E

Index of First Lines.

	PAGE
Two Miltons in separate ages were born	150
Two of a name—both great in their way	94
Two of a trade can ne'er agree	273
"Two trades can ne'er agree"	95
Underneath this sable hearse	274
Under this stone, reader, survey	133
Unlike my subject now shall be my song	260
Upon the cabin stairs we met—the voyage nearly over	213
Urles had the gout, so that he could not stand	188
Vagus, advanced on high, proclaims his skill	122
Vane's speeches to an hour-glass	45
Venus whipt Cupid t' other day	289
View Delia's toilet, see the borrowed plumes	206
Virgil, whose magic verse enthrals	256
Virtue we praise, but practise not her good	242
Ward has no heart, they say; but I deny it	27
We everyday bards may "Anonymous" sign	307
We know not why you for the fair	324
We men have many faults	196
We pledged our hearts, my love and I	256
"What a frail thing is beauty!" says Baron Lebras	211
"What a sad world we live in!" Scandal cries	181
"What bringest thou from the sermon, Jack? Declare that"	190
What! Darès made a knight! No; don't be frighted	181
What dost thou in that mansion fair?	144
What god, what genius, did the pencil move	282
What is a Unionist? One who has yearnings	194
What is lighter than a feather?	197
What is the reason, can you guess	245
"What makes you think the world is round?"	233
What mean ye by this print so rare	254
What news to-day?—"Oh, worse and worse"	30

	PAGE
What num'rous lights this wretch's corpse attend	185
What rivalry in magic power is this!	337
What thanks do we owe, what respects and regards	76
What with briefs and attending the court, self and clerk	167
What woes must such unequal union bring	171
Whatever Rome may strive to fix	339
"What's fashionable, I'll maintain	245
When Adam slept, Eve from his side arose	345
When Alma Mater her kind heart enlarges	110
When ambition achieves its desire	20
When Anacreon would fight, as the poets have said	73
When at the head of our most gracious king	33
When beauteous Helen left her native air	300
When Billy found he scarce could stand	13
When, by some misadventure crossed	210
When Chloe's picture was to Chloe shown	210
When Cupid did his grandsire Jove entreat	279
When Dacier, jointly with his learned wife	341
When Dido found Æneas would not come	261
When dress'd for the evening, girls, now-a-days	203
When each points out a different way	102
When Emily, sweet maid, appears	301
When Eve brought woe to all mankind	197
When Eve upon the first of Men	268
When Frank was poor, the lad was frank and free	193
When Gifford commenced his attack on the Queen	26
When haughty Gallia's dames, that spread	280
When he holds forth, his reverence doth appear	104
When I meet Tom, the purse-proud and impudent blockhead	160
When I resign this world so briary	79
When I was young and débonnaire	299
When in your mimic scenes I view'd	67
When lately Pym descended into Hell	1
When Lesbia first I saw, so heavenly fair	201
When Limerick once, in idle whim	73
When Lovelace married Lady Jenny	227

Index of First Lines.

	PAGE
When man and wife at odds fall out	230
When Mead reach'd the Styx, Pluto started and said	313
When men a dangerous disease did 'scape	120
When Milton was blind, as all the world knows	215
When Nell, given o'er by the doctor, was dying	217
When one good line did much my wonder raise	55
When Orpheus play'd, he touch'd the rocks and trees	155
When Palmerston begins to speak	41
When Paris gave his voice, in Ida's grove	298
When Parliament people petition their friends	264
When people 's ill, they comes to I	117
When Pennington for female ills indites	124
When Priscus, rais'd from low to high estate	192
When quacks, as quacks may by good luck, to be sure	122
When Rusticus from Watercresses	111
When Tadlow walks the streets, the paviours cry	106
When the versatile Bishop of Oxford's famed city	40
When the young Greek for Atalanta sigh'd	197
When thunder rumbles in the skies	158
When Willis of Ephraim heard Rochester preach	90
When would-be Suicides in purpose fail	192
When you with High-Dutch Heeren dine	239
Whence comes it that in Clara's face	173
Whence deathless Kit-Cat took its name	53
Where'er a hatchment we discern	221
Whether tall men, or short men, are best	199
Whig and Tory scratch and bite	43
While faster than his costive brain indites	82
While here the poet paints the charms	292
While Secker liv'd he show'd how seers should live	301
While she pretends to make the graces known	276
Whilst Butler, needy wretch! was yet alive	50
Whilst holy prayers to heav'n were made	120
Whilst in the dark on thy soft hand I hung	319
Whilst petty offences and felonies smart	300
Who only in his cups will fight is like	242
"Who Wrote Eikon Basilike?"	79

Index of First Lines. 421

	PAGE
Whoe'er he be that sojourns here	253
Whoe'er you are, tread softly, I entreat you	143
"Who's up?" inquired Burke of a friend at the door	14
Why durst thou offer, Marcus, to aver	326
Why is a pump like Viscount Castlereagh?	29
Why should Honesty seek any safer retreat	127
Why should we explain that the times are so bad	18
Why walks Nick Flimsy like a malcontent?	176
"Wife, from all evil, when shalt thou delivered be?"	215
"Wife, I perceive thy tongue was made at Edgeware"	215
With a Patten to wife	220
With death doom'd to grapple	15
With eyes of wonder the gay shelves behold	83
With lace bedizen'd comes the man	186
With language dispers'd, men were not able	7
With nose so long and mouth so wide	314
With women and apples both Paris and Adam	305
Within this monumental bed	306
Witty as Horatius Flaccus	76
Wise Solomon, with all his rambling doubts	61
Womankind more joy discovers	198
Would you get to the House through the true gate	25
Ye politicians, tell me, pray	22
Ye sons of Westminster, who still retain	57
Yes, in debate, we must admit	45
Yes! there are her features! her brow, and her hair	309
Yes! 'twas polite, truly, my very good friend	118
Yes, yes, you may rail at the Pope as you please	97
You always are making a god of your spouse	297
You are so witty, profligate, and thin	134
You ask me, Edward, what I think	152
You ask me if I think your poems good	84
You ask me why Pontefract borough should sully	37
You ask me, your servant, to give you in rhyme	204
You beat your pate, and fancy wit will come	165
You feed so fast, and run so very slow	314

	PAGE
You never dine at home at all, but sponge upon your friends	344
You say, without reward or fee	336
You see the goodly hair that Galla wears	318
Young Clinton has set me a difficult task	333
Young Courtly takes me for a dunce	178
Your compliments, dear lady, pray forbear	302
Your dressing, dancing, gadding, where's the good in?	206
Your homely face, Flippanta, you disguise	205
Your lower limbs seem'd far from stout	307
Your poem must eternal be	84
"Your servant, sir," says surly Quin	136
"You see," said our host, as we entered his doors	185